Sunna's Journey

Norse Ritual
Through the Wheel of the Year

Nicholas Egelhoff

Published by Garanus Publications 2013

For more books, see http://www.lulu.com/garanus

Or visit The Magical Druid
http://www.magicaldruid.com

Garanus Publishing
C/o Three Cranes Grove, ADF
PO Box 3264
Columbus, OH 43210

Table of Contents

Nicholas Egelhoff

Introduction

"Every man needs a ritual."[1]

Insightful words from comedian-*cum*-philosopher Lewis Black, but just because he spoke them in jest (his ritual, after all, was the Super Bowl) does not rob them of their truth. Every human being needs ritual. Ritual, whether sacred or profane, helps us to order the world around us, to give us a sense of control and a feeling that all is right with the universe: from brushing our teeth in a certain way, to having our coffee at a specific time with a specific amount of sugar or cream, to participating in religious work to feeling the presence of the divine in our lives. Human beings are ritualistic animals.

This work seeks to help people with ritual, specifically polytheistic religious ritual of an Old Norse bent. Within these pages you will find a liturgical script and a description of a magical working appropriate to a specific time of the year. There are also appropriate ritual stories in both prose and Eddic poem forms that you can perform during the rite. And though the format of the ritual is presented in the Core Order of Ritual of Ár nDraíocht Féin (ADF), it is intended to serve as a source of inspiration and ideas for all pagans and heathens looking for ritual material to mine.

This book consists of four sections:

- An **Introduction** that explains Ár nDraíocht Féin and the Core Order of Ritual for those unfamiliar with either.
- The **High Days**, which contain liturgies for each of the core eight Neo-Pagan High Days.
- The **Devotionals**, which presents liturgies and ideas for other, non-High Day devotional work.
- And the **Appendices** containing a prayer-cycle called "Freyr Learns the Virtues" and a glossary listing all of the non-English terms and phrases, including pronunciation and a short definition.

Ár nDraíocht Féin (ADF)

Just what *is* ADF? Started in 1983 by Isaac Bonewits as a network of independent, religiously-minded scholars interested in the

---

[1] Lewis Black, *The End of the Universe*

Celtic druids and the wider Indo-European cultural and religious traditions[2] Ár nDraíocht Féin[3] (modern Irish for "Our Own Druidry" or "Our Own Magic") has grown into one of the largest Neopagan Druidic organizations in the world. ADF has congregations in the United States, Canada, Britain, New Zealand, and Australia as well as having individual members in many other countries. Three things set it apart from other Neopagan organizations: 1) its inclusion of all documented pre-Christian, Indo-European cultural traditions – from the Celts in the West all the way to the Indo-Iranians and the Vedics in the East; 2) a heavy emphasis on academic scholarship, using the most current and verifiable knowledge of how our ancestors practiced *their* religion so as to better inform our own; and 3) a focus on orthopraxy ("right practice") as opposed to orthodoxy ("right belief"). Among ancient Indo-European cultures it was much more important to perform rituals at the proper time in the proper way, as handed down by tradition, than it was to have the same "correct" theological understanding of the Cosmos as everybody else. Like those pre-Christian ancestors, ADF prescribes a standard ritual format called the "Core Order of Ritual" that unites all congregations ("groves") and keeps them on the same page, freeing individual members to understand the universe in whatever way makes sense to them.[4]

While this book mainly provides ideas and suggestions accessible to all Norse-oriented practitioners of Neopaganism, all of the liturgical scripts follow **ADF's Core Order of Ritual**:

- **Initiation of the Rite**
- **Purification**
- **Honoring the Earth Mother**
- **Statement of Purpose**
- **(Re)Creating the Cosmos**
- **Opening the Gate(s)**

---

[2] *Questions and Answers about ADF*, http://www.adf.org/about/basics/qa.html

[3] Pronounced "arn ree-ocht fane"

[4] Though, it should be noted, that while the working theological understanding of the deities during ritual is a hard polytheistic one – after all, it does not make too much sense to offer gifts/sacrifices to something that is only an archetype or an abstract concept – ADF definitely has members who are soft polytheists, duotheists, monists, atheists, *etc.*; again, it is not theological belief that unites members, but ritual practice.

- **Inviting the Three Kindreds**
- **Key Offerings**
- **Prayer of Sacrifice**
- **Omen**
- **Asking for/Hallowing/Affirmation of the Blessings**
- **Workings**
- **Thanking the Beings**
- **Closing the Gate(s)**
- **Thanking the Earth Mother**
- **Closing the Rite**

Obviously for those not familiar with ADF ritual require a little more elucidation.

The **Initiation of the Rite** consists of a signal, usually audible though visual and other sensory cues can work, that lets those gathered know that ritual is beginning; that profane time has ended and sacred time has begun. This simple step, common to many religious traditions (think the ringing of a church bell or the Muslim call to prayer) often includes a processional from some spot outside of the ritual area into the ritual space. This procession from profane space into sacred space accompanies the change from profane time to sacred time.

Purification in ADF ritual can include the asperging of the ritualists and congregants with water and smudging with sage or some form of incense, but it also includes a purification of the ritual space. Again, this can take the form of aspergation and smudging of the ritual area, but more specifically it involves an entreaty with what is known as the "Outdwellers." ADF theology classifies the Outdwellers as those beings who might be at cross-purposes to the working being done, i.e. benevolent deities who might object (due to whatever mores they might observe) to the working at this particular rite or malicious spirits completely at odds with the Kindreds themselves. The term "Outdweller" does not specify a dualistic approach or imply that the beings referenced are by necessity evil or immoral (although they could be). They just will not be helpful to the ritual working at hand. And unlike some other Neopagan traditions, ADF does not employ a "hard" demarcation between ritual and profane space (e.g. – a circle, etc.) – hence the need for purification and entreaty.

Honoring the Earth Mother is just that: honoring the Earth Mother. One of the few required theological symbols in ADF ritual is the acknowledgement of an Earth Mother. How one understands this symbol/being is left up to the individual: some prefer to think of Her as the spirit of the Land where they live, as one of the ancient goddesses (such as Jorð or Nerðus among the Norse, Gaia or Demeter among the Hellenes, etc.), or as the consciousness of the entire geo- and biosphere (such as in the "Gaia Hypothesis"). Again it is much more important for all practitioners to actually *perform* the honoring of the Earth Mother, than to agree on what She is.

The **Statement of Purpose** describes for the ritualists and congregation just why they have gathered at that time and in that place, performing the ritual that they are performing.

(Re)Creating the Cosmos is much simpler than it might initially sound. In some ways a continuation of the purification stage of the ritual, this step focuses on the hallowing of three ritual symbols: the Fire, the Well, and the Scared Center, most commonly represented as a Tree. In fact, the core idea of this step is the creation of the "Sacred Center": a point – "outside of time" – where all worlds meet and where the deities, the spirits, and the ancestors can commune with the mortal practitioners. Representing common Indo-European cosmological motifs, along with an acknowledgement of a multiplicity of worlds/realms, such as the Norse "Nine Worlds" or the Celtic "Land, Sea, and Sky," the ritual hallowing of these symbols seeks to reenact the ordering of the Cosmos as performed by the deities or ancestors at the beginning of the world, further inculcating the idea of sacred time and space in the minds of the ritualists and the congregation.

Opening the Gate(s) is a ritual step that is, admittedly, not of Indo-European origin. It is a syncretistic appropriation made by Isaac Bonewits in the earliest days of ADF that he found useful for ritual. Taken from Vodoun practice, the opening of a Gate or Gates, focused on the three hallows (Fire, Well, Tree), helps establish the Sacred Center even more fully by opening conduits between the Middle World of mortality with the Underworld (*via* the Well) and the Overworld (*via* the Fire) with all three connected by the World Tree (or Pillar or Mountain, etc., depending on the Indo-European culture in question). Generally the Hallows and Gates act as *foci* for sacrificial offerings, as well: gifts for the ancestors are given to the Well, gifts to the deities are given to the Fire, and gifts to the spirits of the land are laid by the Tree. Though the demarcation of hallow/symbol with each specific class of beings is not a hard, one-to-one division.

The Gatekeeper is more a "title" than anything else, and any appropriate being of the Kindreds (e.g. – Heimdallr, Ratatask, Askr, etc.) can be called upon to lend their spiritual power to the ritualists in the act of opening the Gate(s). The being need not necessarily be a psychopomp or a figure particularly associated with *travel* between worlds, as long as you can make the reasonable association between them and the role of Gatekeeper.

Inviting the Three Kindreds is the invocation of the previously mentioned three classes of beings: the spirits of our ancestors, the spirits of the land, and the spirits of the deities. We do not summon or *command* them to appear in the classic Ceremonial sense but rather invite these beings to join us in ritual as equals – as kith and kin – and give them gifts/sacrifices in the Indo-European tradition of *ghosti*.[5]

The **Key Offerings** are the gifts/sacrifices given to the central being(s) being worshipped/worked with in the ritual. We use a similar form of invocation as in the previous section regarding the Three Kindreds themselves, but more tightly focused and tailored to the specific being(s).

The **Prayer of Sacrifice** is a cap-stone to the previous ritual step: it is the prayer to whatever being(s) being worshipped that they accept the offering being made by the ritualists and the congregation.

An **Omen** is taken by one of the ritualists (the Seer), and while there are a variety of ways to take the omens, the main questions asked generally are in regards to whether the offerings given to the principle beings (and the Three Kindreds in general) were accepted, what they give to us in return, and what they ask of us going forward. Should the Seer receive negative omens (especially in regards to whether or not

---

[5] "*[G]hostis is a [Proto-Indo-European] word which means 'one with whom one has a reciprocal obligation of hospitality.' Our words 'guest' and 'host' both come from this word, and that is just what the ghosti-principle implies. There is an interaction among people, and between people and the gods, according to the laws of hospitality. Society is bound together by an exchange of gifts, by acting as guest on one occasion and host on another. In the same way, we are bound to the gods through the giving of gifts and the receiving of blessings. This is the origin of the Indo-European version of sacrifice." - http://www.ceisiwrserith.com/pier/whatwasreligion.htm

the offerings were accepted) a piacular offering is often given to make up for this short-fall.

Asking for/Hallowing/Affirmation of the Blessings complements the several rounds of sacrificial offerings given to the Kindreds prior to the omen being taken. The old Indo-European sentiment "a gift calls for a gift" sums up this step. We have given to the Kindreds and so custom dictates that they give something to us in return. This is not some paltry economic transaction where we have given such-and-such "payment" in return for some kind of merchandise or service from the Kindreds, but is more of a community-weaving, relationship-building practice. We can look at it in a more prosaic way: when you're moving and you ask your friends to help, you generally give them pizza in return (and maybe throw some beer on top, too), since it would be bad form to not repay them in some sort of way. It is *not required* for you to do so (as in a business transaction), but if you're going to be a good friend, you show your appreciation for their kindness and doing so ultimately strengthens your friendship.

The **Working(s)** section is self-explanatory: should the ritualists and congregation have any kind of non-worship-related work to do (e.g. – blessing of tools, an initiation, etc.), they do it in this section – or, at the very least, after the ritualists and the congregation have received the Blessings of the Kindreds in the previous step.

Thanking the Beings, **Closing the Gate(s)**, and **Thanking the Earth Mother**, too, are fairly self-explanatory. We thank the principle being(s) of the rite for their presence, along with the Three Kindreds in the reverse order that they were called. We again call upon the Gatekeeper to help close the Gate(s) between the Worlds, and finally we thank the Earth Mother.

Closing the Rite is just that: the ritualists make a declaration that the ritual is over thereby re-instituting profane time and space.

While these are the bare-bones, *required* steps of ADF liturgy, there are other steps that most congregations and solitary practitioners include:

- The invocation of a spirit of inspiration, whether that be an abstract concept (simply "Inspiration") or a specific spirit(s) (e.g. – Bragi, the Nine Muses, Brighid, etc.).

- An attunement meditation, generally the "Two Powers" meditation,[6] as a means of spiritually "grounding and centering" and to helping establish a group-mind among the ritualists and the congregation.
- The aforementioned "piacular offering".
- Any others that a congregation or individual decides is appropriate and workable.

I should also explicitly note that **ADF does not endorse nor perform blood-sacrifices of *any* kind in its public rituals.** Whatever individual members do on their own is up to them, but any congregation doing public ritual is exhorted to refrain from that practice.

Now, after having read all of that, one might ask "What are these 'hallows' things and where do I get them?" Well, the answer is easy: use whatever makes sense to you. If you have an actual plot of land with a tree and a well and you can (safely!) make a small fire in their vicinity, then by all means do so. But, should you only have a small room, then you can definitely get by with just three bowls and a stick.[7] I, personally, have used a painting of the Norse cosmos and the image of a fully set-up altar (displayed on a TV screen – modern technology is *wonderful*) at various different times to great effect. There is absolutely no need to be grandiose or break-the-bank in the effort to perform an ADF-style ritual.

All you need is piety.

That being said, you may find it useful to at least have a couple of bowls to hold offerings in (especially if you're indoors and have to deposit them elsewhere post-ritual), maybe a few candles (for a representation of the Fire or for votive lights), etc. Again, go as grand as you think is necessary/affordable, but always remember that sometimes working within a minimal budget can yield pleasantly surprising and inventive results.

---

[6] *Two Powers Meditation*, http://www.adf.org/rituals/meditations/two-powers.html

[7] *Three Bowls and a Stick, or: Creating a Homeshrine on a Budget*, http://www.adf.org/members/training/dp/articles/3-bowls.html

Norse Lore

Of course, all of this requires a caveat regarding artistic license (or, perhaps, "skaldic license"): it was definitely taken. While I used the preserved lore of the Norse as my compass-bearing for all these works, I should explicitly state that I do not present any of these stories or practices, nor should you understand them as, being one-hundred-percent historical or accurate representations of Norse religious practice. They are my variations on seasonal themes taken from the historically attested materials and updated for modern Neo-Pagan, and especially ADF, practice.

Hopefully, you will look upon these stories and liturgical ideas in the same way that our ancestors would have looked upon the variants of common ritual and myth that cropped up and mutated in specific ways according to the conditions of the region in their cultural orbit. After all, the myths we have today are amalgamations of dozens, if not hundreds, of tribal stories told and re-told and worked and re-worked by our ancestors down the generations. Just because they happened to be written down in a book at some point does not mean that those versions are the final ones. And if we are to (re)birth modern versions of our ancestors' religions – tailored to our needs and environs – we must allow those myths and rituals to evolve with us – otherwise we are just historical re-enactors.

The High Days

For many Neo-Pagans, the eight High Days represent the most important liturgical times of the year. The eight recognized High Days – Yule, Imbolc, Ostara, Beltaine, Midsummer, Lughnassadh, Mabon, and Samhain – have their oldest roots in various ancient Celtic and Germanic folk festivals, but their modern forms are no older than the beginning decades of the Twentieth Century with the emergence and development of Wicca in Britain. Various other culturally-focused reconstructionist groups will celebrate other holy days, some – like Hellenic or Roman reconstructionist groups celebrating either the Athenian or Roman festival calendar – will celebrate many more than the eight High Days. But the eight High Days are the most commonly observed holy days among Neo-Pagans, and thus serve as a good common ground.

So, what are the eight High Days? As stated, the High Days have their roots in pre-Christian folk festivals of the Celts and the Germanics. Four of the High Days – Yule, Ostara, Midsummer, and Mabon – are obviously very solar in their focus, as they mark the progression of the seasons throughout the year: Winter moves in to Spring, which moves in to Summer, which moves in to Autumn, which moves back in to Winter. These four "quarters", as they're generally known, celebrate the year's transition through the seasons, while their opposite number (known as the "cross-quarters" in Wicca) – Imbolc, Beltaine, Lughnassadh, and Samhain – are loosely based off of the Celtic fire festivals, which are much more agricultural and cultural in focus: the beginning of Earthly and human fertility, the reaping of the harvests, the honoring of the ancestors, etc.

Let's look at each of the High Days individually:

Yule: Midwinter, the celebration of the Longest Night of the Year. Yule is Germanic in its origin and actually shares some similarities to the Celtic "Samhain" (or "Halloween" as most Westerners know it today), particularly the belief that the barrier between the mortal world and those which lie beyond it is thinnest on this night, and that the restless dead and other unruly spirits roam about; this is particularly manifested in legends regarding the Wild Hunt. But, Yule also celebrates the bonds of community (through gift-giving) and the idea that even in the deepest, darkest night there is the promise of the coming dawn.

Imbolc: Among the Irish, this was a festival that heralded the first glimmers of Spring after a long winter. The name Imbolc comes from Old Irish "i mbolg" and the medieval Irish "oimelc" which refer to the pregnancy and lactation of ewes, respectively. The festival itself was, most likely, originally dedicated to the goddess Brighid, a goddess of smithcraft, healing, and poetry.

Ostara: The Vernal Equinox, marking the seasonal waxing of daylight and heat toward towards their zenith at Midsummer. The name of the High Day is related to the word "east" and is likely tied to a goddess most well-attested to in the Anglo-Saxon "Eostre" – her name being a cognate to the Hellenic goddess "Eos", who was the goddess of the dawn. Like Imbolc before it and Beltaine after, there is a strong focus on fertility and the growth of life, especially since the iconic animal images associated with the High Day (and its Christian descendant, Easter) are the rabbit and the chicken's egg. These being due to the fact that this is the time of year that many animals start giving birth and that, in a pre-industrial society, Ostara marks the first time in the year that there is enough daylight for chickens to begin producing eggs.

Beltaine: Among the ancient Celts, this marked the beginning of the Summer season; in fact, the name of the High Day derives from the Gaelic name for the month of May, and many of the modern traditions of Beltaine (e.g. – dancing around the May Pole, etc.) derive from the more Germanic traditions associated with this time of year. Again, the fertility of the Land and its occupants (plant, animal, and human) is one of the main foci of this High Day.

Midsummer: The celebration of the Longest Day of the Year, when the Sun waxes to its height and the life-giving and -affirming nature of daylight and warmth are celebrated. In the Germanic countries, one tradition at this time of year was to set a wagon wheel on fire and let it roll swiftly down through the fields, imparting them with the blessing of the Sun's *main*, or spiritual power.

Lughnassadh: The third of the "fire festivals" and the first of the festivals celebrating the harvest season. Among the Celts, it marked the funeral of the foster-mother of the god Lugh and was celebrated with games and feasting. In the wider Indo-European orbit, though, this time of year often marked the end to the summer war season, since able hands were needed back home to bring in the crops – so victories were celebrated and good harvests rejoiced in.

Mabon: The Autumnal Equinox marks the second of the harvest festivals and is generally marked as a day of thanksgiving for the gifts of (hopefully) good harvest season up until that point. The recognition of the need to share those bounties throughout the community is a common theme, as well, since winter is coming and that can spell hard times if the Folk don't band together.

Samhain: Samhain (pronounced "Sow-won") marks the last of both the "fire" and "harvest" festivals, and to the Celts it was the beginning of the Winter season. The transition between seasons was a liminal time for them, reflected in the belief that the boundary between worlds was thinnest and that wandering specters of the restless dead and other less-than-benevolent spirits needed to be offered to in order to avert their wrath.

So, how do these modern Neo-Pagan festival days relate to pre-Christian Norse practice, if at all? As noted, Yule, Ostara, and Midsummer have strong Germanic roots, as do certain aspects of the modern Beltaine and Lughnassadh (the holding of games and feasts at the end of the war and viking season). Imbolc has a Germanic analog in the festival of Disting/Disablot or the Anglo-Saxon holiday of "Éowemeolc" (or "Ewe's Milk"). However, in some cases – such as the Autumnal Equinox – there is little if any evidence of Germanic analogs in antiquity and festivals have been (re)constructed to fit the modern Neo-Pagan calendar[8].

But, this fact doesn't make the modern festivals any less valid – so as long as they're honest about their mostly recent invention.

[8] A good resource for this whole subject is the *Our Troth* books (specifically *Volume 2*), edited by Kveldulf Gundarsson and published by The Troth.

Yule

The deepest, darkest time of the year. The weather is harsh and freezing, the wind howls outside the walls of our homes and...other things may be howling as well during those stark, black nights. This is the time of year to kindle a light in the darkness and to take refuge in the bonds of kith and kin.

Working

Materials Needed:

- 3 candles or tea-lights
- The last section of Sun-Pole

The working for Yule is the blessing of the Yule Log. The Log itself is to be made from the last section of the Sun-Pole (see the working for *Midsummer*), halved length-wise, and three circle sections large enough to fit candles or tea-lights carved or drilled into the rounded surface of the Log.

The Log itself is meant to be a focus and store-house for the Grove's (or individual ritualist's) *hamingja* and *wyrd*, the Kindreds' blessings, and Máni's *main*; adding to and combining with the blessings from the Midsummer ritual. Once the Log is hallowed and blessed during the Yule ritual, the ritual fires for Disting, Ostara, and Maitag will all be kindled from the Log's candles. And, finally, the Log itself will be used to make the ritual fire for the Midsummer ritual, where its spiritual potency will be put into *that* Sun-Pole; causing the cycle to continue.

Now, since one half of the last Sun-Pole section will be used to make the Yule Log itself, the other half will be used to make the ritual fire for this ritual.

Variation for Solitaries: much like with the Midsummer ritual, a solitary practitioner does not need to really make any alterations to this working. Just scale it down to a level with which you feel comfortable.

Script

Processional

[Insert song/chant here]

Outdweller Entreaty

Those of the Furious Host: Forfeður and Vættir who ride with the Old Man, Helblindi. We offer you this token of treaty and ask that you will not harry our Hall this evening. *[give offering]*

To all others – those whose voices do not harmonize with our own, whose purposes may be cross with ours, accept this token of treaty and leave our working be. *[give offering]*

Purification

[cense and asperse the Folk]

Opening Statement

[ring sleigh-bells three times to signal beginning of the rite]

As our ancestors once did, so we do today, and so our children will do in the future. Children of Earth, we are here to honor the Kindreds on this, the Winter Solstice. When the Night is deepest and darkest, when furious vættir ride the bone-chilling wind and howl outside the Hall…when the hope of a New Year is kindled and nurtured. So let us join together as one folk to make our offerings in joy and reverence.

Opening Prayer

The skull of Mighty Ymir stretches out above us.
The bones of Mighty Ymir support the land about us.
The blood of Mighty Ymir flows under and around us.
All things are of His flesh,

Our *wyrds* woven together,
May we pray with a good fire.

Inspiration

Worlds-renowned Bragi, silver-tongued skald of the Halls of Asgarð, you who delight the gods with wit, wisdom, and a well-turned phrase; I pray that you find this offering acceptable *[give offering]* and that you will bless our speech with honeyed words. Praise and thanks be upon you.

Honoring the Earth Mother

The Children of the Earth call out to Blessed Jorð - Birther of Storms, Consort of the Shaper, Mother of All. We who walk upon you, who take sustenance from you, who find comfort and rest within your bosom, remember you this day. *[give offering]* May you find this offering acceptable, for it is given in love and gratitude. Earth Mother, accept this offering!

(Re)Creating the Cosmos

In the earliest days, the Cosmos was empty and there was naught but the Void. In time though, a light grew in the south and the flickering fires of Muspelheim illuminated the Void; it's orange glow reflecting off the northern, rimy ice-fields of Niflheim. The fires of Muspelheim grew, its heat melting the ices of the North and birthing the Elivagar, eleven mighty rivers that spread out across the Great Gap between the two realms. In time, the Ur-Jotun Ymir formed from the rimy-eitr, and he was eventually slain and quartered by the grandsons of the Ur-Guð, Búri, the cosmos re-shaped from his corpse.

"The descendants of Ymir survived the catastrophic deluge of blood that resulted from the sacrifice of the First Being, and they were displeased with - what they felt - was a murderous act. In recompense, the sons of Bor gave them the new lands to the East and the eyes of their late progenitor. These were taken by the Jotun, Mundilfari, to the south where they were infused with the fires of Muspelheim and launched into the sky, where they became his children: Sunna, the Sun, and Máni, the Moon. Seeing these two new lights in the Heavens, the Æsir set a wolf behind each, an incentive to make sure that the twins kept to their allotted tasks. And so, round and round the two children sped, measuring out the days, the weeks, the months, the years.

[hallow the Hallows by censing and aspersing them]

As well, we hallow the Yule Log, a symbol and trove of our Grove's wyrd, making it sacred once more for the coming year.

[the Yule Log is hallowed like the Hallows]

Grove Attunement

[perform the Two Powers meditation]

We are shaped from driftwood at the Shore of the Worlds,
Grown from the Land,
Washed in the Sea,
Dried by the Sky.
We are tied together by the gifts of the Three Brothers,
By the weavings of the Nornir.
May we be just and true to each other.
May our worship be pious and pure.
Verði það svo.

The Gates

See now in your mind's eye a winter forest – it's floor carpeted with thick snow, the branches of trees – both those naked and those clothed in green nettles – swaying and creaking in the cold wind.

You hear the swish-swish-swish of poles and the soft whistle of skis on snow. A woman appears among the trees: her hair dark, her clothes made of fur and leather, her look is hard – like winter ice. You catch her scent on the still, crisp air: fire-smoke, wolf-fur, pines. She is Skaði, Mistress of the Wilds, Maiden of the Winter-wastes.

We call upon her now: Blessed Skaði, you who know the tracks and the paths through the impenetrable forests, you who keep the hearth-fire burning so far from any Hall. Accept this offering and join your power with ours, Noble Jötynja, as we open the Gates Between the Worlds.

[give offering and open the Gates: pull the Two Powers into your hands, feeling the fire and water mix, and draw a clockwise triangle over the Well, saying]

May this well be the Triple Well.

[draw a triangle over the Fire, saying:]

May this fire be Bifrost's undying flame.

[draw a triangle over the Tree, saying:]

May this tree be mighty Yggdrasil, rising high and low before me.

[see the three triangles – water, fire, and growing wood – hang before in the air and then come together in a valknot, while declaring:]

Latið opna hliðin! Let the Gates be opened!

Forfeður Offering

Blessed Forfeður, you who came before us, you who bore us, you who helped to shape the path that lies ahead. Ancient Wise; Honored Einherjar; You Countless Masses who toiled in obscurity, but upon whose backs our society is built. Meet us at the boundaries. Join us at our Sacred Hearth and be warmed by our good fire. Aid us and guide us as we walk the Elder Ways. Forfeður, accept this offering! *[give offering]*

[light the candle for the Ancestors]

Landvættir Offering

Noble Vættir, you who inhabit this Land, who lurk in stone and tree and river. Those of the primal wilds, those of the tilled and planted field, those of cobbled stones and bricked-walls: hear our call. May you join us by our fire, may you share your bounties with us as we share ours with you. Meet us at the boundaries. Join us at our Sacred Hearth and be warmed by our good fire. Aid us and guide us as we walk the Elder Ways. Blessed Vættir, accept this offering! *[give offering]*

[light the candle for the Land-Spirits]

Guðir Offering

Shining Guðir, you who shaped the Cosmos, you who guard and guide the World's wyrd, you who teach us and bless us with bounty. May your radiance light our hall, may your warmth stoke our fire, and may your presence alongside us this evening make the Long Night that much more pleasant. Meet us at the boundaries. Join us at our Sacred Hearth and be warmed by our good fire. Aid us and guide us as we walk the Elder Ways. Shining Guðir, accept this offering! *[give offering]*

[light the candle for the Deities]

Key Offering

[tell Yule story/poem]

Brother of Sunna, Evader of Hati, Lune, Gleamer, Hastener, Year-Counter, Waxer and Waner. Pale-Face.

Máni.

We call out to you, Shining One. You who guide us through this, the Darkest of Nights. Many-Faced one, protect us and guide us with your silvery light; and please, accept these offerings that we give to you. Máni, accept our offerings! *[give offering]*

Omen

[make an offering to the Norns, saying:]

Wise Sisters, Tenders of the Great Tree, Weavers of That-Which-Is and That-Which-Is-Becoming. Accept this offering, please, and let me peer into your Sacred Well.

[take the omens, preferably with runes]

The seer for this rite will ask four questions:
Have our offerings been accepted?
What do the Forfeður give in return?
What do the Vættir give in return?
What do the Guðir give in return?

Calling for, Hallowing, and Affirmation of the Blessings

Holy Ones, we have given in friendship and love, so that you might give in return. Kindreds, we ask that you give us the Blessed Waters: the Waters of Wyrd, the Waters of Wisdom, the Waters of Life!

Mighty Ones, give us the Waters!

Noble Ones, give us the Waters!

Shining Ones, give us the Waters!

[pass the pitcher of Water over the Yule-log's candles, charging the Waters by intoning the rune associated with the specific Kindred during their part of the call-and-response, while pushing energy into the pitcher; when Waters are charged, hold them up to the congregation, saying:]

Sjáið vatn lífsins!

Children of the Earth, before you is the holy cup. Do you wish to share in these blessings?

All: We do!

Then, as the waters are poured out, know that they hold blessings for you and this grove and this community. Work well with these blessings, Children of the Earth.

[pass out the Waters to the Folk; a portion of the Waters is sprinkled on the Yule Log while saying:]

May Máni's light,
Main and might,
Fill these flames in the darkness.
May the blessings of the Kindreds
On this Hallowed Grove
Shine throughout the Long Night.

Thanking

[thank the assembled Kindreds in reverse order: Deities, Land-Spirits, and Ancestors]

Closing the Gates

Noble Skaði, Blessed Giantess of the Wild-Lands, we call out to you once more. Give us the power of your frigid winds, give us the might of your evergreen forests – join your power with ours as we close the Gates Between the Worlds.

[give an offering and close the Gates: draw the Two Powers back into your hands, feeling the water and fire turn to ice within you, drawing a counter-clockwise triangle over the Tree, saying:]

May this Tree be just a tree.

[draw a triangle over the Fire, saying:]

May this Fire be just flame.
[draw a triangle over the Well, saying:]

May this Well be just water.

[as you draw the triangles, see the them form from ice, hanging in the air by the Hallows; declare:]

Latið loka hliðunum! Let the Gates be Closed!

[clap your hands firmly together and see the icy triangles shatter, the cosmic powers keeping the Gates open dispersing; then say:]

Blessed Skaði, we thank you.

Thanking Inspiration

Silver-tounged Bragi, skald of skalds, poet of poets, we thank you.

Thanking the Earth Mother

Jorð, beauteous and bountiful mother, we thank you.

Closing the Rite

Go now, Children of Earth, in peace with the blessings of the Kindred and a Fire in your Heart. This rite is ended.

Story & Poem

"Máni's Aid"

This story is true.

Long after the gods had shaped humanity from two pieces of drift-wood found on a beach, it happened that a man was braving the bitter chill and snow of a darkened, Mid-Winter's night on his way home. He had supped with friends and made merry with them – which was only fitting on the darkest and loneliest night of the year – but now had to fare on to his own home.

It was a prospect that he did not relish.

As he traveled across snowy fields, the wind picked up, its soft sighs increasing to dreadful moans that chilled the man's bones in more ways than just the physical. It was then that he noticed sounds behind him, seeing dark silhouettes moving toward him across the snow. Fearing marauders, the man made for a near-by wood, hoping to lose his pursuers in the darkness of the trees.

But, as it turned out, the man himself became lost in the thick woods. In no time, he could not tell which direction was which, the silvery-light of the Full Moon was ambient and omnipresent beneath evergreen boughs, and was no aid to the man. As he searched for a way out, he saw the dark forms coming closer, catching up to him in their pursuit. And the man gasped when he saw them, for they were not bandits or brigands or highwaymen.

No, for they were all - to a one - dead-men.

The man fled mindlessly from the skeletal, rotting figures, not caring what direction he fled as long as it was away from those frightful creatures. He called out to every god he could think of, pleading for aid and mercy. But none came.

The man's flight came to an abrupt end as he skidded to a stop at the edge of a cliff over-looking a nearly frozen river; its banks shaded in the darkness of pines and firs. Desperate, the man called out once more to any who would listen and help.

It was then that he saw the Moon appear from behind the trees, a light guiding him out of the woods. The man slid down to the river's edge and followed it out, slowing only when he no longer saw the dead men pursuing him. He thanked Blessed Máni for his aid and continued home, shaken but none the worse for wear.

The wind picked up more as the man approached the edge of the forest, but he did not care: he knew which way home was now and had only thoughts of a warm fire and steaming cider dancing in his head. The wind howled and screamed through the boughs of the trees, but he paid those protests no mind.

That is, until the wind died momentarily, but the howling continued.

Dogs. Hounds. Wolves, even. Their howls rose from far behind the man, but they made the hairs on his neck stand. For he could tell even then, that the howls were getting closer. The man sprinted through the snow as fast as he could making it to the tree-line and out into open field as he sought to lose his four-legged pursuers.

Not long after the man himself exited the wood, the first of the hounds did, as well. And the sight of them chilled the man to his very core. Glowing eyes they had, like bale-fires; and each was at least twice the size of any dog he'd seen. A fresh howl arose on the wind as the hunting-dogs caught sight of their prey. Fear pushed the man further on across the field, despite the burning of his lungs and legs at the exertion.

"Máni!" the man cried out to the clear, empty night sky where that silvery orb shone. "Máni! Silver-Eye, you have helped me once already this night! Please, Blessed One, do not let me fall to these hounds!"

It was then that the winds picked up to horrendous gales and the light of the Full Moon dimmed almost to nothingness, thick clouds rolling in to obscure its shining face. And despite the viciousness of the wind, the man found no difficulty in making progress forward. Indeed, he quickly out-paced his pursuers once again, as the darkness and wind confused the spectral-hounds.

The wind died, eventually, and a cold silence fell upon the snow-laden field. As the man pressed onward – desiring more than ever the warmth of his hearth fire and the safety of his home's walls – he heard the soft, lethargic gurgle of a nearly frozen river break the silence. His heart jumped joyously in his chest: just across the river were his lands. He was nearly home. His pace increased and within a few moments he sighted the bridge that spanned the icy gap.

He set one foot on the wooden bridge and stopped, his heart turning to ice within his chest. There was the soft whinny ahead, and against the deeper darkness of the now cloud-filled skies, he could see the subtle silhouette of a horse and hooded-rider standing sentry at the mid-point of the bridge.

The man's heart caught in his throat, and he silently whispered another desperate prayer to the Moon.

"Little fox, little fox: you have out-run my huntsmen. You have out-run my hounds." The horseman said softly. "For that, you have my respect. But, you will not out-run me." The words hung in the frozen air for a moment that seemed like eternity to the man standing at the foot of the bridge. As the silence stretched, light slowly shone down upon them, as the Moon's cloak of clouds slipped away.

"You have your choice now," the horseman said, and in the moonlight, only one eye could be seen gazing out from under his hood. "Join my retinue. Or die."

The man took a frightened step backward, his booted foot slipping ever so slightly on a patch of ice. His gaze darted down, seeing the moonlight gleam like diamonds off the ice beneath his feet, before he returned to the horseman. "I cannot, good sir," he said to the hooded-rider. "I have a family, a home, a life. To those I must return this night." The horse neighed, and the rider's posture straightened.

"Then you travel to my niece's hall," came the rider's response before he spurred his horse forward.

As the horse charged, the man threw himself to the side, latching onto the bridge's railing to keep himself upright. The horse landed where he'd been standing a moment before…and its hooves skidded on the ice. The mount slipped and lost its balance, throwing the hooded-rider from his seat and into a tall bank of snow.

The man ran for his very life.

He sprinted across the bridge. He sprinted across the field. He kept his gaze forward, not even sparing a quick glance over his shoulder once his front-door was in sight. He slammed the door open and then slammed it shut tight, locking and barring it, making sure none could enter. He stayed up until morning, until he saw Sunna's glorious face once more, and then he retired to his bed.

And after that night, he never tarried about on Yule. And he always lit three candles in memory of Máni's divine aid.

This story is true   that some years ago
During a dark Midwinter's night,
A man braved the chill   to make his way home
After supping 'n' making merry with friends.
The night: dark and cold;   and home many miles off;
The man longed to lounge by his fire.
Hurry, he did; he was chilled and impatient;
Wanting to be back home and resting.

The wind blew harder,   its sighs turned to howls,
And the man saw silhouettes behind him.
Fearing marauders he made for a nearby wood,
Hoping to lose his pursuers.
But, he got turned around,   lost among the trees,

Des'prate to find his direction home.
The dark forms grew closer   and he gasped when he saw them clear;
For they were all – to a one – dead men.
Mindlessly he fled   from the skeletal, rotting figures
Not caring which direction he dared travel.
His flight came to a stop   as he faltered at a cliff's edge
Over-looking a languid, frozen river.
Sliding down its banks   in the dark shadows of fir trees
He pleaded for the aid of any god.
It was then the cold Moon shone,   sliding out from the clouds
Its light guiding him down the river's length.

The dead men disappeared   in the dark night behind him
And he thanked Blessed Máni for his aid.
He emerged in a field, the wind howling fiercely,
But the man only thought of his home.
Of warm fire, steaming cider he thought as he strode
Across the field's snow-laden acres.
Until the wind died,   with the howling unabated;
Chill fear spiked up the man's spine.

Dogs, hounds, and wolves,   their howls rising up,
Coming ever closer to the man.
Sprinting across the snow,   lungs and legs aching,
He hoped to lose his bestial pursuers.
Not long after he saw the hounds,   the sight chilled his bones:
Monstrous beasts with eyes like bale-fire.
A fresh howl arose as the hounds saw their prey;
The sound spurred him onward.

"Máni!" he cried out   to the clear night sky
Where that silv'ry orb shone brightly.
"Silver-Eye, you have helped me once   so far this fear-filled night!
"Lend me aid and save me from these hounds!"
The winds grew stronger   and thick clouds rolled in,
The Land descended into darkness.
The dogs lost the scent,   and despite the gales,
The man ran on quite rapidly.

The man pressed on   and progressed steadily
Toward resting in his own home.
He soon heard the gurgle   of a nearly-frozen stream,
And recognized the river near his land.
He soon saw the bridge   that spanned the icy gap;
But stopped with one foot upon its bulk.
His heart turned to ice and his legs trembled fearfully
At the sight that greeted his eyes.

The silhouette of a rider   and the house he sat astride
Stood steadfast upon the bridge.
"Little fox, little fox: you have   out-run my honored huntsmen;
And my hounds languishing alone.
"You have my respect: such prey is a rarity;
"Only you will not out-run me."
At the rider's words   the man whispered quietly,
Praying to Máni once more.

"You have your choice now," the horseman rumbled.
"Join my retinue or die most swiftly."
"I cannot go with you, good sir," the man said.
"I have a home, a family, to which I must return."
"Then to my niece's hall   you travel this night,"
Came the rider's reply.
He spurred the horse forward and swiftly it surged,
Charging fast at the chilled man's form.

To the side of the bridge   the man leapt with all speed,
Out of the horseman's path.
And where the horse landed   its hooves skidded on ice,
Tossing the rider toward a snowbank.
The man ran for his life,   sprinting 'cross the land;
Not stopping 'til he was locked inside his home.
Not until Sunna's first light   spread rosy 'cross the snow
Did he relax and retire to bed.

The memory of that night,   most terrifying and deadly,
Stayed with the man many years.

Sunna's Journey

Being hunted by dead men,   chased by bale-hounds,
And harried by the leader of the Hunt.
He would always remember   with gratitude and thanks,
Máni's multiple blessings.
Every Yule he would light   three warm, sil'vry candles
In memory of the Moon's divine aid.

Disting

The darkness of Winter is slowly ebbing away, the frozen ground is thawing. It is during this time that we rejoice in the first lengthening days of the year, of the first glimmers of fertility and life in the World.

Working

Materials Needed:

- 1 bowl
- 1 table
- 4 paper-maché *völsi*
- Brown acrylic paint

The working for Disting is focused on fertility and the potency of tools. A common tradition for this time of year is called the "Charming of the Plow" during which various tools – in the vein of the eponymous "plow" – are blessed and hallowed for their use in the coming year. One way of doing this, described in *Völsa þáttr*, is by using a preserved horse phallus to confer the blessing.

Obviously, using a real, honest-to-the-gods horse phallus is not exactly convenient to most modern pagans (unless you live on a horse farm, but even then…). So, replacements will be used for this working. Use whatever materials you feel are adequate, but for this example I suggest simple paper-maché. Once the phalli are made and dry, paint them with the brown acrylic paint, and when the paint has dried you will have your four *völsi* for use in the ritual.

In the ritual itself, the *völsi* will be laid out on the table upon which the Folk's tools to be blessed will sit upon. The *völsi* should be laid in each corner of the table, with the head of each phallus pointing in toward the tools. A Blessing Bowl will need to be kept on the main altar for the rite, and partially filled with water (water from the Blessings will be poured in, as well, prior to the working; thus hallowing the water already in the Blessing Bowl), which will be aspersed on to the *völsi* and then the tools during the working.

When the ritual is finished, the *völsi* can be planted at home for an extra blessing of fertility.

Variation for Solitaries: no alteration needs to be made for solitary practitioners.

Script

Processional

[Insert song/chant here]

Outdweller Entreaty

To all those whose voices do not harmonize with our own, whose purposes may be cross with ours, who may seek to harm and harrow with no legitimate grievance, accept this token of treaty and leave our working be. *[give offering]* Blessed Disir, noble women of our lineages, protectresses and grand-mothers, we ask that you stand watch over this space and make sure that the treaty is upheld. *[give offering]* Praise and thanks be upon on you all, *verði það svo.*

Purification

[cense and asperse the Folk]

Opening Statement

[ring bells three times to signal beginning of the rite]

As our ancestors once did, so we do today, and so our children will do in the future. Children of Earth, we are here to honor the Kindreds on this, the Festival of Disting. The Night of the Year has stretched long and deep, the winter has been bitterly cold. But a hope glimmers on the horizon, as this was the time of the year when our ancestors would first begin to plow their fields and sow the seeds of harvests to come. So let us join together as one folk to make our offerings in joy and reverence.

Opening Prayer

The skull of Mighty Ymir stretches out above us.
The bones of Mighty Ymir support the land about us.

The blood of Mighty Ymir flows under and around us.
All things are of His flesh,
Our wyrds woven together,
May we pray with a good fire.

Inspiration

Noble Alvíss, most wise and erudite of the Dvergar, we call out to you this day. Please, stand with us this day as we invite the Kindreds in frið and kinship. Accept this offering given in gratitude and honor, *[give offering]* and bless our speech with wise words. Praise and thanks be upon you.

Honoring the Earth Mother

The Children of the Earth call out to Blessed Jorð - Birther of Storms, Consort of the Shaper, Mother of All. We who walk upon you, who take sustenance from you, who find comfort and rest within your bosom, remember you this day. *[give offering]* May you find this offering acceptable, for it is given in love and gratitude. Earth Mother, accept this offering!

(Re)Creating the Cosmos

In the primal times, the Great Hrímthurs was slain and quartered by the Sons of Búri: his Skull became the Sky, his Blood became the Sea, his Body became the Land. And from his Flesh grew a Great Tree, which connected all of the Worlds. May we recreate that Holy Sacrifice this day as we emulate the ordering of the worlds.

[hallow the Hallows while the Folk sing the "Portal Song"]

Grove Attunement

[perform the Two Powers meditation]

We are shaped from driftwood at the Shore of the Worlds,
Grown from the Land,
Washed in the Sea,

Dried by the Sky.
We are tied together by the gifts of the Three Brothers,
By the weavings of the Nornir.
May we be just and true to each other.
May our worship be pious and pure.
Verði það svo.

The Gates

See now in your mind's eye a darkened, wintry road. Snow falls and obscures your vision, the scent of hearth-fires drifts on the air. You hear the soft crunching of footsteps nearby, a dark, indistinct figure approaches on the road. The figure's form resolves into that of a man wearing a thick cloak with a deep, deep hood pulled up hiding his face from the cold. In one hand he carries a tall, thick staff, which gives off a muffled *clack!* every time it touches the snow-covered road.

As he grows closer, you can see within the shadow of his hood, and from within that darkness gleams one, sparkling eye. You recognize him now - the Wise Wanderer, the High One, the Hooded One, the God of the Mysteries: Oðinn.

We call upon him now: Blessed Alfoðr, Shaper of Worlds, and Counselor to those wise enough to listen; you who know all the roads and ways through-out the Worlds, we call out to you and ask a boon. Accept this offering and join your power with ours, Wisest of the Æsir, as we open the Gates Between the Worlds.

[give offering and open the Gates: pull the Two Powers into your hands, feeling the fire and water mix, and draw a clockwise triangle over the Well, saying]

May this well be the Triple Well.

[draw a triangle over the Fire, saying:]

May this fire be Bifrost's undying flame.

[draw a triangle over the Tree, saying:]

May this tree be mighty Yggdrasil, rising high and low before me.

[see the three triangles – water, fire, and growing wood – hang before in the air and then come together in a valknot, while declaring:]

Latið opna hliðin! Let the Gates be opened!

Forfeður Offering

Blessed Forfeður, you who came before us, you who bore us, you who helped to shape the path that lies ahead. Ancient Wise; Honored Einherjar; You Countless Masses who toiled in obscurity, but upon whose backs our society is built. Meet us at the boundaries. Join us at our Sacred Hearth and be warmed by our good fire. Aid us and guide us as we walk the Elder Ways. Forfeður, accept this offering! *[give offering]*

Landvættir Offering

Noble Vættir, you who inhabit this Land, who lurk in stone and tree and river. Those of the primal wilds, those of the tilled and planted field, those of cobbled stones and bricked-walls: hear our call. May you join us by our fire, may you share your bounties with us as we share ours with you. Meet us at the boundaries. Join us at our Sacred Hearth and be warmed by our good fire. Aid us and guide us as we walk the Elder Ways. Blessed Vættir, accept this offering! *[give offering]*

Guðir Offering

Shining Guðir, you who shaped the Cosmos, you who guard and guide the World's wyrd, you who teach us and bless us with bounty. May your radiance light our hall, may your warmth stoke our fire, and may your presence alongside us this evening make the Long Night that much more pleasant. Meet us at the boundaries. Join us at our Sacred Hearth and be warmed by our good fire. Aid us and guide us as we walk the Elder Ways. Shining Guðir, accept this offering! *[give offering]*

Key Offering

[tell Disting story/poem]

Noble Gefjon: Blessed Maiden, Giver of Prosperity and Happiness, You who toiled so our Ancestors might have sustenance. We remember you this day and give you praise and thanks. May we have your strength and fortitude in these cold times to work toward the bounty that comes with warmth and light. Gefjon, Handmaiden of Frigga and Bringer of the Plow, accept our offerings! *[give offering]*

Omen

[make an offering to the Norns, saying:]

Wise Sisters, Tenders of the Great Tree, Weavers of That-Which-Is and That-Which-Is-Becoming. Accept this offering, please, and let me peer into your Sacred Well.

[take the omens, preferably with runes]

The seer for this rite will ask four questions:
Have our offerings been accepted?
What do the Forfeður give in return?
What do the Vættir give in return?
What do the Guðir give in return?

Calling for, Hallowing, and Affirmation of the Blessings

Holy Ones, we have given in friendship and love, so that you might give in return. Kindreds, we ask that you give us the Blessed Waters: the Waters of Wyrd, the Waters of Wisdom, the Waters of Life!

Mighty Ones, give us the Waters!

Noble Ones, give us the Waters!

Shining Ones, give us the Waters!

[charge the Waters by intoning the rune associated with the specific Kindred during their part of the call-and-response, while pushing energy into the pitcher; when Waters are charged, hold them up to the congregation]

"Sjáið vatn lífsins!"

Children of the Earth, before you is the holy cup. Do you wish to share in these blessings?

All: We do!

Then, as the waters are poured out, know that they hold blessings for you and this grove and this community. Work well with these blessings, Children of the Earth.

[pass out the Waters to the Folk; a portion of the Waters is poured into the Blessing Bowl for the working]

Working

[take the Blessing Bowl and walk to the table where the Folk's tools have been laid out. Sprinkle the four völsi with water from the Bowl, saying the following for each faux-phallus]

May the Mörnir receive this blessing, and in return give us the strength of their fertility.

[once the phalli have been asperged, sprinkle the Folk's tools with water from the Blessing Bowl, singing the following galdr]

Blessings of bounty, fecundity, and fruitfulness,
Be upon these tools of trade and toil.

[draw the rune Berkano over the collected tools with the asperger, repeating the stanza one last time as you do so; once finished, say the next lines of the galdr while sprinkling the tools, again:]

Bubbling over with the brawn and bellipotence
Of mighty Mother Jörð,
May these instruments and implements be invested
With the might and main of the Hallowed Mother.

[draw the rune Uruz over the collected tools with the asperger, repeating the last stanzas one last time as you do so; once finished return the Blessing Bowl to its original seat]

Thanking

[Thank the assembled Kindreds in reverse order: Deities, Land-Spirits, and Ancestors]

Closing the Gates

Wizened Alfoðr, Noble Wanderer of the Nine Worlds, we call out to you once more. Give us the power of your fortuitous foresight, give us the might of your hard-won Mysteries – join your power with ours as we close the Gates Between the Worlds.

[give an offering and close the Gates: draw the Two Powers back into your hands, feeling the water and fire turn to ice within you, drawing a counter-clockwise triangle over the Tree, saying:]

May this Tree be just a tree.

[draw a triangle over the Fire, saying:]

May this Fire be just flame.

[draw a triangle over the Well, saying:]

May this Well be just water.

[as you draw the triangles, see the them form from ice, hanging in the air by the Hallows; declare:]

Latið loka hliðunum! Let the Gates be Closed!

[clap your hands firmly together and see the icy triangles shatter, the cosmic powers keeping the Gates open dispersing; and say:]

Blessed Oðinn, we thank you.

Thanking Inspiration

Quick-witted Alvíss, most discerning and discriminating of all Dvergar, we thank you.

Thanking the Earth Mother

Jorð, beauteous and bountiful mother, we thank you.

Closing the Rite

Go now, Children of Earth, in peace with the blessings of the Kindred and a Fire in your Heart. This rite is ended.

Story & Poem

"Gefjon's Gift"

This story is true.

In the early days of Humankind – after Askr and Embla had been quite fruitful and multiplied, spreading their progeny across the Miðgarð like trees casting forth seeds onto the wind – there came a hard winter. Stores of hunted meat and gathered fruits and vegetables dwindled and dwindled and dwindled, until the stores were bare. Starving, the hosts of Men called out to the Shining Guðir – the Æsir and the Vanir – pleading for help and mercy.

The cries were heard by a young Ásynja, a maiden-goddess by the name of "Gefjon." On a sojourn at the behest of her mistress, Frigga, Gefjon was troubled by the sights she witnessed during her furlong through the Miðgarð. When she returned to Asgarð, she questioned her mistress, explaining her deep worries for Men. Frigga listened patiently and was silent, deep in thought, for a long time. Finally, she told her handmaiden that there was no solution that she could think of, but advised Gefjon to visit her wise husband for counsel.

To Valaskjálf the maiden traveled, seeking an audience with the wisest of the Æsir: the Alfoðr, Oðinn. The Old Man welcomed her into his hall and listened to her worries and her questions, before excusing himself to ponder a solution. When finally he returned, it was with long face.

"Back to Miðgarð you must travel," he told the young Ásynja. "To a certain grove on a certain mountain you must travel, and there, seek the wisdom of the most powerful of the Jötynjur: she who is known as Jörð."

And so, guided by the High One's instructions, Gefjon returned to the world of Men. She traveled through field and wood, across streams and oceans, until she came to the forested mountain that Oðinn had described. Finding the mouth of a cave within small glade, she traveled deep into the Earth, until the maiden-goddess entered a vast, rock chamber. Within the chamber she found a lovely, matronly woman who welcomed Gefjon warmly. The young Ásynja explained her worries and her desire to help Humankind to the ancient Jötynja, pleading for her help. The woman held up a calming hand and spoke soothingly to Gefjon, explaining that she had the answer that the maiden sought.

Humankind's problem was that it did not know how to work the Earth and grow their own food – they were unable to secure their own future, simply because they relied on the ebbs, flows, and whims of wyrd to make sure their stomachs were full and their children grew strong. But, they would not be able to work the Earth on their own, so the ancient etin-woman promised that she would assist Gefjon in this work.

Deep in the Earth, Jörð said, there dwelled the Dvergar, ancient smiths and masters of metal-work and invention. The Dvergar would craft for her a device – a "plow" – that could be used in the effort of helping Humanity feed themselves, all Gefjon had to do was go get it. Thanking the ancient Jötynja, Gefjon set off deeper into the Earth, eager to find the Dvergar who would help her.

However, when the Dvergar heard from their sentries that a comely young goddess was approaching their territory, the four who were to help her devised a plan. Though they were bound to help Jörð in whatever she asked, there was nothing stopping them from reaping some bounty off this client of hers.

When Gefjon finally arrived in the realm of the Dvergar, she was greeted by the first of the four. The Dverg was like most of his kind: Man-sized and –shaped, with deathly pale skin and black hair and beard. He told the nubile Ásynja that he had for her the frame of the device, but his brothers were working on the three other parts for it.

"Please, sir Dverg, give me your piece," Gefjon asked.

Smiling, the Dverg told her that he would be more than happy to do so, but his aid was not free, and that he would require payment for his services. Unsure at first, Gefjon soon realized that he meant to lay with her. Though she found the creature repellent for many a reason, the maiden-goddess decided that her goal was the more important thing. And so, she lay with him. When they were done, the Dverg gave her the frame for the plow and sent her on her way. His laughs echoed along the rock tunnels behind her.

Gefjon finally came to the second Dverg, who said that he had fashioned the coulter of the plow. But, he, too, required a payment much like his brother. Somewhat crest-fallen, Gefjon gave herself to this Dverg, as well. Taking the coulter he'd crafted, the Ásynjur bit back tears as more laughs echoed behind her as she left.

The third Dverg – who had fashioned the plow's mouldboard – and the fourth Dverg – who had fashioned the ploughshare – required payment just like their two brothers. But, reminding herself that so many depended upon her help, Gefjon submitted herself to the payment that had been deemed necessary. As she returned to the Jötynja's cavern, the maiden-goddess wept openly, feeling debased and ashamed.

Seeing the Ásynja's tears, Jörð questioned the young woman as to why she wept. Gefjon responded by asking the etin-woman why she had required her servants to reap payment from her in that way. Surely, there was something else she could have done to settle her debt? Angered, Jörð took Gefjon by the hand and led the maiden-goddess out from the caves and down to plain in the shadow of the mountain. Jörð stomped her foot four times and the Earth shook down to its very roots.

Gefjon stood there, watching fearfully, as four mounds grew out of the Earth, and from them erupted the four Dvergar brothers she'd encountered. "How dare you take advantage of one whom I have sent to you?!" the etin-woman roared, her voice threatening to crack the Dome of the Heavens. "For such beastliness, you shall help her finish her task." And with the wave of a hand, the Dvergar began to change. They grew bigger, and huskier, and horns grew from their heads. When all was done, four bulls stood before them.

Jörð tied them to the plow they'd crafted and showed Gefjon how to operate the machine. Giving the Ásynja a whip to encourage her beasts, the etin-woman wished her good luck before Gefjon set to her task.

All through the Miðgarð she traveled, driving the plow into the hard, cold earth and tilling up the soil. She showed Humankind how to make their own plows and how to use them, and how to go about raising crops for eating. And as she departed to continue onward, praises were sung at Gefjon's back.

Finally, Gefjon returned to the ancient Jötynja's mountain and gave her back the plow. Jörð unhooked the bulls and then castrated them, handing the phalli over to the maiden-goddess. Gefjon took them to the first furrows that she'd plowed in each corner of the Garð and planted them, the organs lending great fertility to the growing crops. The bulls themselves were kept as draught animals by Jörð, as punishment for their misdeed.

The plowed fields brought forth many a crop that kept Humankind fed. Thanks to Gefjon, never again was there a famine as bad the one that had brought Humanity the plow.

In the early days of Man after Askr 'n' Embla had been shaped
And their progeny spread past the horizons,
There came a hard winter, food stores had dwindled,
And many a mortal starved.
Their bellies were empty and their prospects were bleak,
No game they could find to feed on.
Despondent and weak they wallowed in misery
Giving cries of mercy to the Guðir.

Their sobs were heard by a shining, young Ásynja,
A maiden-goddess named "Gefjon."
At the behest of her mistress, the honored lady, Frigga,

She sojourned through the Miðgarð.
She witnessed the ill-fortune fallen upon Mankind,
And the sights troubled her soul.
Returning to Asgarð she asked of her mistress
Why Men must suffer so.

Frigga was silent, thinking deeply for a while,
Before bidding Gefjon to seek Oðinn.
To Valaskjálf she traveled to query the Alfoðr,
Wisest in all the Worlds.
He welcomed her warmly to his great hall,
Listening to her concerns 'n' lamentations:
"Mortal Men are starving, their stomachs are hollow,
"Surely something can be done."

"To the Miðgarð you must travel," replied the mighty Alfoðr,
"And seek the Jötynja, Jörð."
Thanking wise Oðinn for his words of counsel,
Gefjon made haste for the Miðgarð.
Across field and stream, through forest and vale,
The goddess sought the wise giantess.
Finally, on a mountain, found deep in cave,
Gefjon bowed before Jörð.

To the *dvergar* she must go, Jörð said to Gefjon,
To the deep-dwelling smiths of old.
The prodigious offspring of old Ymir's flesh
Knew how to help Mankind.
A device called a "plow" the *dvergar* could make
That would help Men feed themselves.
Too long they relied on the good grace of wyrd
To keep themselves whole and hale.

Four of the smiths would shape her device,
Jörð told youthful Gefjon.
Off she was sent to seek the dvergar
And obtain the object she sought.
But when the four *dvergar* heard of the beautiful Ásynja
They devised a dastardly plan.

Help her they would as they were bound by Jörð,
But bounty they would reap, as well.

Each required payment for the pieces they crafted,
Seeking to sample her flesh.
To lie with her in bed was the price they levied;
Gefjon reluctantly gave in.
For many relied on her, the mission paramount,
And so she submitted to their lust.
The dwarves took their payment and gave her the plow,
Their laughs humiliating her deeply.

Returning to Jörð, the young goddess in tears,
The Jötynja was quite concerned.
When Gefjon explained the payment each *dverg* took,
The giantess grew quite angry.
She led the goddess to a plain and planted her foot four times,
Rocking the Earth to its roots.
Four mounds appeared and the four *dvergar* emerged,
And Jörð glared at them angrily.

"How dare you take advantage of one whom I've sent to you,"
The etin-woman roared, enraged.
"For the beastliness you showed you shall help her finish."
And the smiths began to change shape.
Bigger 'n' huskier they grew, horns jutting from their heads;
Finished, four bulls stood before the pair.
Jörð handed her a whip and yoked the bulls to the plow,
Showing the Ásynja how to handle it.

All throughout the Miðgarð she traveled with the plow,
Tilling the soil for the masses.
She showed Humankind how to make such machines;
How to plant, how to raise crops for eating.
Finally she returned to Jörð's snow-capped home,
Before unhooking the bulls from the plow.
The Jötynja took up a sickle and used it quite quickly,
Swiftly castrating the cattle.

The *phalli* she gave to Gefjon for planting
In the four far corners of the Garð.
In the first furrows she'd plowed for the benefit of Man,
She set the severed organs.
Great fertility they gave to the fields that they'd plowed,
Giving much food for Men to eat.
Thanks to Gefjon, never again was there such a famine
As the one that brought the plow.

Ostara

The Dawn of the Year, the birth of Spring. During Ostara, we celebrate the end of the Year's Long Dark Night and the return of warmth and the light. Birth and life are rejoiced in, and we come together as a community to share in the waxing of life.

Working

Materials Needed:

- Blessing Bowl
- Bowl or basket for eggs
- Hard-boiled eggs (as many as needed)

The working for Ostara revolves around the archetypal Spring icon: the chicken egg. As mentioned previously, one of the reasons why eggs are so associated with this time of the year (i.e. – Easter) is because in pre-industrial societies lacking electric lights, this is the first time in the year that there is enough sunlight for chickens to begin ovulating. And these eggs could often times be the first opportunity for fresh protein after a long Winter of preserved food stores.

The preparation for the working is simple: hard-boil as many eggs as you can reasonably assume you'll need for the rite (this is based on previous estimates of ritual attendance; if this is your first Ostara ritual, then make as many as you think you can – even if you make too many, they're a good snack). Once you're ready for ritual, make sure the eggs are in a bowl or a basket and set upon the altar. You'll need another bowl, a Blessing Bowl, to hold some of the Waters of Life and during the working portion of the rite, the eggs will be aspersed and a *galdr* spoken over them as a blessing. The eggs will then be given out to the gathered Folk to consume and bring the blessings of Ostara more fully into their lives.

Variation for Solitaries: not much alteration needs to be done for this ritual, aside from making fewer hard-boiled eggs.

Script

Processional

[Insert song/chant here]

Outdweller Entreaty

To all those whose voices do not harmonize with our own, whose purposes may be cross with ours, who may seek to harm and harrow with no legitimate grievance, accept this token of treaty and leave our working be. *[give offering]* Blessed Disir, noble women of our lineages, protectresses and grand-mothers, we ask that you stand watch over this space and make sure that the treaty is upheld. *[give offering]* Praise and thanks be upon on you all, *verði það svo.*

Purification

[cense and asperse the Folk]

Opening Statement

[ring bells three times to signal beginning of the rite]

As our ancestors once did, so we do today, and so our children will do in the future. Children of Earth, we are here to honor the Kindreds on this, the Festival of Ostara. The Dawn of the Year is upon us – the Sun's nascent, rosy light dances on the horizon. New young are birthed and life blooms in full. So let us join together as one folk to make our offerings in joy and reverence.

Opening Prayer

The skull of Mighty Ymir stretches out above us.
The bones of Mighty Ymir support the land about us.
The blood of Mighty Ymir flows under and around us.
All things are of His flesh,

Our wyrds woven together,
May we pray with a good fire.

Inspiration

Blessed Sága, Mistress of the Sunken Benches, weaver of stories and chanter of tales, we call out to you. Please stand with us with us this day as we invite the Kindreds in frið and kinship. Accept this offering given in gratitude and honor, *[give offering]* and share with us your ability to enthrall an audience this day. Praise and thanks be upon you.

Honoring the Earth Mother

The Children of the Earth call out to Blessed Jorð – Birther of Storms, Consort of the Shaper, Mother of All. We who walk upon you, who take sustenance from you, who find comfort and rest within your bosom, remember you this day. *[give offering]* May you find this offering acceptable, for it is given in love and gratitude. Earth Mother, accept this offering!

(Re)Creating the Cosmos

In the primal times, the Great Hrímthurs was slain and quartered by the Sons of Búri: his Skull became the Sky, his Blood became the Sea, his Body became the Land. And from his Flesh grew a Great Tree, which connected all of the Worlds. May we recreate that Holy Sacrifice this day as we emulate the ordering of the worlds.

[hallow the Hallows by censing and aspersing them]

Grove Attunement

[perform the Two Powers meditation]

We are shaped from driftwood at the Shore of the Worlds,
Grown from the Land,
Washed in the Sea,
Dried by the Sky.

We are tied together by the gifts of the Three Brothers,
By the weavings of the Nornir.
May we be just and true to each other.
May our worship be pious and pure.
Verði það svo.

The Gates

See now in your mind's eye the mighty ramparts of a great, walled city. Made of cyclopean blocks of granite, the wall is strong and tall, capable of rebuffing any host who might dare to breach it. But, along the ramparts walks the figure of a man, his gaze ever outward beyond the city's bounds. He is tall and of a noble bearing, with long, white hair that resembles the foam of the sea in its color and the way it moves; his skin is white, as well, pale like alabaster and one could almost mistake him for an albino.

He wears the raiment of a guardsman and carries with him two horns: one in his hand and worn from use, the other slung by his side and pristine as it awaits its purpose. The man squints towards the horizon – where he sees figures, small as ants at that distance – moving toward the city. He cocks an ear toward them, nods satisfactorily after a moment, and peals out a call on his weathered horn.

The gates of this great city open and close upon the signal of this man – this noble gatekeeper and vigilant watchman – known as Heimdall.

We call upon him now: Noble Heimdall, Eagle-Eye, Blower of the Gjallarhorn, we call out to you and ask that you open the Gates for us. We come in frið and friendship, and seek to commune with the Kindreds. Accept this offering and join your powers with ours, Vigilant Watchman of the Gods, as we open the Gates Between the Worlds.

[give offering and open the Gates: pull the Two Powers into your hands, feeling the fire and water mix, and draw a clockwise triangle over the Well, saying]

May this well be the Triple Well.

[draw a triangle over the Fire, saying:]

May this fire be Bifrost's undying flame.

[draw a triangle over the Tree, saying:]

May this tree be mighty Yggdrasil, rising high and low before me.

[see the three triangles – water, fire, and growing wood – hang before in the air and then come together in a valknot, while declaring:]

Latið opna hliðin! Let the Gates be opened!

Forfeður Offering

Blessed Forfeður, you who came before us, you who bore us, you who helped to shape the path that lies ahead. Ancient Wise; Honored Einherjar; You Countless Masses who toiled in obscurity, but upon whose backs our society is built. Meet us at the boundaries. Join us at our Sacred Hearth and be warmed by our good fire. Aid us and guide us as we walk the Elder Ways. Forfeður, accept this offering! *[give offering]*

Landvættir Offering

Noble Vættir, you who inhabit this Land, who lurk in stone and tree and river. Those of the primal wilds, those of the tilled and planted field, those of cobbled stones and bricked-walls: hear our call. May you join us by our fire, may you share your bounties with us as we share ours with you. Meet us at the boundaries. Join us at our Sacred Hearth and be warmed by our good fire. Aid us and guide us as we walk the Elder Ways. Blessed Vættir, accept this offering! *[give offering]*

Guðir Offering

Shining Guðir, you who shaped the Cosmos, you who guard and guide the World's wyrd, you who teach us and bless us with bounty. May your radiance light our hall, may your warmth stoke our fire, and may your presence alongside us this day make it that much more pleasant. Meet us at the boundaries. Join us at our Sacred Hearth and be warmed by our good fire. Aid us and guide us as we walk the Elder Ways. Shining Guðir, accept this offering! *[give offering]*

Key Offering

[Tell the Ostara story/poem]

Blessed Ostara: Shining Maiden of the Dawn, Youthful Light of the East, and Herald of the Glorious Sun. We remember your bravery, your wit, and your struggle to bring us the Golden Light of Sunna after the Long Darkness of Winter. May your blessings of fertility and light be with us this day. Shining Ostara, Blessed Light of the Rosy Dawn, accept our offerings! *[give offering]*

Omen

[make an offering to the Norns, saying:]

Wise Sisters, Tenders of the Great Tree, Weavers of That-Which-Is and That-Which-Is-Becoming. Accept this offering, please, and let me peer into your Sacred Well.

[take the omens, preferably with runes]

The seer for this rite will ask four questions:
Have our offerings been accepted?
What do the Forfeður give in return?
What do the Vættir give in return?
What do the Guðir give in return?

Calling for, Hallowing, and Affirmation of the Blessings

Holy Ones, we have given in friendship and love, so that you might give in return. Kindreds, we ask that you give us the Blessed Waters: the Waters of Wyrd, the Waters of Wisdom, the Waters of Life!

Mighty Ones, give us the Waters!

Noble Ones, give us the Waters!

Shining Ones, give us the Waters!

[charge the Waters by intoning the rune associated with the specific Kindred during their part of the call-and-response, while pushing energy into the pitcher; when Waters are charged, hold them up to the congregation, saying:]

Sjáið vatn lífsins!

Children of the Earth, before you is the holy cup. Do you wish to share in these blessings?

All: We do!

Then, as the waters are poured out, know that they hold blessings for you and this grove and this community. Work well with these blessings, Children of the Earth.

[pass out the Waters to the Folk; a portion of the Waters is poured into the Blessing Bowl for the working]

Working

[*take the Blessing Bowl and stand before the bowl of eggs; asperse the eggs – drawing the rune dagaz in the air over them – as you speak the following galdr:]*

Ostara's opulent, gorgeous glow

Emerges from the world's eastern edge.
Bringing new beginnings to bear and to form,
Birthing new life for the world.

[set down the Blessing Bowl and pick up the bowl of eggs, saying:]

The Blessings of Ostara – of new life and new beginnings – is upon these eggs, take them and let the gifts of the Goddess of the Dawn be with you.

[take the bowl of eggs around to the congregants and let them each take one egg; when finished, return to the altar area]

Thanking

[thank the assembled Kindreds in reverse order: Deities, Land-Spirits, and Ancestors]

Closing the Gates

Noble Watchman, Guardian upon the Walls of Asgarð, Vigilant Heimdall: we call out to you once more. Give us the power of your unrivalled sight, give us the range of your inescapable hearing. Give us your authority to close the Gates Between the Worlds.

[give an offering and close the Gates: draw the Two Powers back into your hands, feeling the water and fire turn to ice within you, drawing a counter-clockwise triangle over the Tree, saying:]

May this Tree be just a tree.

[draw a triangle over the Fire, saying:]

May this Fire be just flame.

[draw a triangle over the Well, saying:]

May this Well be just water.

[as you draw the triangles, see the them form from ice, hanging in the air by the Hallows; declare:]

Latið loka hliðunum! Let the Gates be Closed!

[clap your hands firmly together and see the icy triangles shatter, the cosmic powers keeping the Gates open dispersing; and say:]

Vigilant Heimdall, we thank you.

Thanking Inspiration

Soul-stirring, story-weaving, audience-enchanting Sága: we thank you.

Thanking the Earth Mother

Jorð, beauteous and bountiful mother, we thank you.

Closing the Rite

Go now, Children of Earth, in peace with the blessings of the Kindred and a Fire in your Heart. This rite is ended.

Story & Poem

"Ostara's Prize"

This story is true.

In the Old Times, as the Deep Darkness of Yule passed, Sunna would slowly begin to show her face to the Worlds again – being that, though the bitter chill of Winter was not to her liking, she would grow stir-crazy secluded in her Hall. Her golden face would thaw the ices of Winter and slowly begin to warm the Worlds, bringing the flowering of life that was Spring. And so, Sunna's re-emergence was always looked forward to by the gods and Men and all the spirits, as it meant an end to the cold and the darkness.

One year, though, Yule passed and the festival of Disting came and went, but Sunna was nowhere to be seen. Some of the gods despaired that this heralded the six years of Winter before the conflagration of Ragnarök. The Alfoðr quickly tried to allay these fears, so that panic would not run rife through Asgarð, and sent a messenger to Sunna's Hall to check on the etin-maiden. The messenger was a cousin to Sunna and her twin brother, Máni, a young maiden-goddess named Ostara – chosen by Oðinn for her wits and her courage.

When Ostara arrived at Sunna's Hall, she found the place in shambles. The doors were knocked in, furniture was broken and tossed about, and – most disturbing of all – the Hall was empty. Not a one of Sunna's servants nor, especially, Sunna herself was to be found. Befuddled, Ostara wandered through the wreckage for some time, before seating herself in the Hall's yard to think. As she pondered what this all meant, a cock wandered into the yard.

"All gone," the cock crowed.

"Indeed," Ostara responded. "Pray tell, did you happen to see what took place here?"

The cock nodded and crowed, "Giants came. Giants came and scattered the servants. They took Lady Sunna and retreated from this place."

Ostara's heart fell as she heard this. "Which way did they go?" she asked the cock.

"East," the cock replied. "They traveled to the East."

Ostara thanked the cock for its aid and set off to the East. It did not take long for her to find the Jotnar's tracks – they were giants, after all – and she followed all the way to the borders of Jotunheim. Fearful, she summoned her courage and entered Giant-Home, but took care to disguise herself, lest she be discovered.

In the form of a hare Ostara traveled the craggy land of Jotunheim, staying with the tracks of Sunna's abductors. The tracks led to a Hall, high in the mountains of the East, around which Ostara found many Jotnar standing guard. She circled the Hall in her hare-skin, surveying the land and trying to find a way in. Smiling, she spotted a clutch of chickens feeding not far from the Hall's eastern door. Slipping from her hare-skin, she donned the guise of a chicken and blended with the group that was feeding.

From the Hall she heard the hearty, wall-shaking laugh of a mighty Jotun. Ostara drew closer, hopping up onto the sill of a window, and peeked a glimpse inside. She saw her radiant cousin, Sunna, bound upon the floor of the Hall, and standing around her were a circle of Jotnar. The largest of them was still laughing.

"You are ours now, Mundilfari's Daughter," the Mighty Jotun said. "You will stay here and give us light and life and delight us with your rapturous beauty until the Worlds come to an end."

Sunna simply glared at the Jotun – for she was gagged – and attempted to gift the him with an obscene gesture, but her hands were bound behind her. Though, by the Jotun's deep grimace, her look was sufficient to communicate her feelings on that particular prospect.

"That is not Mundilfari's Child," Ostara clucked from the window-sill.

The gathered Jotnar looked at the chicken in the window, surprised by the intrusion. "Who are you?!" questioned the Mighty – and displeased – Jotun.

"I am but a chicken," Ostara responded, "but even I can see that that is not the Lady Sunna."

"We should wring its neck, sire," said one of the other Jotnar, indicating the chicken, but the Mighty Jotun held up a hand.

"What do you mean by this?" asked the Jotun. "How do you know that she is not the Sun?"

Ostara hopped down from the window and stepped over to the circle of Jotnar. She sidled up next to her bound cousin and inspected the etin-maiden with several bobs of her avian head. "She must be one of the Lady's handmaidens," Ostara replied absently. "Indeed, she has the look of Sunna's household, but surely she cannot be the Glorious Sun Herself."

"Again: how do you know this?" the Mighty Jotun rumbled angrily.

Ostara cocked her head toward the Mighty Jotun, looking at him with one eye. "If she was the Lady Sunna, would not this room but overflowing with the glorious radiance of her light? Would not this Hall be sweltering in the heat of the Summer Solstice?" Ostara turned back to the captive. "Besides," she clucked, "Sunna's not a redhead."

Some of the Jotnar began chattering in confusion at this last statement, peering down to get a closer look at the tied-up maiden. With them distracted, she turned to their Leader.

"I have a test!" she crowed suddenly, as if hit by inspiration.

"A...test?" the Mighty Jotun repeated back, uncertain of this skeptical chicken before him.

"Yes, a test," Ostara said, nodding. She squatted and clucked loudly, producing an egg. "We put her in the egg," Ostara said. "If she can light it from within, then you've truly captured the Sun – and deserve all the accolades for doing so."

Somewhat confused, the Mighty Jotun agreed to the test. Ostara walked several times around her bound cousin, clucking out a galdr she'd once heard performed by the Alfoðr, shrinking the etin-maiden down until she could fit inside the egg. Once Sunna was inside, Ostara took a step back. "Gather close," she said to the Jotnar, "so that you can properly see."

As the Jotnar bunched together around the egg, leaning into watch it, Ostara switched her hamr back into the form of a hare. "One...two...," she said, making sure that the Jotnar were focused on the egg, "Three!"

At that, she bounded into the center, snatched the egg and made for the window. Swallowing the egg, Ostara hopped out of the Hall's window and made for the wilderness. The angry roar of the Mighty Jotun followed her as she fled, and though the Jotnar chased – she felt the ground quake mightily beneath their hurried footsteps – Ostara stayed hidden and traveled quick until she had re-entered the walls of Asgarð.

She made for Valaskjálf, where the Alfoðr and the other Guðir were waiting. Still in the shape of a hare, Ostara entered the Hall, coming to a rest before Oðinn himself. Not waiting a moment longer, she birthed the egg that she'd swallowed and from it erupted Sunna in her glory.

The gods all cheered the return of the Sun and bestowed upon Ostara, Goddess of the Dawn, many an honor.

In the Spring of the Worlds   when the gods were young

And the seasons newly shaped,
During the bitter chill of Yuletide – that deep, dark night –
Sunna would hide her face from the Worlds.
The dark and the cold she did not like,
Only rarely did she leave her hall.
When spring-time came, and her shining visage returned,
Greeted with great cheer by all.

One year, though, Yule came and went,
But Sunna was nowhere to be seen.
Disting passed, too, but the darkness persisted;
Some o' the gods despaired deeply.
Would winter last six years? Would this herald Ragnarök?
Could the end come so soon?
The Alfoðr acted quickly to allay such fears
And keep them from gripping the Guðir.

The Wise One decided that he would send a messenger
To seek Sunna within her hall.
A cousin to the goddess and her twin brother, Great Máni,
The Herald of the Dawn, hight Ostara.
When she arrived at the hall, the place was in shambles;
Not one of Sunna's servants was found.
Befuddled, Ostara wandered some before sitting in the yard
To think and to ponder her findings.

A cock wandered by, "All gone!" it crowed loudly
And the lady nodded a reply.
"Indeed. Pray tell, did you happen to see what took place?"
The cock nodded and crowed its response.
"Giants came 'n' scattered the Folk, they came and took Lady Sunna.
"They fled far to the East with her bound."
Ostara thanked the cock and took off to the East
Following the Jotnar's footsteps.

To Giant's-Home the tracks did lead her
Winding and turning all the way.
Fearful and cautious Ostara was, she took care to disguise herself,
Donning the hide of a hare.

She traveled the craggy landscape   letting the tracks guide her way
'Til she came to a high mountain hall.
Well-guarded by Jotnar   she sought a way in,
To slip past the giants' presence.

Seeing chickens in the yard   she changed shape to blend in
And hurried close to the hall.
Spying in through a window   she spotted Sunna on the floor,
In the midst of her cretinous captors.
They laughed quite victoriously,   their voices quite mocking,
As they stood over Sunna's bound form.
The Sun goddess wasn't happy,   she glared at them hatefully,
Giving them a gesture obscene.

"Make no mistake,   Mundilfari's Daughter: you're ours!"
Cried the large leader of the Jotnar.
Perched on the window   Ostara peeked in,
And clucked loud to catch their attention.
"'Tis not Mundilfari's Child,"   she chided from the window,
Peering down upon the prone goddess.
The Jotnar were surprised,   the sight was unexpected:
They glared and gaped at the chicken.

"Who are you?!"   roared the lead Jotun,
Growling and glaring at the chicken.
"I am but a chicken,"   Ostara clucked back,
"Even I can see that's not Sunna."
The Jotnar were furious,   they threatened to fight;
But their leader desired to learn more.
"Pray tell, little chicken,   enlighten me, please:
"How do you know she's not Sunna?"

"She has the look of Sunna's household,   that is not debated,
"But she is not the Sun herself.
"Would not this hall be sweltering?   Would it not be overflowing
"With her glorious, golden light?"
The chicken continued clucking   at the confused and burly Jotun.
"Besides, Sunna's surely not a redhead."
Confused, the other Jotnar   looked curiously at the goddess,

Dumbfounded and indecisive.

“A test!” the chicken clucked over the Jotnar’s chattering,
Looking steadily at their leader.
“We put her in an egg,   and if she lights it from within,
“We’ll surely know she’s Sunna!”
The confused Jotun leader   laconically agreed as
Ostara popped out an egg.
The Jotnar then gathered   around the bound goddess
As Ostara clucked out a galdr.

Sunna then shrank   so quickly that she
Fit easily within the egg.
The Jotnar slid closer   at Ostara’s sly urging,
While shifted back to a hare.
Swiftly stealing the egg   Ostara eagerly fled,
Leaving the hall long behind her.
Safely back home, Ostara   freed Sunna from the egg
To the cordial cheering of all.

Maitag

The fullness of the Sun's warmth and light begins to suffuse the World at this time of year, and we rejoice as Spring comes into full bloom. We kindle fires to symbolize the kindling of life and love in this season.

Working

Materials Needed:

- Amber
- Rose
- Raspberry leaves
- Sandalwood
- Mortar & Pestle
- 2 Braziers or Fire-Pits

The crux of the Maitag ritual working is the "Freyja Incense", a special offering to the goddess and a conduit of her blessing to the Folk. *How* to make incense will not be covered here, as there are plenty of books and websites[9] out there giving step-by-step instructions for how to accomplish it. What you will need, though, for this particular incense is some amber (for the resin), rose and jasmine (for the herbs), and sandalwood (for the wood). Mix these together using a mortar and pestle according to the instructions you find, into either combustible or non-combustible incense. Combustible incense would be like any kind of cone or stick incense that you can buy in any variety of pagan, New Age, or religious shops. Non-combustible incense is the type used in the old days and even in the present by such institutions like the Catholic Church: it is fairly crumbly and is burned by setting it atop a burning charcoal. The script for the ritual assumes the use of modern, combustible incense – but if you can integrate non-combustible incense successfully, use it if you like.

You will also need two braziers or metal fire-pits in which to build the purifying need-fires. The combustible incense will be

[9] Just google "how to make incense"

scattered into these fires and the Folk will walk between them, being smudged by the blessed smoke of the incense and the fires.

Variation for Solitaries: One fire will do – or even just a few tea-lights and a couple cones of the Freyja Incense should suffice.

Script

Processional

[Insert song/chant here]

Outdweller Entreaty

To all those whose voices do not harmonize with our own, whose purposes may be cross with ours, who may seek to harm and harrow with no legitimate grievance, accept this token of treaty and leave our working be. *[give offering]* Blessed Disir, noble women of our lineages, protectresses and grand-mothers, we ask that you stand watch over this space and make sure that the treaty is upheld. *[give offering]* Praise and thanks be upon on you all, verði það svo.

Purification

[cense and asperse to purify the Folk]

Opening Statement

[ring bells three times to signal beginning of the rite]

As our ancestors once did, so we do today, and so our children will do in the future. Children of Earth, we are here to honor the Kindreds on this, the Festival of Maitag. The Flowering of Spring is in full force – love is in the air, and the World's fertility is growing toward its zenith for the Year. So let us join together as one folk to make our offerings in joy and reverence.

Opening Prayer

The skull of Mighty Ymir stretches out above us.
The bones of Mighty Ymir support the land about us.
The blood of Mighty Ymir flows under and around us.
All things are of His flesh,

Our wyrds woven together,
May we pray with a good fire.

Inspiration

Worlds-renowned Bragi, silver-tongued skald of the Halls of Asgarð, you who delight the gods with wit, wisdom, and a well-turned phrase; I pray that you find this offering acceptable *[give offering]* and that you will bless our speech with honeyed words. Praise and thanks be upon you.

Honoring the Earth Mother

The Children of the Earth call out to Blessed Jorð - Birther of Storms, Consort of the Shaper, Mother of All. We who walk upon you, who take sustenance from you, who find comfort and rest within your bosom, remember you this day. *[give offering]* May you find this offering acceptable, for it is given in love and gratitude. Earth Mother, accept this offering!

(Re)Creating the Cosmos

In the primal times, the Great Hrímthurs was slain and quartered by the Sons of Búri: his Skull became the Sky, his Blood became the Sea, his Body became the Land. And from his Flesh grew a Great Tree, which connected all of the Worlds. May we recreate that Holy Sacrifice this day as we emulate the ordering of the worlds.

[hallow the Hallows while the Folk sing the "Portal Song"]

Grove Attunement

[perform the Two Powers meditation]

We are shaped from driftwood at the Shore of the Worlds,
Grown from the Land,
Washed in the Sea,
Dried by the Sky.
We are tied together by the gifts of the Three Brothers,

By the weavings of the Nornir.
May we be just and true to each other.
May our worship be pious and pure.
Verði það svo.

The Gates

See now in your mind's eye a beautiful orchard coming into bloom. The scent of flowering apple-trees is strong on the air, and already, the growing fruit can be seen among the branches of the trees. The wind blows softly, bringing petals and pollen with it. And not far off, you can hear the soft lilting of a feminine voice as it sings.

Following the voice into the depths of the orchard, you find a young woman at work, tending to the trees. She goes from tree to tree, checking on their growth and pruning where necessary; in the crook of her arm hangs a wicker basket, waiting for its payload of apples to ripen and fill it. The young woman is Iðunna, the Keeper of this Orchard, and it is from her that the Youth of the Gods is given.

Generous Iðunna, Eternally Young, Giver of the Apples, Guardian of the Way of Immortality, whose beauty inspires the Greatest of Skalds, we call upon you this day. Without your wise and careful tending, without your generosity, without your potent and fecund might and main, the Guðir themselves would have withered away long ago. We pray that you accept this offering and in return join your power with ours as we open the Gates Between the Worlds.

[give offering and open the Gates: pull the Two Powers into your hands, feeling the fire and water mix, and draw a clockwise triangle over the Well, saying]

May this well be the Triple Well.

[draw a triangle over the Fire, saying:]

May this fire be Bifrost's undying flame.

[draw a triangle over the Tree, saying:]

May this tree be mighty Yggdrasil, rising high and low before me.

[see the three triangles – water, fire, and growing wood – hang before in the air and then come together in a valknot, while declaring:]

Latið opna hliðin! Let the Gates be opened!

Forfeður Offering

Blessed Forfeður, you who came before us, you who bore us, you who helped to shape the path that lies ahead. Ancient Wise; Honored Einherjar; You Countless Masses who toiled in obscurity, but upon whose backs our society is built. Meet us at the boundaries. Join us at our Sacred Hearth and be warmed by our good fire. Aid us and guide us as we walk the Elder Ways. Forfeður, accept this offering! *[give offering]*

Landvættir Offering

Noble Vættir, you who inhabit this Land, who lurk in stone and tree and river. Those of the primal wilds, those of the tilled and planted field, those of cobbled stones and bricked-walls: hear our call. May you join us by our fire, may you share your bounties with us as we share ours with you. Meet us at the boundaries. Join us at our Sacred Hearth and be warmed by our good fire. Aid us and guide us as we walk the Elder Ways. Blessed Vættir, accept this offering! *[give offering]*

Guðir Offering

Shining Guðir, you who shaped the Cosmos, you who guard and guide the World's wyrd, you who teach us and bless us with bounty. May your radiance light our hall, may your warmth stoke our fire, and may your presence alongside us this day make it that much more pleasant. Meet us at the boundaries. Join us at our Sacred Hearth and be warmed by our good fire. Aid us and guide us as we walk the Elder Ways. Shining Guðir, accept this offering! *[give offering]*

Key Offering

[tell Maitag story/poem]

Blessed Freyja, Beauteous and Ravishing One, She of Gold and Amber, She who Enflames Passions and Sows the Seeds of Love. We honor and remember you this day, thankful for the fire you help to kindle in our hearts and our loins, bringing lovers together in joyous union. May your blessings of love, fertility, and growth be with us this day. Golden Freyja, Blessed Lady of Love, accept our offerings! *[give offering]*

Omen

[make an offering to the Norns, saying:]

Wise Sisters, Tenders of the Great Tree, Weavers of That-Which-Is and That-Which-Is-Becoming. Accept this offering, please, and let me peer into your Sacred Well.

[take the omens, preferably with runes]

The seer for this rite will ask four questions:
Have our offerings been accepted?
What do the Forfeður give in return?
What do the Vættir give in return?
What do the Guðir give in return?

Calling for, Hallowing, and Affirmation of the Blessings

Holy Ones, we have given in friendship and love, so that you might give in return. Kindreds, we ask that you give us the Blessed Waters: the Waters of Wyrd, the Waters of Wisdom, the Waters of Life!

Mighty Ones, give us the Waters!

Noble Ones, give us the Waters!

Shining Ones, give us the Waters!

[charge the Waters by intoning the rune associated with the specific Kindred during their part of the call-and-response, while pushing energy into the pitcher; when Waters are charged, hold them up to the congregation, and say:]

Sjáið vatn lífsins!

Children of the Earth, before you is the holy cup. Do you wish to share in these blessings?

All: We do!

Then, as the waters are poured out, know that they hold blessings for you and this grove and this community. Work well with these blessings, Children of the Earth.

[pass out the Waters to the Folk]

Working

[go to the need-fires and offer some of the Freyja Incense – amber, rose, and jasmine – to them, before holding your hands over the flames and charging them with the Two Powers, saying:]

Lady, Lover, Lighter of Love's Flame
May these flames purify and kindle
The fertile fires of mind, heart, and loin.
Verði það svo.

[have the Folk walk between the fires, being smudged with the smoke of the fires and incense; repeat the galdr as many times is necessary until all the Folk have processed through]

Thanking

[thank the assembled Kindreds in reverse order: Deities, Land-Spirits, and Ancestors]

Closing the Gates

Beauteous Tender of the Orchard, Giver of the Apples of Immortality, Blessed Iðunna we call upon you once again and ask that you join your magic with ours – blend the might and the main that keeps even the Guðir eternally young – so that we might close the Gates Between the Worlds.

[give an offering and close the Gates: draw the Two Powers back into your hands, feeling the water and fire turn to ice within you, drawing a counter-clockwise triangle over the Tree, saying:]

May this Tree be just a tree.

[draw a triangle over the Fire, saying:]

May this Fire be just flame.

[draw a triangle over the Well, saying:]

May this Well be just water.

[as you draw the triangles, see the them form from ice, hanging in the air by the Hallows; declare:]

Latið loka hliðunum! Let the Gates be Closed!

[clap your hands firmly together and see the icy triangles shatter, the cosmic powers keeping the Gates open dispersing; and say:]

Generous Iðunna, we thank you.

All: Iðunna, we thank you!

Thanking Inspiration

Blessed Bragi, Poet of Poets, Greatest of Skalds: we thank you.

Thanking the Earth Mother

Jorð, beauteous and bountiful mother, we thank you.

Closing the Rite

Go now, Children of Earth, in peace with the blessings of the Kindred and a Fire in your Heart. This rite is ended.

Story & Poem

"Freyja's Frozen Heart"

This story is true.

In Olden Days, there was a woman named Gertrude who was a devoted follower of the goddess Freyja. A matchmaker she was and a *seiðkona* – so skilled and mighty, in fact, that she led a sextet of women practitioners.

She was also deeply in love with a man named Klaus.

Klaus was a barkeep at a local tavern, a gregarious man full of life with hair like lustrous bronze. Gertrude had worked hard to make Klaus notice her, but despite her wiles and her wisdom, she found herself always faltering around him and failing to garner his affections. And so, night after night, she prayed to Freyja – a goddess of love – asking for her heart's desire; and when she could, Gertrude offered gifts of amber and wine to the Lovely One.

But, it was not to be.

One night, Gertrude entered the tavern and found handsome, effulgent Klaus fawning over a buxom young woman with luminous golden-brown hair. Gertrude's heart broke, watching the two flirt back and forth shamelessly. But, when the woman turned and Gertrude saw the necklace that she wore – an intricate, four-stranded affair made of gold and silver and bits of amber, with a central piece of gilded-amber cut into the shape of a heart – despair filled her being.

Gertrude fled the tavern, seeking the company of sisters in the Art. She wailed and her tears flowed like a raging river as she told them what she'd seen: her goddess betraying her. Though the other (seiðkonar) tried to comfort and console, nothing could assuage Gertrude's grief. But, her grief soon turned to cold hatred and she vowed that she would get vengeance for the goddess' theft.

Convincing her sisters of her plan, they quickly imbued a talisman risted with runes that would work Gertrude's vengeance.

Returning to the tavern, Gertrude saw that Freyja was still there, toying with handsome Klaus as he tended bar. Gertrude nudged past the goddess as inconspicuously as possible, hanging the talisman – a thing of wood and leaf, its runes stained with blood – from Freyja's heavy belt. She whispered the galdr as she walked away, and immediately the charm took effect.

Though Freyja had been courting Klaus as a possible lover, her interest suddenly died. Klaus had done nothing, and the goddess still understood her previous attraction in an intellectual way, but…the passion was gone. It had died. Looking around the tavern, her eyes sought the most beautiful and handsome of its patrons. And though she did indeed find them, they too did nothing to stoke the flames of her passion.

Confused, Freyja left and wandered the land, looking for someone who would awaken her desire once more. Her searching went on for years and years, until finally she retired to a small home deep in the forest, accepting the fate she'd been given.

It was into this forest that a young man named Óttar came many years later, traveling as he was throughout the land looking for work. Near sunset, the young man came to rest at a stream, seeking to relax and quench his thirst for a short time. As he rested, he took notice of movement upstream and moved toward it to get a closer look. He found a young maiden washing clothes on the river-bank, the sun's waning rays making her golden-brown hair shine. Óttar was immediately taken with her. He approached her cautiously, not wishing to scare her, noticing the intricate necklace she wore and the heavy, chain belt made of gold she wore around her waist, and surmised that she must be some merchant's daughter.

He tried to engage her in conversation and flirtation, and though she seemed more than willing to talk, Óttar could tell that she had not warmed up to him. The sky was darkening and the maiden took her leave, but not before Óttar asked if he could ever see her again.

With a shrug, she responded that he might, should he ever come through this forest again.

The next morning, Óttar continued on, out of the forest and into the next town, but the maiden was the only thought in his head. He found work and saved up some coin, and with it he bought many beautiful, fragrant, and exotic flowers, intent on returning to the forest and giving them to the maiden.

And so he did. After searching for some time, he found the maiden with the golden-brown hair once more and gave her all the flowers he'd bought for her and…she seemed unmoved. She voiced her thanks for the beautiful gifts, but seemed no more warmed to Óttar than she had the first time he'd seen her. They parted ways and Óttar returned to the town, still smitten with the maiden.

Years passed, and as Óttar worked and scrimped and saved, he would return to the forest with gifts of gold and amber and precious jewels. To each of these, the maiden voiced her thanks, but was no more moved than she'd been the first time Óttar had talked to her on the river-bank. But the man – for the years had aged him some, though the maiden seemed as young as ever – was not deterred, and Óttar was determined to find some way to win the maiden's heart.

Now, Óttar's frequent visits to the forest had garnered the notice of the land's native spirits, beings who had been acquainted with the maiden since she first took residence and felt pity for her plight. One such spirit, by the name of Hölderlin, had noticed a peculiar bauble hanging from the maiden's belt, and when Óttar next entered the forest with his newest gift, the spirit appeared to him.

"Perhaps," the spirit said, "instead of trying to win her over with expensive gifts, you should make her dinner, play her some music, and dance around the fire with her. Indeed, you should try jumping the fire with her, as that might impress her with your skill and bravery."

Thinking the advice over, Óttar thanked the spirit and gave it a piece of silver in recompense and headed down to the maiden's home. Along the way he caught some rabbits and gathered some firewood. Now, Óttar had no instrument – and wouldn't have known how to play one, in any case – but he'd always been complimented on his singing voice and he knew many a jaunty song.

When he came to the maiden's home he talked her into letting him prepare dinner for them. The maiden agreed, for while she felt no stirring of passion for Óttar, she'd found him to be a good and honest man, and a friendship had grown between the two over the many years he'd wooed her. The sun was slipping below the horizon by the time the food was ready, and so the two sat to eat by the fire Óttar had made outside the maiden's home. Once filled, Óttar began regaling her with stories and songs he knew, and after a while, the maiden felt like dancing. Around the fire she danced as Óttar sang, until he stood and joined her. Around and around the two of them danced to Óttar's songs, until they reached a point where a song exhorted "JUMP!" and Óttar took the maiden by the hand and the two leapt over the fire.

The talisman burned, old and dry as it was, and nothing of it remained when they landed. So exhilarating was the jump, that when Freyja looked at Óttar once again, she saw the kindness and persistence and the strength of the man before her, and her heart burned once more. She kissed him and revealed herself to the man, and took Óttar as a special lover.

For he had been the man that had returned her passion to her.

In Olden Days, of song and deeds
When gods and giants roamed,
There was a woman wise and skilled
In matters of love and magic.
"Gertrude" her name; match-making her trade,
Seeress and seiðkona her roles.
Her heart, however, hungered for a man,
A lively lad, called Klaus.

Sunna's Journey

To the tavern she would travel
Every evening without fail.
Despite her wisdom and her wiles
Her flirtation always faltered.
Klaus was none the wiser, oblivious every eve',
Bewitched by beer and frivolity.
So, her prayers ascended on pyres of sweetened smoke
Focused on Freyja's ears.

The Lady of Love did hear those pleas
And intended to answer the call
But when she observed the woman's love
Her heart was taken, too.
Seduce she did Gertrude's desire
Naming him hers for the night.
The seiðkona did see this treacherous act,
And despair filled her form.

In her hurt and her anger, vengeance did she vow
Upon she who had shattered her heart.
A talisman, Gertrude crafted; charms did she lay.
A vessel to fulfill her vow.
Returning to the tavern, she saw Freyja flirting more,
Upon her belt the talisman would hang.
The galdr spoken, the vengeance given
Gertrude fled that great hall.

Freyja flirted and fawned over Klaus,
But confusingly her heart went cold.
Perplexed and concerned, her passion had fled
And Freyja despaired its demise.
Wand'ring she traveled, worried for her heart;
Passion's panacea was not found.
Finally, to a forest she fled in dismay
Seeking loneliness' succor.

Many years passed and youth did she keep
As she was swallowed by love's cold silence.
Into the woodsa man came wand'ring,

Searching the land for a livelihood.
"Óttar" was his name, and work he did seek
A trade to build his life upon.
Near sunset he rested by a cool, clear stream
Seeking to soothe his aches.

A young lady he did see doing her laundry in the water
And his heart was instantly hers.
Cautiously he approached taking care not to frighten
For fear that she would flee from his sight.
Richly dressed she was, adorned in gold and amber,
A merchant's daughter she must be.
Óttar spoke, Óttar flirted; she did not warm to him.
But, this did not daunt the man.

Her laundry finished, she stood to leave;
Óttar was sad to see her go.
He pleaded that she stay, he prayed to see her more.
"Perhaps," she said, "if you pass this way again."
On the morrow, Óttar moved on
Traveling to a town nearby.
There he found work and earned a good wage,
Saving for a gift for the girl.

He would return to the forest, with his gifts for her
Hoping to win her affections.
He brought her flowers, he brought her gold,
He brought her beautiful jewels and amber.
To all of these, though, she seemed apathetic,
No more moved than before.
The seasons came and went, the Great Wheel turned,
But, still Óttar's passion burned.

In the forest there were otherswho would see his frequent visits
Spirits of wood, air, stone, and water.
One among their number, by the name of "Hölderlin"
Felt pity for their plight.
During their many meetings he'd spy a marv'lous bauble
Hanging from the fair maid's belt.

When next Óttar entered the deep and dark woods
He manifested before the man.

"Make her dinner, play some music melt her heart with
A delirious dance 'round a fire!" he advised
Óttar thanked the spirit and continued on his way
Collecting firewood and a brace of coneys.
Arriving at the maiden's home he announced he would make dinner
A request she could not refuse.
The fire high and their bellies filled,
Óttar regaled her with songs and stories.

'Round the fire the young maid frolicked
As Óttar serenaded her steps.
She bid him join, and blend their dance together
Jumping the fire in jubilance.
The talisman burned and her passion took flame
Warming her wintry heart.
Óttar and Freyja embraced each other fully
Their love over-flowing their reason.

It was Óttar's loyalty and persistent love
That broke the spell on Freyja's soul.
A heart once frozen burned freely again
And her passion poured forth into the World.

Midsummer

Sunna's might and main are at the height of their power at this time. Light and warmth suffuse the World on the Longest Day, and we celebrate the zenith of the Sun's year-long journey.

Working

Materials Needed:

- 1 wooden pole (~10 feet tall, ~4 inches wide)
- 1 12-spoked wooden wagon wheel
- 12 tea lights and holders

The centerpiece of this working is the Sun-Pole.

Ideally, you should acquire a long, thick log (a Scottish caber would be good, should you be able to get one) or tree trunk – primarily because something along the lines of a caber will be large enough (both in height and girth) to be visually impressive, but it will also provide enough wood for the ritual fires mentioned below. Traditionally, a caber measures around four inches in diameter and ten feet in height, so should an actual caber not be possible to obtain, you should be able to find something along those lines in your local home improvement store or lumber-yard. As well, the wagon-wheel to be placed on top of the pole can also most likely be found at your local home improvement store or from a variety of online retailers.

Once you have acquired the pole and wheel you will need to carve the pole with runes. Since the Sun-Pole serves as a focus and store-house for the Grove's (or individual ritualist's) *hamingja* and *wyrd*, the Kindreds' blessings, and Sunna's *main*, I suggest the runes *ehwaz*, *mannaz*, *perthro*, and *sowilo* – for partnership, humanity (in the senses of both individual personhood and community), luck, and the Sun. Two columns of *mannaz* should be inscribed from top to bottom, spaced evenly around the pole. Two columns of *sowilo* runes will oppose the columns of *mannaz*, so that the runic-columns alternate. Four rows of *ehwaz* should be evenly spaced along the height of the pole, and where the rows intersect the columns, the *ehwaz* runes will be separated from the *mannaz* and *sowilo* by a *perthro* on each side of the vertical runes. As you inscribe the runes, you should sing their names or root sounds – "eh", "mah", "puh", and "suh", respectively – focusing on charging the runes as you sing and carve them (of course, focus on safety first and foremost).

You will need to affix the tea light holders to the wheel on the outer rim at the end of each of the twelve spokes. And the wheel itself will need to be fixed temporarily to the top of the pole – how you do this will depend on the type of pole you use. *Temporarily* is the key-word, as once the ritual is over the pole will be taken down and sawed into five sections. You will make each cut above each row of *mannaz* runes, with enough space left so that the runes are left unmarred. Four of these sections will be used to build the ritual fires of Loaf-Fest, Gleichentag, Dises, and Yule, respectively. The fifth section, the top section, will be sawed in half prior to the Yule ritual and shaped into the Yule Log – but we will cover that in the section on Yule. The previous Yule Log (should the ritualist(s) have already performed the above Yule rite) will be used to build the ritual fire for this rite.

Prior to the beginning of the Solstice rite the tea lights will be lit and placed within their holders on the wagon-wheel symbolizing Sunna's light shining down from the top of the celestial vault.

Variation for Solitaries: Not much alteration needs to be made, though Solitaries may decide to use a smaller pole (both in height and girth).

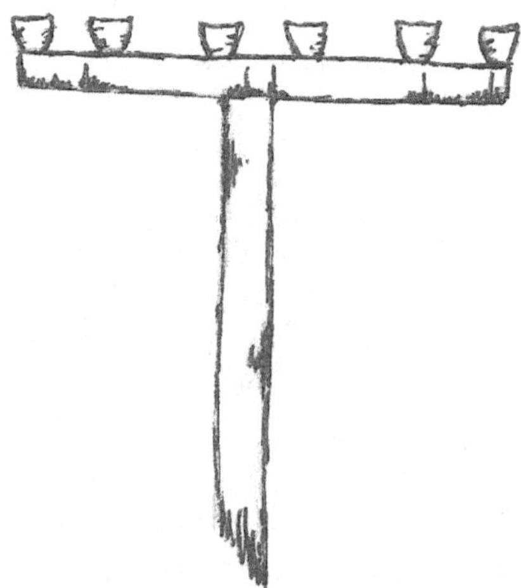

The Wheel & Pole

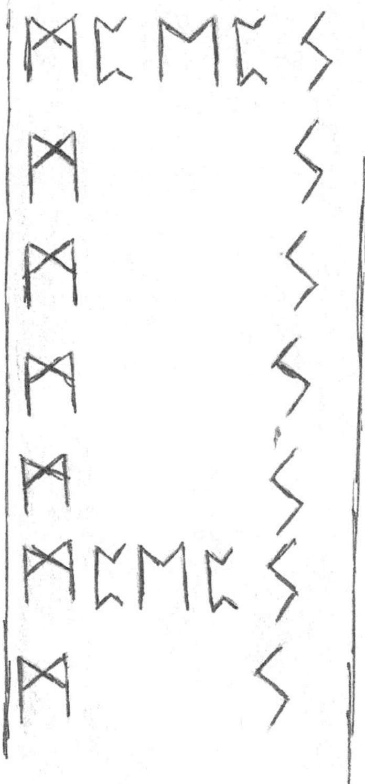

The Runic Inscription

Script

Initiation of the Rite

[Ring bells three times to signal beginning of the rite.]

Outdweller Entreaty

To those whose voices do not harmonize with our own, whose purposes may be at cross with our own, accept this token of treaty and leave our working be. *[give a peace-token]*

Purification

[cense and asperse to purify the Folk]

Honoring the Earth Mother

The Children of the Earth call out to Blessed Jorð - Birther of Storms, Consort of the Shaper, Mother of All. We who walk upon you, who take sustenance from you, who find comfort and rest within your bosom, remember you this day. *[give offering]* May you find this offering acceptable, for it is given in love and gratitude. Earth Mother, accept this offering!

Opening Statement

As our ancestors once did, so we do today, and so our children will do in the future. Children of Earth, we are here to honor the Kindreds on this, the Summer Solstice, when the Day is longest and brightest, when all beings rejoice in the victorious, effulgent glory of Blessed Lady Sunna. So let us join together as one folk to make our offerings in joy and reverence.

Opening Prayer

The skull of Mighty Ymir stretches out above us.

The bones of Mighty Ymir support the land about us.
The blood of Mighty Ymir flows under and around us.
All things are of His flesh,
Our wyrds woven together,
May we pray with a good fire.

Inspiration

Worlds-renowned Bragi, silver-tongued skald of the Halls of Asgarð, you who delight the gods with wit, wisdom, and a well-turned phrase; I pray that you find this offering acceptable *[give offering]* and that you will bless our speech with honeyed words. Praise and thanks be upon you.

(Re)Creating the Cosmos

In the primal times, the Great Hrímthurs was slain and quartered by the Sons of Búri: his Skull became the Sky, his Blood became the Sea, his Body became the Land. And from his Flesh grew a Great Tree, which connected all of the Worlds. May we recreate that Holy Sacrifice this day as we emulate the ordering of the worlds.

[hallow the Hallows by censing and aspersing them]

As well, we hallow the Sun-Pole, a symbol and trove of our Grove's wyrd and hamingja, making it sacred once more for the coming year.

[the Sun-Pole is hallowed by censing and aspersing just like the Hallows]

Grove Attunement

[perform the Two Powers meditation, afterwards say:]

We are shaped from driftwood at the Shore of the Worlds,
Grown from the Land,
Washed in the Sea,
Dried by the Sky.

We are tied together by the gifts of the Three Brothers,
By the weavings of the Nornir.
May we be just and true to each other.
May our worship be pious and pure.
Verði það svo.

The Gates

See now in your mind's eye a summer forest – the canopy is an explosion of green leaves and arboreal flowers in bloom. Birds sing and animals move through the underbrush. At the center of the forest stands an immense, cyclopean tree. Among the Tree's crown of verdant leaves, you can see the silhouette of an immense hawk. Occasionally it flaps its wings, and a moment later a cool breeze reaches you, brushing pleasantly across your skin. Among the Tree's massive roots, in the dark gaps and crevices between them, you sometimes see the slithering form of a snake or serpent; but only for the briefest of moments, before its scaly hide is gone.

You see movement among the branches and along the trunk of the Tree itself, and after a few moments the movement resolves into the form of a squirrel. This is Ratatosk – "Rat-Tooth" – one of the Great Tree's primary inhabitants, a gossip and courier and go-between for all who reside within the Tree's orbit.

Insightful and agile, Ratatosk. Honored Scurrier and Chatterer and Forager, you who know all the branches and roots of the World Tree. You who bear messages between Hawk, Hart, and Wyrm, we call out to you this day. In return for this offering we give in your honor, join your power with ours, so that we might open the Gates Between the Worlds!

[give offering and open the Gates: pull the Two Powers into your hands, feeling the fire and water mix, and draw a clockwise triangle over the Well, saying:]

May this well be the Triple Well.

[draw a triangle over the Fire, saying:]

May this fire be Bifrost's Undying Flame.

[draw a triangle over the Tree, saying:]

May this tree be mighty Yggdrasil, rising high and low before me.

[see the three triangles – water, fire, and growing wood – hang before you in the air and then come together in a valknot, while declaring:]

Latið opna hliðin! Let the Gates be opened!

Forfeður Offering

Blessed Forfeður, you who came before us, you who bore us, you who helped to shape the path that lies ahead. Ancient Wise; Honored Einherjar; You Countless Masses who toiled in obscurity but upon whose backs our society is built. Meet us at the boundaries. Join us at our Sacred Hearth and be warmed by our good fire. Aid us and guide us as we walk the Elder Ways. Forfeður, accept this offering! *[give offering]*

Landvættir Offering

Noble Vættir, you who inhabit this Land, who lurk in stone and tree and river. Those of the primal wilds, those of the tilled and planted field, those of cobbled stones and bricked-walls: hear our call. May you join us by our fire, may you share your bounties with us as we share ours with you. Meet us at the boundaries. Join us at our Sacred Hearth and be warmed by our good fire. Aid us and guide us as we walk the Elder Ways. Blessed Vættir, accept this offering! *[give offering]*

Guðir Offering

Shining Guðir, you who shaped the Cosmos, you who guard and guide the World's wyrd, you who teach us and bless us with bounty. May your radiance light our hall, may your warmth stoke our fire, and may your presence alongside us this day make it that much more joyous. Meet us at the boundaries. Join us at our Sacred Hearth and be warmed by our good fire. Aid us and guide us as we walk the Elder Ways. Shining Guðir, accept this offering! *[give offering]*

Key Offering

[tell Summer Solstice story/poem]

Golden One; Giver of Life, Light, and Warmth. Blessed Sunna, we honor you.

We call out to you, Shining One. You who race through the Heavens – day after day, year after year – giving light and warmth to all of the Nine Worlds. You give so much and receive so little in return for your effort. Blessed Lady, we give you these gifts and pray that you find them acceptable. Sunna, accept our offerings!

Omen

[make an offering to the Norns, saying:]

Wise Sisters, Tenders of the Great Tree, Weavers of That-Which-Is and That-Which-Is-Becoming. Accept this offering, please, and let me peer into your Sacred Well.

[take the omens, preferably with runes, and the seer for this rite will ask four questions:

Have our offerings been accepted?
What do the Forfeður give in return?
What do the Vættir give in return?
What do the Guðir give in return?

Calling for, Hallowing, and Affirmation of the Blessings

Holy Ones, we have given in friendship and love, so that you might give in return. We ask that you give us the Blessed Waters: the Waters of Wyrd, the Waters of Wisdom, the Waters of Life!

Mighty Ones, give us the Waters!

Noble Ones, give us the Waters!

Shining Ones, give us the Waters!

[walk the pitcher of Water around the Sun-Pole three times, charging the Waters by intoning the runes associated with the specific Kindred's blessings during their part of the call-and-response, while pushing energy into the pitcher; when the Waters are charged, hold them up to the congregation, saying:]

Sjáið vatn lífsins!

Children of the Earth, before you is the holy cup. Do you wish to share in these blessings?

All: We do!

Then, as the waters are poured out, know that they hold blessings for you and this grove and this community. Work well with these blessings, Children of the Earth.

[pass out the Waters to the Folk; a portion of the Waters is sprinkled on the Sun-Pole while saying:]

May Sunna's light,
Main and might,
Fill this pole
With the Kindred's blessings
On this Hallowed Grove.

Thanking

[thank the assembled Kindreds in reverse order: Deities, Land-Spirits, and Ancestors]

Closing the Gates

Quick and chattering Ratatosk, we thank you for your aid this day, and ask one more boon from you, before you return to the branches of the Great Tree – join your might and main with ours as we close the Gates Between the Worlds.

[give an offering and close the Gates: draw the Two Powers back into your hands, feeling the water and fire turn to ice within you, drawing a counter-clockwise triangle over the Tree, saying:]

May this Tree be just a tree.

[draw a triangle over the Fire, saying:]

May this Fire be just flame.

[draw a triangle over the Well, saying:]

May this Well be just water.

[as you draw the triangles, see the them form from ice, hanging in the air by the Hallows; declare:]

Latið loka hliðunum! Let the Gates be Closed!

[clap your hands firmly together and see the icy triangles shatter, the cosmic powers keeping the Gates open dispersing; and say:]

Honored Ratatosk, we thank you.

Thanking Inspiration

Silver-tounged Bragi, skald of skalds, poet of poets, we thank you.

Thanking the Earth Mother

Jorð, beauteous and bountiful mother, we thank you.

Closing the Rite

Go now, Children of Earth, in peace with the blessings of the Kindred and a Fire in your Heart. This rite is ended.

Story & Poem

"Sunna's Respite"

This story is true.

In the Earliest of Days, after the Three Brothers had slaughtered and quartered the ur-etin, Ymir, the Sun and the Moon were created from the etin's eyes by a surviving Jotun named "Mundilfari." Mundilfari had taken the eyes south to where the border of Muspelheim met the Miðgarð and infused them with sparks of that fiery realm before casting them into the sky. "Sunna" and "Máni" he named them, and they were as children to him.

But cunning Oðinn, fearing reprisals from the Jotnar despite their acceptance of weregild from the Three Brothers, set two wolves lose in the Heavens, to chase the Sun and Moon, in order make sure that they kept to their duties and had no time to possibly plot revenge. And even though Sunna and her brother felt nothing but friendliness toward the Æsir – after all, if not for their act, the siblings would never had existed – they couldn't help but feel some annoyance at the constant pursuit loosed upon them.

And so this went: day after day, week after week, year after year, age after age.

But one summer's day, as Sunna kept her pace through the Heavens, she desired to rest, even if it was only the briefest of respites. However, her heels were always harried by the wolf set after her: Sköll, one of Fenrir's get. Everywhere in the Nine Worlds she ran, looking for some refuge or haven where the wolf could not get her.

To the Mountains of Jotunheim she ran, but the wolf found her there.

To the icy wastes of Niflheim she ran, but the wolf nearly hamstrung her there.

To the burning deserts of Muspelheim she fled, but even among the fire and the sand the wolf followed.

Across the western waves to Vanaheim she traveled, but the wolf braved the waters and followed in her wake.

Despondent, tired, and fearful, Sunna turned her eyes toward the tallest object in all the cosmos: the World Tree. She raced across the worlds toward the Tree that stood at the center of them all, swiftly climbing the trunk and branches once she arrived. Sköll was not far from her heels, and growled and howled his frustration as the young goddess climbed beyond his reach.

"Get down here!" he growled angrily.

And from up in the branches, Sunna responded: "No! I desire to rest!"

"There is no rest for you," the wolf howled back. "Running is your lot, not resting on your hind-quarters."

"I run all year-round," Sunna replied, "I work myself to near death keeping the worlds lit and keeping myself from your jaws. I deserve at least a few moments of rest!"

The wolf simply growled angrily in response.

"Now, what's all this?" came a voice higher up in the tree. Sunna looked up and saw a squirrel peering down at her from a few branches higher. "You're not supposed to be up here. Are you?"

"Please, Sir Squirrel, that dreadful wolf seeks to run me down and eat me. Can I not have some respite in your tree to regain my strength and breath?"

The squirrel rubbed his eyes blearily and yawned. "I don't know…" he said. "You being up here is disturbing my sleep and all…and I need it to be alert and quick when I'm foraging at night."

"But, I am the Sun," the young goddess said, thinking quickly. "If you help me, I will give you my ægis to forage during the day, when it'll be safer for you to do so!"

The squirrel considered the offer for a moment or two, all while the wolf's growling from his spot among the Tree's roots became louder. "Well, that would be nice," the squirrel finally said. "But, I don't know, you're really not supposed to be up here…"

"Please," Sunna begged, "isn't there something that I can do?"

The squirrel scratched his chin. "Well…if I'm going to be up during the day, there are two animals awake then, too, who could really harm me: the fox and the owl."

"Fine. I will make sure that they are only awake from now on when my brother is running his route."

The squirrel smiled. "Excellent!" He paused a moment in thought. "Stay here," he said, and then scurried off out of sight.

The squirrel was gone a good long while, and during that time Sunna tried to rest as much as she could among the branches of the World Tree. All while Sköll sat beneath her on the ground, growling and howling and barking at her to come down. Finally, the squirrel returned.

"Where did—" Sunna began to ask, but the squirrel held up a paw to silence her, before pointing towards the roots of the Tree. Sunna looked down at the ground and was surprised to see the roots moving and a hole opening near their base. The wolf backed away from the hole cautiously, his hackles rising and a deep growl coming from him as three cloaked women emerged. They spoke briefly to the wolf, one of them pointing up toward where Sunna was perched in the branches of the Tree, and then returned the way they'd arrived – the hole closing up behind them. Sköll glared up at the Tree for a brief moment then stalked off into the woods.

Stunned, Sunna turned to the squirrel. "What did you do? Where did you go?"

"I called in a debt," the squirrel said simply. "But there are conditions: once a year – on this day – you must return here to rest, with your golden light shining brightly from the top of the World Tree for an entire day. Also, once a year – on the day opposite this one – you must descend into the Underworld and spend the day with the Three Sisters. For they desire your company, as well. The rest of the time, though, you must spend running – as is your allotted wyrd."

Beaming brightly from ear to ear, Sunna swept the squirrel up and hugged him as tightly as was safe. Thanking the squirrel for his assistance, Sunna spent the rest of the day relaxing and lounging and letting her tired body recuperate – all from her safe spot at the Top of the World.

In earliest days, after the divine Brothers had butchered
And quartered the ur-etin, Ymir,
The giant's eyes were made into the glorious Sun
And her shining, silv'ry brother
Mundilfari, their father named them "Sunna" and "Máni"
Investing them with the main of Muspelheim.
But, wary Oðinn fearing reprisals, set wolves
To chase them 'cross the Heavens.

And so this went: day after day, week after week
Age following lengthy age.
The wolves were for naught for the children were friendly
To all Æsir and their kin.
The pursuit was tiring, it's fruit: annoyance
For the children felt unduly oppressed.
But still they ran 'round the Dome of the Sky
Sacrificing rest for relationship.

One midsummer's day as Sunna kept pace,
She desired the briefest of respites.
However, her heels were harried by the wolf,
Sköll, of Fenrir's get.
Nowhere she found haven in any o' the Worlds,
None where the wolf could not find her.

Sunna's Journey

Desperate and tired she fled all about
Seeking somewhere to rest.

To the Mountains of Jotunheim she made like the wind,
But found the wolf waiting for her.
The icy wastes of Niflheim gave no respite;
The wolf nearly hamstrung her there.
To the deserts of Muspelheimshe fled quite desp'rate,
But still she was found 'mong the sands.
West to Vanaheim she traveled 'cross the waves,
But the wolf followed in her wake.

Despondent and tired, fearful and desperate
Sunna turned her eyes to the Tree.
Tallest in the Cosmos, 'twas the Center of All
About which the Worlds did dance.
Swiftly up the trunk, she took to the branches;
Sköll's breath hot on her heels.
Tired, exhausted - she eased on a limb
Resting far from his reach.

"Get down here!" he growled,
Voicing his vexation.
But Sunna resisted, reclining on the branches.
"I desire to rest!" she retorted.
The wolf growled angrily; frustrated, annoyed!
At the goddess beyond his grasp.
The two traded words,both testy and sharp;
Neither would choose to concede.

A chittering was heard, coming from high in the Tree
The branches bounced with movement.
Out of the foliage a squirrel's form appeared,
Barking his annoyance at both.
Sunna spoke up, pressing for sanctuary
Asking the squirrel for his mercy.
The squirrel was uncertain, being sleepy n' not-quick,
He had to think over her words.

Her day-time ægis she offered to him,
In return for rest in the Tree.
The squirrel seemed thoughtful, but not sold on her offer,
Presenting two problems he had.
"During the day, the fox and the owl do roam,
Fixed on feasting on me."
Her word she gave that under Máni's watch only
They'd hunt from that day hence.

Excited, appreciative, the squirrel disappeared,
Bounding off into the branches.
Sunna was alone, on her branch solitary,
With the wolf waiting below.
Sköll kept growling, goading her descent,
Off'ring threats to make her drop down.
Nervous, unsure, nestled on a branch
She awaited the squirrel's arrival.

When the squirrel came back, quickly he shushed her,
Pointing to the roots of the Tree.
Move they did, making an opening
Deep down into the earth.
Three women emerged - wrapped in cloaks, faces hidden
The wolf backed fearfully from them.
Their words she heard not, but Sunna did smile
When the wolf sourly slunk off.

When the women retreated back among the roots,
Sunna spoke to the squirrel.
The squirrel then described the deal he had made
With the Three Sisters below:
Once a year on this day she would ascend the Great Tree,
Resting at the Roof of the World.
But one day six months after, she'd descend to the Norns
Gracing them with her golden light.

Jubilant Sunna beamed and thanked him joyfully,

Hugging the squirrel to her bosom.
Safe on the Tree's boughs at the Top of the World,
Sunna rested and relaxed.

Loaf-Fest

The first harvest of the year, a time for the celebration of plenty and the victories of the previous months. The crops, whether they're actual or figurative, are brought in and we as a community revel in their bounty.

Working

Materials Needed:

- Torc (or other suitable "trophy")

The Loaf-Fest working is two-fold: the Games that are held prior to the Rite and the blessing of and presentation of the Champion's Torc. The Games themselves can be held at any point between Midsummer and Loaf-Fest, though the closer to the ritual that they occur the better (including the day of, just prior to the ritual taking place). The blessing of the Champion's Torc is fairly simple, and the most difficult part may be acquiring a torc. There are plenty of "celtic jewelry" websites online (Crafty Celts[10] is one of the better merchants) from which you can buy a torc, but what it comes down to is what you want to have. A torc is the recommended example, but honestly, the object can be whatever you and your Grove decide that you want to use (with only minor changes to the wording of the blessing).

Now, one may ask, "Why are we even holding these games? What is the point?"

It's a good question.

In modern Neo-Paganism, the most common form of this holiday is that of *Lughnassadh*[11], based on the traditional Gaelic holiday known as "Lammas" in Britain. In Celtic mythology, the festival was begun by the god Lugh in memory of his foster-mother, Tailtiu, who died of exhaustion after clearing the fields of Ireland so that they could be farmed. During the festival, there was a great

[10] www.craftycelts.com

[11] Pronounced "Loo-nah-sah"

funeral feast and games were held in celebration of the memory of the god's foster-mother.

But, among the Norse, we see similar sorts of celebration during this time of the year (during which the previous grain stores would have become very low and the first harvests of the year were coming in from the fields). In Iceland, we see horse-fights being held at this time of the year[12]; as well, there were usually celebrations of victory[13] throughout the cultural orbit of the Norse, as this marked the end of the war/viking[14] season. So the use of ritual games – such as wrestling, archery, stone-throws, foot-races, etc. – is more than appropriate to mark this time of year as one of victorious celebration.

The types of games that you hold depend on what you and your Folk feel are appropriate and safe (after all, someone accidentally breaking their collar-bone can put a damper on the festivities). But, as mentioned above, such events as simple wrestling, archery, or foot-races can be done quite economically and safely. Be creative and experiment. Remember, this is for the enjoyment of the Folk, so see what they want to compete in.

Variation for Solitaries: For a solitary, giving oneself a "blue ribbon" for excelling at games in which you're the only contestant might seem…pointless (and, honestly, a little sad). Instead, one will likely want to adapt the text of the liturgy to have the torc (or whatever object is used) be a talisman to imbue the wearer with strength, might, and excellence. The text of the charm need not be changed, but the wording of the rest of the text should reflect this change of intent.

---

[12]Gundarsson, *Our Troth, Volume 2: Living the Troth*, pp. 401-405

[13] *Ibid*

[14] The Old Norse word "viking" refers directly to overseas exploration, but grew to connote trading/piracy/raiding expeditions.

Script

Processional

[Insert song/chant here]

Outdweller Entreaty

To those whose voices do not harmonize with our own, whose purposes may be cross with ours, accept this token of treaty and leave our working be. *[give offering]*

Purification

[cense and asperse to purify the Folk]

Honoring the Earth Mother

The Children of the Earth call out to Blessed Jorð - Birther of Storms, Consort of the Shaper, Mother of All. We who walk upon you, who take sustenance from you, who find comfort and rest within your bosom, remember you this day. *[give offering]* May you find this offering acceptable, for it is given in love and gratitude. Earth Mother, accept this offering!

Opening Statement

[ring bells three times to signal beginning of the rite]

As our ancestors once did, so we do today, and so our children will do in the future. Children of Earth, we are here to honor the Kindreds on this, the first harvest of the season, Loaf-Feast. On this day we commemorate the marriage of Thor and Sif, god of the thunder-storm and goddess of the bountiful fields. Because of their union, we have food in our bellies and reason to celebrate. So let us join together as one folk to make our offerings in joy and reverence.

Opening Prayer

The skull of Mighty Ymir stretches out above us.
The bones of Mighty Ymir support the land about us.
The blood of Mighty Ymir flows under and around us.
All things are of His flesh,
Our wyrds woven together,
May we pray with a good fire.

Inspiration

Blessed Sága, Mistress of the Sunken Benches, weaver of stories and chanter of tales, we call out to you. Please stand with us with us this day as we invite the Kindreds in frið and kinship. Accept this offering given in gratitude and honor, *[give offering]* and share with us your ability to enthrall an audience this day. Praise and thanks be upon you.

(Re)Creating the Cosmos

In the primal times, the Great Hrímthurs was slain and quartered by the Sons of Búri: his Skull became the Sky, his Blood became the Sea, his Body became the Land. And from his Flesh grew a Great Tree, which connected all of the Worlds. May we recreate that Holy Sacrifice this day as we emulate the ordering of the worlds.

[hallow the Hallows by censing and aspersing them]

Grove Attunement

[perform the Two Powers meditation]

We are shaped from driftwood at the Shore of the Worlds,
Grown from the Land,
Washed in the Sea,
Dried by the Sky.
We are tied together by the gifts of the Three Brothers,
By the weavings of the Nornir.
May we be just and true to each other.

May our worship be pious and pure.
Verði það svo.

The Gates

See now in your mind's eye the mighty ramparts of a great, walled city. Built of cyclopean blocks of granite, the wall stands strong and tall, capable of rebuffing any host who might dare to breach it. But, along the ramparts walks the figure of a man, his gaze cast ever outward beyond the city's bounds. He is tall and of a noble bearing, with long, white hair that resembles the foam of the sea in its color and motion; his skin is white, as well, pale like alabaster and one could almost mistake him for an albino.

He wears the raiment of a guardsman and carries with him two horns: one clasped in his hand and worn from use, the other slung by his side and pristine as it awaits its purpose. The man squints towards the horizon where he sees figures, small as ants at that distance – moving toward the city. He cocks an ear toward them, nods satisfactorily after a moment, and peals out a call on his weathered horn.

The gates of this great city open and close upon the signal of this man – this noble gatekeeper and vigilant watchman – known as Heimdall.

We call upon him now: Noble Heimdall, Eagle-Eye, Blower of the Gjallarhorn, we call out to you and ask that you open the Gates for us. We come in frið and friendship, and seek to commune with the Kindreds. Accept this offering and join your powers with ours, Vigilant Watchman of the Gods, as we open the Gates Between the Worlds.

[give offering and open the Gates: pull the Two Powers into your hands, feeling the fire and water mix, and draw a clockwise triangle over the Well, saying:]

May this well be the Triple Well.

[draw a triangle over the Fire, saying:]

May this fire be Bifrost's undying flame.

[draw a triangle over the Tree, saying:]

May this tree be mighty Yggdrasil, rising high and low before me.

[see the three triangles – water, fire, and growing wood – hang before in the air and then come together in a valknot, while declaring:]

Latið opna hliðin! Let the Gates be opened!

Forfeður Offering

Blessed Forfeður, you who came before us, you who bore us, you who helped to shape the path that lies ahead. Ancient Wise; Honored Einherjar; You Countless Masses who toiled in obscurity, but upon whose backs our society is built. Meet us at the boundaries. Join us at our Sacred Hearth and be warmed by our good fire. Aid us and guide us as we walk the Elder Ways. Forfeður, accept this offering! *[give offering]*

Landvættir Offering

Noble Vættir, you who inhabit this Land, who lurk in stone and tree and river. Those of the primal wilds, those of the tilled and planted field, those of cobbled stones and bricked-walls: hear our call. May you join us by our fire, may you share your bounties with us as we share ours with you. Meet us at the boundaries. Join us at our Sacred Hearth and be warmed by our good fire. Aid us and guide us as we walk the Elder Ways. Blessed Vættir, accept this offering! *[give offering]*

Guðir Offering

Shining Guðir, you who shaped the Cosmos, you who guard and guide the World's wyrd, you who teach us and bless us with bounty. May your radiance light our hall, may your warmth stoke our fire, and may your presence alongside us this day make it that much more pleasant. Meet us at the boundaries. Join us at our Sacred Hearth and be warmed by our good fire. Aid us and guide us as we walk the Elder Ways. Shining Guðir, accept this offering! *[give offering]*

Key Offering

[tell Loaf-Feast story or poem]

Thunderer and Golden-Hair, you whose union is our blessing and bounty, we remember and honor you this day. Your marriage ensures a good harvest – of grain, of work, of life – and so, we thank you and we honor you. Blessed Thor and Sif, givers of great bounty, we pray you find these offerings acceptable. Thor, Sif: accept our offerings!

Omen

[make an offering to the Norns, saying:]

Wise Sisters, Tenders of the Great Tree, Weavers of That-Which-Is and That-Which-Is-Becoming. Accept this offering, please, and let me peer into your Sacred Well.

[take the omens, preferably with runes]

The seer for this rite will ask four questions:
Have our offerings been accepted?
What do the Forfeður give in return?
What do the Vættir give in return?
What do the Guðir give in return?

Calling for, Hallowing, and Affirmation of the Blessings

Holy Ones, we have given in friendship and love, so that you might give in return. Kindreds, we ask that you give us the Blessed Waters: the Waters of Wyrd, the Waters of Wisdom, the Waters of Life!

Mighty Ones, give us the Waters!

Noble Ones, give us the Waters!

Shining Ones, give us the Waters!

Sjáið vatn lífsins!

Children of the Earth, before you is the holy cup. Do you wish to share in these blessings?

All: We do!

Then, as the waters are poured out, know that they hold blessings for you and this grove and this community. Work well with these blessings, Children of the Earth.

[pass out the Waters to the Folk; a portion is kept for the Working]

Working

[take the Pitcher and sprinkle the Champion's Torc with some of the remaining Waters and sign the runes Thurisaz and Berkano, while saying:]

The strength of giants/ the fertile fields
Fill this ring of champion's might

The strength of giants/ the fertile fields
Fill the wearer, day and night.

May the might and main of the Thunderer, winner of the hand of Sif, be imparted upon the wearer of this Torc for one year.

[give the Torc to the winner of the games held before the ritual]

Thanking
[thank the assembled Kindreds in reverse order: Deities, Land-Spirits, and Ancestors]

Closing the Gates

Noble Watchman, Guardian upon the Walls of Asgarð, Vigilant Heimdall: we call out to you once more. Give us the power of your unrivalled sight, give us the range of your inescapable hearing. Give us your authority to close the Gates Between the Worlds.

[give an offering to the Gatekeeper and close the Gates: draw the Two Powers back into your hands, feeling the water and fire turn to ice within you, drawing a counter-clockwise triangle over the Tree, saying:]

May this Tree be just a tree.

[draw a triangle over the Fire, saying:]

May this Fire be just flame.

[draw a triangle over the Well, saying:]

May this Well be just water.

[as you draw the triangles, see the them form from ice, hanging in the air by the Hallows; declare:]

Latið loka hliðunum! Let the Gates be Closed!

[clap your hands firmly together and see the icy triangles shatter, the cosmic powers keeping the Gates open dispersing; and say:]

Vigilant Heimdall, we thank you.

Thanking Inspiration

Soul-stirring, story-weaving, audience-enchanting Sága: we thank you.

Thanking the Earth Mother

Jorð, beauteous and bountiful mother, we thank you.

Closing the Rite

Go now, Children of Earth, in peace with the blessings of the Kindred and a Fire in your Heart. This rite is ended.

Story & Poem

"The Nuptial Games"

This story is true.

In the Early Days, after the Cosmos had been re-formed from the body of Ymir and the Guðir were still quite young, it happened that Thor was off on a hunting trip. In those days, the Jotun's-Bane had no hammer with which to slay his foes, instead, using only his powerful hands to wring the life from them. But, he enjoyed the sport of hunting Jotnar with but his bare hands, despite the difficulty of it.

As he traveled through the wilds, he happened upon a farmstead, its fields filled with rippling, golden wheat and its lawns filled with all kinds of livestock. He was stopped in his tracks, though, by the sound of singing. Entranced by the golden voice – so sweet that it must have been dipped in honey – Thor tracked it back to its source: a golden-locked young woman who was out touring the fields.

Thor was immediately taken with the young woman, who named herself as "Sif" when the red-haired god introduced himself. Hearing her simply speak her name was as beautiful as when she sung, so the mighty giant-slayer thought, and he knew then and there that he had to have her as his. He asked for her hand, but Sif was reluctant, despite the look in her eyes that said she found the hunter enticing, as well.

"There are two others who wish to have me as their wife," she said. "Already, I know not how to choose between the two of them. How would choose with a third involved?"

His mind working quickly, Thor blurted out: "A contest! Yes, a series of trials. Who ever comes out as the over-all champion, he shall be your husband!"

Sif thought for a moment and then nodded. "Yes, that sounds acceptable. I will agree to a series of trials." With that decided, she sent out word for the other two suitors to come to her farmstead.

As word travels quickly – even back then it did – the whole host of the Guðir arrived with the two suitors. Both were known to the red-haired hunter: Freyr, son of Njorð, and Loki, son of Laufey. As the Guðir assembled to watch the trials, the suitors prepared themselves for the first contest: horse-fighting.

The suitors were given the skins of mustangs, so that they might change their hamr and combat each other in an appropriate form, and battled each other one-on-one. Each fought valiantly, but Njorð's son was declared the winner, having emerged victorious in two out of the three matches.

The second test was one of aim and skill, and the suitors took up their places on the archery field. First they shot at targets on bales of hay, then they shot at geese, and finally they shot at flies. Each time, it was the mighty hunter of Jotnar that hit his targets dead-on – even the fly was cut in twain by the steel head of his arrow. Freyr congratulated the giant-slayer on his skill, but Loki simply grumbled his mounting displeasure.

The final test was administered by the Wise One, Oðinn, and was deemed to be a test of wits. Freyr was questioned first, and he was asked what was the greatest gift gained by the truce between Áss and Van. "Peace," the young Van replied. "An end to fighting!" The All-Father shook his head and replied: "Peace and war come and go, the greatest gift we gained was Kvasir's Blood."

Loki, the Old Man's blood-brother, was questioned next, and he was asked what the first thing was. "That is easy!" Laufey's son replied: "Muspelheim was the first thing to blaze into existence, after it was Niflheim." The All-Father shook his head once again. "There was one thing before it: the 'No-Thing' – the Void of Ginnungagap." Loki frowned and spat out a curse at the Wise One, stomping off in anger.

Finally, it was Thor's turn to answer the High One's riddle. "What is it that ripens the grain?" he was asked. The giant-slayer thought long and hard, before answering. "It is…the Fire of the Heavens and…and the Waters of the Sky!" The Old Man smiled and nodded his head. "Verily, it is."

With a cheer, the Guðir hailed Thor as the winner of Sif's hand and plans were immediately made to have the two wed. But, that night, angered and resentful, Loki stole into Sif's bed-chamber and cut the long, lustrous golden locks from the goddess' head. When she woke in the morning, Sif was distraught and inconsolable, fearful that her groom would no longer want to wed her. It did not take the Guðir long to figure out who among them committed the vicious deed, and with his life threatened by the furious bridge-groom, Loki was quick to make recompense.

After all, the son of Laufey had been feeling spiteful, not suicidal.

Quickly, Loki descended into Svartalfheim where the Dvergar dwelled deep within the Earth. Bartering with the subterranean smiths, he quickly made a deal that would not only assuage Sif, but hopefully win back the good-will of the other Guðir, as well. Returning on the morning of the wedding ceremony, Loki made straight for Sif's chambers, presenting the goddess with a wig made from spun-gold. Sif was delighted by the piece, and as she was presented to her groom, she shone like the golden face of Sunna herself. But, Loki's generosity was not done there, at the feast that followed he presented the bridge-groom with a mighty steel hammer that would command the very Fire of the Heavens – along with gloves and a belt with which to wield the great weapon. And he gave others gifts to restore his favor among the Guðir: he presented Freyr with a great mechanical boar sheathed in gold-leaf and a wondrous ship that would fold small enough to fight in the Van's pocket; and to the All-Father himself Loki gave a spear that never missed its target and a ring that produced nine copies of itself on every ninth night.

With that, Loki was forgiven his rash and vicious act, and welcomed back into the fold of the Guðir, where he joined in the celebration of the marriage of Thor and Sif. Their union was a joyous one and their main spread far on the summer rains, filling the Land with growth and fertility, bringing prosperity to all its Folk.

In Early Days, when the Deities were young,
And the Worlds still fresh from shaping,
It occurred that Thor, Thunderer, Jotun's bane,
Happened to be out a-hunting.
No Hammer he had then, for he used his hands
To throttle trolls and giants.
Despite the difficulty, he delighted in the sport,
Laughing as he laid them to rest.

Through trackless wilds he wandered, joyful,
Happy to be trav'ling the Worlds.
A golden voice, though, glided to his ear
Bewitching him with its beauty.
"So delightful and sweet! Surely," he thought,
"It had to have been dipped in honey!"
Led by his ears, entranced by the song,
Thor tirelessly tracked its source.

A farmstead he found, its fields rippling
With golden grains and livestock.
Wand'ring the wheat fields, he found a young woman
Whose song enthralled his ears.
Golden hair she had, shining like Sunna;
She was a beauty like none he'd seen.
"Sif" she named herself to the spell-bound god,
Her speech as lovely as her song.

His heart taken by her beauty and her kind, gentle nature
Thor hastily asked for her hand.
"Two others there are who wish me their wife,"
Sif hesitantly said.
"Already I know not how to choose 'tween the two;
How could I choose with a third?"
"A contest!" Thor countered,

"Test us with a series o' trials!"

Silent for some moments, Sif signaled her consent:
Trials would determine who won.
Word traveled swiftly, sweeping through the land
The Host of the Guðir hurried to watch.
The other suitors soon arrived,
Their names known to Thor.
Njorð's son, Freyr, was the first, joined by
Loki, son of Laufey.

In the form of mustangs the three met in combat,
The first challenge championed by Freyr.
The second trial proved to be a test of true aim,
All three given archer's bows.
First they had to hit simple bales of hay,
Followed by geese 'n' buzzing flies.
Only the Jotun-hunter could hit all three,
Even the flies ended in twain.

Loki grumbled mightily as they met a final time,
Displeased at his poor performance.
Before the aged Wise One - the Runatyr, the Alfoðr
They stood for their final challenge.
The first to be tested was the handsome Freyr Ingvi,
To whom was set a sly riddle.
"What was the greatest gift that we all did gain
From the treaty between Áss and Van?"

"Peace!" Freyr answered, "An end to hostilities!"
But Oðinn simply shook his head.
"Blessed mead brewed from Kvasir's blood
Was the great boon won for all."
To Loki he turned, continuing the trial, asking,
"What was the first thing to exist?"
"Muspelheim and Niflheim! Fire and Ice!"
Loki crowed quite confidently.

His head shook again, and the Alfoðr frowned,

"Ginnungagap, the No-Thing, was before all."
Cursing and spitting, Loki stomped off
Leaving the field to the Thunderer.
"What is it that ripens the wheat?"
The grizzled sage asked his son.
"The Fire of Heavens, falling from on high…
And…the Waters of the Sky streaming down!"

The Old Man nodded, smiling immensely; "Verily it is," he said;
The Guðir hailed Thor the winner.
Preparations were made, and plans arranged,
To immediately have the two wed.
But, angered and resentful, Loki snuck into
Sif's silent bed-chamber that night.
Smiling cruelly, with scissors he did cut
The long, lustrous locks from her head.

In Dawn's rosy light, Sif was distraught
Lamenting the loss of her hair.
The Guðir did quickly venture forward a guess
As to who was responsible for the reaping.
Facing Thor's wrath, Loki sued for peace:
He'd been spiteful, not suicidal.
He promised recompense, to repay what he'd stolen
From the beautiful goddess of the grain.

Swiftly he descended to where the Dvergar dwelled
Within the halls of their home, Svartalfheim.
Loki bartered and dealed with the deep-dwelling smiths
Winning gifts of good-willing for the gods.
Returning on the morning of the marriage ceremony,
He hurried to deliver his presents.
To Sif he did give hair spun of gold,
More lustrous by far than her old locks.

The generosity continued as the feasting began,
Loki looking to mend hurt feelings.
To the mighty Thor he gave a great hammer of steel,
With a belt and gloves of bull-hide.

Blessed Freyr received a boar filled with gears 'n' gold-sheathed
And a folding ship that fit in his pocket.
Finally, to the Alfoðr: a spear with unerring aim,
And a ring that reproduced e'ry ninth night.

Delighted and grateful, the Guðir forgave him,
Inviting Loki to live with them once more.
And so went the marriage of mighty Thor 'n' blessed Sif,
The Thunderer 'n' She of the Golden Grain.

Gleichentag

The Dusk of the Year, we celebrate the second harvest at this time, giving thanks for all the bounties that the Kindreds have given to us, and coming together to share in the bonds of kin and kith.

Working

Materials Needed:

- Food
- Drink
- Friends

This Gleichentag ritual is most definitely one of thanksgiving. Between the first and second harvest festivals, it celebrates the not only the bounty of the Land itself, but the uniting effect that that bounty can have on the community. The working for the ritual, though, actually takes place after the ritual itself is finished during a communal meal or potluck. For this reason, it will be extremely helpful to inform the Folk ahead of time that bringing an item of food or drink to the ritual will be, if not completely required, a very good idea at the very least.

During the portion of the rite where the Blessings of the Kindreds are received by the Folk, some of the Waters will be sprinkled upon the food and drink brought, as well the dining area to be used after the rite will be aspersed. Once the meal has begun, the Folk are encouraged to voice their thanks for anything in the past year, to reconcile with one another (or other pertinent individuals in their life), and to meditate upon true wealth and bounty.

Variation for Solitaries: Prepare a meal for yourself, setting aside portions for the your ancestors and the spirits of the land. While you eat, think over the previous year and give thanks for all the boons that you've received. As well, consider those relationships which may be strained and how they may be fixed. If they can be, resolve to bury the hatchet with the other parties. When finished with the meal, dispose of the portions set aside for the ancestors and the spirits in a place suitable for offerings.

Script

Processional

[Insert song/chant here]

Outdweller Entreaty

To those whose voices do not harmonize with our own, whose purposes may be at cross with ours, accept this token of treaty and leave our working be. *[give offering]*

Purification

[cense and asperse to purify the Folk]

Opening Statement

[ring bells three times to signal beginning of the rite]

As our ancestors once did, so we do today, and so our children will do in the future. Children of Earth, we are here to honor the Kindreds on this, Gleichentag, the day when light and dark are of equal lengths. So let us join together as one folk to make our offerings in joy and reverence.

Opening Prayer

The skull of Mighty Ymir stretches out above us.
The bones of Mighty Ymir support the land about us.
The blood of Mighty Ymir flows under and around us.
All things are of His flesh,
Our wyrds woven together,
May we pray with a good fire.

Inspiration

Blessed Freyr Ingvi: Lord of Plenty and Protector of the Peace. We make you this offering *[give offering]* and ask that you inspire us to keep your frið-stead in our hearts, in our homes, and in our community. Praise and thanks be upon you, Freyr!

Honoring the Earth Mother

The Children of the Earth call out to Blessed Jorð - Birther of Storms, Consort of the Shaper, Mother of All. We who walk upon you, who take sustenance from you, who find comfort and rest within your bosom, remember you this day. *[give offering]* May you find this offering acceptable, for it is given in love and gratitude. Earth Mother, accept this offering!

(Re)Creating the Cosmos

In the primal times, the Great Hrímthurs was slain and quartered by the Sons of Búri: his Skull became the Sky, his Blood became the Sea, his Body became the Land. And from his Flesh grew a Great Tree, which connected all of the Worlds. May we recreate that Holy Sacrifice this day as we emulate the ordering of the worlds.

[hallow the Hallows while the Folk sing the "Portal Song"]

Grove Attunement

[perform the Two Powers meditation, afterwards say:]

We are shaped from driftwood at the Shore of the Worlds,
Grown from the Land,
Washed in the Sea,
Dried by the Sky.
We are tied together by the gifts of the Three Brothers,
By the weavings of the Nornir.
May we be just and true to each other.
May our worship be pious and pure.
Verði það svo.

The Gates

See now in your mind's eye the sandy expanse the marks the border between Land and Sea. White-capped waves flow up onto the beach as the tide reaches its height. Feel the spray of sea-water on your skin, the wind moves over and around you, the sounds of sea-birds in your ears. Not far off, you see a man standing on the beach, one foot on the dry sands, the other placed just so that when the tide rolls in it gets submerged. He has the look of an old sailor: sun-bleached hair, skin made tan and leathery from years of salt-spray and clear, sunny skies out on the open water. This is the Vanic Lord of the Seas, Njorð.

Njorð, father of Freyr and Freyja, Master-Sailor and Captain of the Waves, we call out to you this day and give you this offering [give offering]. In return, we simply ask that you join your power with ours, so that we might open the Gates Between the Worlds this day.

[give offering and open the Gates: pull the Two Powers into your hands, feeling the fire and water mix, and draw a clockwise triangle over the Well, saying:]

May this well be the Triple Well.

[draw a triangle over the Fire, saying:]

May this fire be Bifrost's undying flame.

[draw a triangle over the Tree, saying:]

May this tree be mighty Yggdrasil, rising high and low before me.

[see the three triangles – water, fire, and growing wood – hang before in the air and then come together in a valknot, while declaring:]

Latið opna hliðin! Let the Gates be opened!

Forfeður Offering

Blessed Forfeður, you who came before us, you who bore us, you who helped to shape the path that lies ahead. Ancient Wise; Honored Einherjar; You Countless Masses who toiled in obscurity, but upon whose backs our society is built. Meet us at the boundaries. Join us at our Sacred Hearth and be warmed by our good fire. Aid us and guide us as we walk the Elder Ways. Forfeður, accept this offering! *[give offering]*

Landvættir Offering

Noble Vættir, you who inhabit this Land, who lurk in stone and tree and river. Those of the primal wilds, those of the tilled and planted field, those of cobbled stones and bricked-walls: hear our call. May you join us by our fire, may you share your bounties with us as we share ours with you. Meet us at the boundaries. Join us at our Sacred Hearth and be warmed by our good fire. Aid us and guide us as we walk the Elder Ways. Blessed Vættir, accept this offering! *[give offering]*

Guðir Offering

Shining Guðir, you who shaped the Cosmos, you who guard and guide the World's wyrd, you who teach us and bless us with bounty. May your radiance light our hall, may your warmth stoke our fire, and may your presence alongside us this day and make it that much more pleasant. Meet us at the boundaries. Join us at our Sacred Hearth and be warmed by our good fire. Aid us and guide us as we walk the Elder Ways. Shining Guðir, accept this offering! *[give offering]*

Key Offering

[tell Gleichentag story/poem]

Blessed Nerðus, Generous Goddess of the Land, you who helped broker peace between the Guðir – we honor you this day. Your bounty sustains and comforts us, and we thank you. You give so much and receive so little in return for your effort and we pray, Blessed Lady, that you find these gifts that we give acceptable, for they are given in love, honor, and thanksgiving. Nerðus, accept our offerings!

Omen

[make an offering to the Norns, saying:]

Wise Sisters, Tenders of the Great Tree, Weavers of That-Which-Is and That-Which-Is-Becoming. Accept this offering, please, and let me peer into your Sacred Well.

[take the omens, preferably with runes]

The seer for this rite will ask four questions:
Have our offerings been accepted?
What do the Forfeður give in return?
What do the Vættir give in return?
What do the Guðir give in return?

Calling for, Hallowing, and Affirmation of the Blessings

Holy Ones, we have given in friendship and love, so that you might give in return. Kindreds, we ask that you give us the Blessed Waters: the Waters of Wyrd, the Waters of Wisdom, the Waters of Life!

Mighty Ones, give us the Waters!

Noble Ones, give us the Waters!

Shining Ones, give us the Waters!

Sjáið vatn lífsins!

Children of the Earth, before you is the holy cup. Do you wish to share in these blessings?

All: We do!

Then, as the waters are poured out, know that they hold blessings for you and this grove and this community. Work well with these blessings, Children of the Earth.

[pass out the Waters to the Folk, save some for the Working, though. When the Folk have drank the waters, walk the pitcher of Water around the feasting area and asperse the food and drink with the Blessings, saying:]

May the peace and wisdom of the Guðir bless this feast,
And be in our hearts and minds, in our words and actions.
Verði það svo.

Thanking

[thank the assembled Kindreds in reverse order: Deities, Land-Spirits, and Ancestors]

Closing the Gates

Wise and experienced, Njorð, we thank you for your aid this day, and ask one more boon from you, before this rite is ended – join your might and main with ours as we close the Gates Between the Worlds.

[give an offering and close the Gates: draw the Two Powers back into your hands, feeling the water and fire turn to ice within you, drawing a counter-clockwise triangle over the Tree, saying:]

May this Tree be just a tree.

[draw a triangle over the Fire, saying:]

May this Fire be just flame.

[draw a triangle over the Well, saying:]

May this Well be just water.

[as you draw the triangles, see the them form from ice, hanging in the air by the Hallows; declare:]

Latið loka hliðunum! Let the Gates be Closed!

[clap your hands firmly together and see the icy triangles shatter, the cosmic powers keeping the Gates open dispersing; and say:]

Blessed Njorð, we thank you.

Thanking Inspiration

Freyr Ingvi, King of the Alfar and Keeper of the Peace, we thank you.

Thanking the Earth Mother

Jorð, beauteous and bountiful mother, we thank you.

Closing the Rite

Go now, Children of Earth, in peace with the blessings of the Kindred and a Fire in your Heart. This rite is ended.

Post-Ritual Working

Children of the Earth, though the rite is ended, there is still work to be done. As we break bread with each other now, we must remember the lessons of the Guðir: the forgiveness of grievances, the richness of peace, and the importance of community. While we dine, you are all encouraged to share with the community that which you are thankful for, to forgive one another for slights made in the past year, and to remember that true wealth lies in peace both within and without.

Story & Poem

"The Spite of Gullveig"

This story is true.

In the Early Days, after the Cosmos had been re-formed from the corpse of that Ur-Etin, Ymir, and the Guðir were still quite young, it happened that a young goddess was wandering near the border of a deep, wild forest. Auburn-haired and quite comely, the Vanic maiden was none other than Freyja, twin to her brother, Freyr Ingvi, and one of the most passionate of the Vanir tribe.

As she traveled by the forest, movement among the trees caught her eye. She traveled closer to the tree-line and peered into the dark, green shadows of the wood, searching for the source of motion. Finally, after several moments' gazing, she beheld the mover: a tall man, broad of chest and shoulder, clad in the raiment of a woodsman, with the most handsome of face and form. Freyja's breath was taken from her as she gazed upon the man and her heart longed for him. He was too far into the forest for her grab his attention, so she followed him as he traveled. All through the forest he ranged, with Freyja shadowing him from afar, until the man emerged on the other side, near a community of long-houses and halls.

She followed the man into the village, where she was stopped by a pale-skinned man with hair as white as sea-foam, who asked her who she was.

"My…my name is Freyja, one of the Vanir," she said. "I saw a handsome man in the forest today and followed him here. Do you know him?"

"That sounds like Viðarr Oðinnson," the pale man said. "For what do you want with him?"

Freyja smiled and almost swooned as she heard the handsome man's name, and immediately babbled to the pale man how she loved him and sought to be his. The man was silent for a moment…and then burst out laughing.

"Go back to your people, girl," he said. "Such a union between Áss and Van will never happen, nor would Viðarr's father be inclined to bless it. Now go, before I call the rest of the guard to make you go."

Hurt and confused, Freyja wandered back into the forest, tears welling in her eyes and her heart near broken. As she traveled, though, her hurt and confusion slowly turned to anger and spite. How dare those men of the other village – those Æsir - deny her the man that she loved, deny her heart its joy? She would show them, Freyja determined, and she hatched a plan of vengeance.

Using what small knowledge she had of the hidden workings of the World, she set a glamour upon herself: a disguise of robes of gold-leaf and she made her hair shining and lustrous like the rays of the Sun; her eyes beguiling and her curves enchanting, bedecked in wondrous golden jewelry. The following day she wandered into the village of the Æsir and announced that she sought a husband. All the men's attention she immediately grabbed with her beauty, and the women's with her adornments.

"I am Gullveig," she said, "and I will only wed he who proves himself worthy of my hand."

Immediately, the men set upon competing with one another, all lusting after the rapturous Gullveig. They brought her their wealth, they composed poems and epics to her loveliness, they promised her fertile lands that would be the envy of all others. And, finally, they set upon each other with blows and curses; bloodying themselves to be the one that Gullveig picked.

On this went, with the pleased look on Gullveig's face becoming more and more apparent. Finally, a booming voice rang out through the village, calling a halt to the fighting, and all stared at an old man who stood opposite Gullveig across the village commons. Liar, he called her. Deceiver and strife-sower and inflicter-of-sorrows, he labeled her. With a chant like the singing of ravens, the old man dispelled Gullveig's enchantment and the Æsir found themselves freed.

They found themselves angered, as well.

Grabbing her up, they took her to the old man's hall and built up a pyre. Lashing Gullveig to the stake, and piercing her side with the old man's spear, they burnt her. Her screams echoed through the old man's longhouse as she burned. Finally, her voice died out, and then so did the flames. But what the Æsir found confused them: they found Gullveig, naked as the day she was born, healthy and whole among the ashes.

Again, they built up a pyre and burnt her on it. But, among the ashes they found her whole and hale; so they burnt her for a third time. Yet, again, they found her body renewed when the flames died away. "Oðinn," the Æsir said to the old man, "what can we do? There is no way to punish this spell-weaving deceiver!" The old man counseled that they take her to the forest and leave her. As the Æsir returned to their home, leaving the young woman naked and alone in the forest, Oðinn wove a spell commanding that no decent, honorable man would have any truck with Gullveig.

Alone and naked Frejya found herself once the Æsir had gone. She stumbled through the forest, dirtying herself in mud and muck, twigs and brambles catching themselves in her hair. Trapping several animals and skinning them, Freyja made clothes from their fur, and once again plotted vengeance. They had stabbed her! And burnt her! That could not go unpunished. Returning to the village's edge, she coaxed the spirits of the land into turmoil and wove enchantments to twist the minds and hearts of the Æsir.

But the old man, Oðinn – wily and cunning – was waiting for her and sung his own songs to counter-act Freyja's magic. At his command, the pale man and the other guards of the Æsir snatched her up and brought her once again to the village commons. "Though dressed like a wretch and the lowest and impoverished of wild-folk," Oðinn said as he studied the young goddess, "you glow with an inner light brighter than the Sun. What is your name – your true name – child?"

Spitefully, Freyja would only give them the name that the old man had just given her: *Heiðr*, "the Gleaming One". It was then that the pale man stepped forward and wiped the dirt and mud from her face and pronounced that he recognized her: she was none other than the young Vanic woman who had followed Viðarr from the forest a few days prior. A council was then called among the Æsir as Freyja was kept under watch, in regards to who should pay for the damages that she had caused. They finally decided to send a messenger to the Vanir to sue for reparations; but when the messenger returned, they were shocked to find that the Vanir had laughed at him and simply demanded that Freyja be returned.

Angered, the Æsir took up their swords and spears, their shields and their helms, and brought war down upon the Vanir. For years both sides fought, any advantage one gained over the other was quickly toppled and lost. As the seasons passed, the land was ravaged as the two tribes of deities waged their war upon one another. Finally, one of the Vanir, the goddess Nerðus – one who loved the land itself and the growing things, both plant and animal, that it bore – looked out upon the ravaged World and wept. She pleaded with her people that they come to a truce, to an armistice, with the Æsir, and after many long days, the Vanir finally agreed.

They called a halt to the combat and invited the host of the Æsir to a feast and proposed a peace between their tribes. Though the Æsir were not averse to a cessation of hostilities, they still felt aggrieved for all that had been done to them by Freyja. So, the Vanir agreed to an exchange of hostages to ensure peace and make up for the impetuous actions of their young tribeswoman: the Æsir would keep Freyja, who would be joined by her brother, Freyr Ingvi, and their father, Njorð; and the Vanir received Oðinn's brother, Hoenir, and the wise-etin Mimir.

Agreeing to the terms, both tribes sealed their truce with an oath made over a cauldron of ale, from which resulted the god Kvasir.

But *that* is another story.

In Early Days when the worlds were young,
Newly carved from the Etin's corpse,
A goddess was wand'ring near the edge of a wood;
Beautiful and wily was she.
Auburn-haired and comely, with curves like an hour-glass,
Her beauty surpassed by few.
Freyja, she was, twin to Freyr Ingvi,
Most passionate of the Vanir, verily.

As she traveled by the forest a shape among the trees
Caught her eye as she chanced to see it.
A tall and strapping man it showed itself to be;
A woodsman, of handsome face and form.
Shadowing the man, she followed through the forest;
Longing to make him her own.
Through the wood they traveled and out the other side,
To a village of halls and long-houses.

Stopped, the goddess was, by a pale man with white hair,
Asking who she was, what she wanted.
A man she'd seen and followed, Freyja to the guard,
Asking if he knew the handsome woodsman.
"Sounds like Viðarr Oðinnsson," opined the albino guard,
And Freyja almost swooned to hear his name.
The guard asked her business with broad-shouldered Viðarr,
And Freyja confessed her desires.

The white god erupted with gut-shaking laughter,
Wiping tears from his eyes as he chortled.
"No union 'tween Áss and Van is likely to happen,
"Doubtedly would Viðarr's father deign to bless it."
The white guard waved her off, and she wandered away
Hurt and confused, her heart nearly broken.
Tears burned her cheeks, confusion turned to anger;
She determined to seek her vengeance.

Using what small knowledge she had regarding magic,
Freyja crafted a clever glamour:
Robes of richest gold-leaf, hair shining like the Sun,
And bedecked in wond'rous jewelry wrought from gold.
The next day she traveled to the village of the Æsir,
Announg that she sought a husband 'mong their men.
"Gullveig" she named herself, glorious and beautiful,
And the Æsir fought ferociously to win her hand.

On went these battles, cruelly and bloodily,
Before Oðinn could end the bewitchment.
"Deceiver," he labeled her, "Liar" and "strife-sower";
Commanding that she be punished for her crimes.
Three times they burnt her, three times they stabbed her;
Each time she emerged hale and whole.
Hesitant and fearful, the Æsir expelled her,
Leaving her naked 'neath forest's boughs.

Alone in the forest, forced to survive on her own,
Freyja's anger burned bright within her.
They had stabbed her! They had burnt her!
The Æsir must pay for their crimes!
From the skins of animals she fashioned crude cluthes
And ventured back to the edge of the village.
Calling upon the spirits, she set a spell upon the Æsir;
Twisting their hearts and their minds.

It was Oðinn's quick wits and cunning wiles that
Averted the Æsir's disaster.
He sung back at her, songs like those of ravens,
Ending Freyja's enchantments.
The village guards took her, binding her arms,
As Oðinn looked over her.
"Dressed like a wild-thing, yet you glow with an inner light.
"Tell me your true name, child."

Spitefully, Freyja gave the name just granted her:
"Heiðr", the Gleaming One; the Shining One.
It was then that the pale god as he had some days prior

And announced her as Freyja of the Vanir.
Into custody she was taken as the Æsir called a council
To determine how best to deal with her.
It was decied that the Vanir should pay a weregild,
To make amends for their trouble-making kin.

But the herald they sent had returned empty-handed;
The Vanir had laughed in his face.
Angered and wrathful, the Æsir made war
Seeking justice for the strife they'd endured.
For years both sides fought, bitter and hate-filled,
Neither tribe gained any ground.
Their lands were ravaged, crops razed to the ground,
Possessions and wealth plundered horribly.

It was one of the Vanir who ventured a truce:
Nerðus, who so loved the Land.
Weapons were dropped, hands were shaken in peace;
Hostages exchanged by both tribes.
A great feast was then held by the gathered deities,
Their truce sealed by Kvasir's birth.
So it was then, and so shall it be ever after:
Peace 'tween the tribes of the gods.

Dises

Darkness sets upon the World as winter grows closer; we come together at this time to remember those that came before us, those whose blood and love flows within us, who helped to shape the World that we now shape.

Working

Materials Needed:

- Drinking horns (or vessels)
- Mead or beer
- Water

The working of this rite is one of remembrance and honor. The Ancestors are the most human of the Kindreds (having formerly been mortals themselves, after all) and keeping their memories alive is one of the best ways of giving them honor. The working will require drinking horns (or other appropriate drinking vessels, though horns are ideal), liquids to drink, and time.

Drinking horns can be found online, but should they be outside of your price range, use any appropriate drinking vessel. "Appropriate" referring to size and appearance. Depending on the expected size of the Folk you will want vessels that will be comparable (e.g. – if you have sixty people, using two small Dixie cups probably won't be the most efficient and effective idea); as well, try and use vessels that look nice. This is a ritual, number one, but it is also a ritual honoring your ancestors. Use something that you think they would respect.

The liquids depend on at least two factors: location and preference. If you are holding this rite at a location that prohibits alcohol (e.g. – a state or municipal park, etc.), then don't use mead or beer or any other type of alcoholic beverage. As well, if any of the Folk have issues with alcohol (such as being in recovery or just not liking it) than the best option might be to go with water. In a case like this, one can not only asperse the drinking horns with the Blessings, but also pour some in to mix with the drinking-water already within them. Should the rite be held in a place where alcohol is prohibited and the Folk don't have any major issues with alcohol, then a good compromise is one horn filled with mead (or beer, etc.) and one horn filled with water.

Lastly: time. Depending on the number of Folk expected to arrive, this working could take a while. Should it go on for a good amount of time, perhaps utilize drummers or others versed in the bardic arts (music, singing, etc.) to provide some background entertainment so that the Folk don't get bored. And, honestly, this doesn't mean they're being disrespectful or anything: we're all human. Sometimes we get bored. Even in ritual. But, having some soft drumming in the background can mitigate some of the negative factors of these kinds of down-time moments (e.g. – the valkyries refilling the horns, etc.) and make the rite that much more enjoyable.

Script

Processional

[Insert song/chant here]

Outdweller Entreaty

To those whose voices do not harmonize with our own, whose purposes may be at cross with ours, accept this token of treaty and leave our working be. [give offering]

Purification

[cense and asperse purify to the Folk]

Opening Statement

[ring bells three times to signal beginning of the rite]

As our ancestors once did, so we do today, and so our children will do in the future. Children of Earth, we are here to honor the Kindreds on this, Dises, the twilight of the year, when we remember those who came before us. So let us join together as one folk to make our offerings in joy and reverence.

Opening Prayer

The skull of Mighty Ymir stretches out above us.
The bones of Mighty Ymir support the land about us.
The blood of Mighty Ymir flows under and around us.
All things are of His flesh,
Our wyrds woven together,
May we pray with a good fire.

Inspiration

Wise and cunning Oðinn – you who know how to write, to read, to paint, to prove; to ask, to offer, to send, to spend – God of the Mysteries we call upon you this day. Inspire us with your holy ecstasy, open our eyes to see what is hidden, give us ears to hear the secret whisperings - so that we might come closer to our Ancestors and all the Kindreds. Oðinn, accept this offering! *[give offering]*

Honoring the Earth Mother

The Children of the Earth call out to Blessed Jorð - Birther of Storms, Consort of the Shaper, Mother of All. We who walk upon you, who take sustenance from you, who find comfort and rest within your bosom, remember you this day. *[give offering]* May you find this offering acceptable, for it is given in love and gratitude. Earth Mother, accept this offering!

(Re)Creating the Cosmos

In the primal times, the Great Hrímthurs was slain and quartered by the Sons of Búri: his Skull became the Sky, his Blood became the Sea, his Body became the Land. And from his Flesh grew a Great Tree, which connected all of the Worlds. May we recreate that Holy Sacrifice this day as we emulate the ordering of the worlds.

[hallow the Hallows while the Folk sing the "Portal Song"]

Grove Attunement

[perform the Two Powers meditation, afterwards say:]

We are shaped from driftwood at the Shore of the Worlds,
Grown from the Land,
Washed in the Sea,
Dried by the Sky.
We are tied together by the gifts of the Three Brothers,
By the weavings of the Nornir.
May we be just and true to each other.

May our worship be pious and pure.
Verði það svo.

The Gates

See now in your mind's eye this very room, the Mists of Magic cover the floor – cool, wet tendrils snaking between those gathered here. Among the gathered, you see a woman appear, moving slowly between man and woman, adult and child. Her hair is as pale and white as moonlight, her skin white as bones, though tinged here and there with a blue reminiscent of bruising. As she passes by, you catch the smell of flowers, incense, and rotting meat – and you see that while she is, indeed, exceedingly beautiful, parts of her are in a constant state of decay and rot. This woman, embodying the fullness and fleeting nature of life and the cold permanence of the grave, is the Blessed Lady Hella, Queen of the Underworld.

Blessed Hella, we call out to you this day and give you this offering [give offering]. In return, we simply ask that you join your power with ours, so that we might open the Gates Between the Worlds this day.

[give offering and open the Gates: pull the Two Powers into your hands, feeling the fire and water mix, and draw a clockwise triangle over the Well, saying]

May this well be the Triple Well.

[draw a triangle over the Fire, saying:]

May this fire be Bifrost's undying flame.

[draw a triangle over the Tree, saying:]

May this tree be mighty Yggdrasil, rising high and low before me.

[see the three triangles – water, fire, and growing wood – hang before in the air and then come together in a valknot, while declaring:]

Latið opna hliðin! Let the Gates be opened!

Forfeður Offering

Blessed Forfeður, you who came before us, you who bore us, you who helped to shape the path that lies ahead. Ancient Wise; Honored Einherjar; You Countless Masses who toiled in obscurity, but upon whose backs our society is built. Meet us at the boundaries. Join us at our Sacred Hearth and be warmed by our good fire. Aid us and guide us as we walk the Elder Ways. Forfeður, accept this offering! *[give offering]*

Landvættir Offering

Noble Vættir, you who inhabit this Land, who lurk in stone and tree and river. Those of the primal wilds, those of the tilled and planted field, those of cobbled stones and bricked-walls: hear our call. May you join us by our fire, may you share your bounties with us as we share ours with you. Meet us at the boundaries. Join us at our Sacred Hearth and be warmed by our good fire. Aid us and guide us as we walk the Elder Ways. Blessed Vættir, accept this offering! *[give offering]*

Guðir Offering

Shining Guðir, you who shaped the Cosmos, you who guard and guide the World's wyrd, you who teach us and bless us with bounty. May your radiance light our hall, may your warmth stoke our fire, and may your presence alongside us this evening make the Long Night that much more pleasant. Meet us at the boundaries. Join us at our Sacred Hearth and be warmed by our good fire. Aid us and guide us as we walk the Elder Ways. Shining Guðir, accept this offering! *[give offering]*

Key Offering

[tell Dises story/poem]

First among Humanity, Ancestors of all Peoples; First Man and Woman, crafted from the trees: Askr and Embla we honor you this day. Honored Asker and Embla, shaped by the Guðir themselves on some lonely beach at the edge of the Miðgarð, without you none of us would be here. Though we owe a debt to the gifts given to us by all of our Ancestors, our debt to you is greatest of all. We give you these offerings today in gratitude, love, and remembrance: Askr and Embla, accept our offerings!

Omen

[make an offering to the Norns, saying:]

Wise Sisters, Tenders of the Great Tree, Weavers of That-Which-Is and That-Which-Is-Becoming. Accept this offering, please, and let me peer into your Sacred Well.

[Take the omens, preferably with runes]

The seer for this rite will ask four questions:
Have our offerings been accepted?
What do the Forfeður give in return?
What do the Vættir give in return?
What do the Guðir give in return?

Calling for, Hallowing, and Affirmation of the Blessings

Holy Ones, we have given in friendship and love, so that you might give in return. Kindreds, we ask that you give us the Blessed Waters: the Waters of Wyrd, the Waters of Wisdom, the Waters of Life!

Mighty Ones, give us the Waters!

Noble Ones, give us the Waters!

Shining Ones, give us the Waters!

Sjáið vatn lífsins!

Children of the Earth, before you is the holy cup. Do you wish to share in these blessings?

All: We do!

Then, as the waters are poured out, know that they hold blessings for you and this grove and this community. Work well with these blessings, Children of the Earth.

[pass out the Waters to the Folk, save some for the Working, though. When the Folk have drank the waters, walk the pitcher of Water over to the table holding the drinking horns and asperse the horns, saying:]

May the blessings of the Kindred fill this drink,
May they fill our hearts and minds.
May the Well of Memory not run dry,
So that those who have passed are not forgotten.
Verði það svo.

Working

[the valkyries take up the drinking horns and walk them around to the Folk; each individual – who agrees to do so – is prompted by the valkyrie saying:]

Peer into the Well of Memory
And speak of what you see.
Tell us of those gone before you;
Remembered, so they might always be.

[the individual then speaks briefly of their Ancestors before taking a drink from the horn; repeat the process with the entire Folk, using as many rounds as is deemed necessary; when finished, the valkyries return the horns to their table, before taking their place among the Folk]

Thanking

[thank the assembled Kindreds in reverse order: Deities, Land-Spirits, and Ancestors]

Closing the Gates

Blessed, generous, and hospitable Lady Hel, we thank you for your aid this day, and ask one more boon from you, before this rite is ended – join your might and main with ours as we close the Gates Between the Worlds.

[give an offering and close the Gates: draw the Two Powers back into your hands, feeling the water and fire turn to ice within you, drawing a counter-clockwise triangle over the Tree, saying:]

May this Tree be just a tree.

[draw a triangle over the Fire, saying:]

May this Fire be just flame.

[draw a triangle over the Well, saying:]

May this Well be just water.

[as you draw the triangles, see the them form from ice, hanging in the air by the Hallows; declare:]

Latið loka hliðunum! Let the Gates be Closed!

[clap your hands firmly together and see the icy triangles shatter, the cosmic powers keeping the Gates open dispersing; and say:]

Blessed Hel, we thank you.

Thanking Inspiration

Wise Alfoðr, Walker Between the Worlds, Shaper of the Miðgarð – Honored Oðinn, we thank you.

Thanking the Earth Mother

Jorð, beauteous and bountiful mother, we thank you.

Closing the Rite

Go now, Children of Earth, in peace with the blessings of the Kindred and a Fire in your Heart. This rite is ended.

Poem & Story

"The First Ancestor"

This story is true.

Long ago, after the worlds had been shaped from the body of that Ancient Etin, Oðinn and his two brothers were walking along the shore of Miðgarð. As they traveled, they came across two pieces of drift-wood that had washed up on the sands. The trio decided to make something from the wood, and so they crafted the first human beings - Askr and Embla - giving them form, speech, reason, and spirit.

The two begat many children and lived quite long; longer than most of their children and grandchildren, for they had come from trees, of course, and shared in some of that longevity. But one day, after many years, Askr woke to feel a stirring in his aged-being, but knew not what it might be.

The elderly patriarch felt compelled to go walk in the fields and forests near his home, and so he set out that day with a thick staff of Ash in hand to help him in his meandering. He walked for several hours, up and down hills, across streams and through meadows. And after a time, he began to feel tired. He had a hard time catching his breath. His chest and arm ached. Askr decided to sit down on a smooth, rounded boulder that lay near a stout, ancient tree, if only to try and catch his wind again.

He closed his eyes briefly, feeling the weight of his lids growing heavier, and when he opened them again, Askr saw that he was no longer alone. A man stood nearby, in the shade of the trees. He wore a long, hooded cloak and had a thick, grey beard. In his hands, he held a staff similar to the one that Askr carried.

Askr leapt to his feet in surprise, but the other held up a pacifying hand. The bearded man greeted him, and when he spoke, Askr caught a glimpse of the man's one eye.

"Blessed Alfoðr, Mighty Shaper, for what reason do you grace me with your presence?" Askr said.

"I am here to guide you on to your new home, Askr," Oðinn replied.

"'New home'?" the man questioned.

The Hooded-One nodded. "Indeed. You have passed beyond the mortal world this day, and cannot return. Not as you once did, in any case."

"I do not understand," Askr replied.

Oðinn nodded passed the mortal man's shoulder. "Turn and look."

When Askr turned, he found himself staring at…himself. Slumped on the boulder, still and unmoving. Fearful, he looked at Oðinn.

"You have died, Askr. As all things do. Come with me now." And with that, Oðinn turned and walked off into the trees. Numbly, Askr followed. Oðinn led the man to the entrance of a cave in the side of a hill and produced a lamp from within the shadows of his long cloak. They walked deep within the cave in silence, descending through tunnels, and though it must have become colder the further they traveled, Askr felt no chill upon his skin.

Suddenly, the silence was broken by the sound of a low growling in the darkness. Oðinn stopped and held the lamp outward, reaching into his cloak once more. In the darkness, two eyes appeared, reflecting the light of the All-Father's lamp, and the growling continued. Oðinn withdrew two honey-cakes and set them at his feet. A moment passed, the growling ceased, and a form slunk into the circle of lamp-light. It was a dog, a massive beast, and jet-black in color. It gobbled up the honey-cakes and before long was sitting at Oðinn's feet, looking expectantly upward at the Hooded-One, as if waiting for more. The hoary-bearded god placed one more cake on the ground in front of the dog, patted the beast on the head, and lead Askr onward.

"What was that dog doing here, so deep within the bosom of the Earth?" the man asked.

"Garm guards the Gate, keeping the dead within and the living without, and making sure that none - at least, none who are not supposed to - cross the boundary," Oðinn replied.

They continued downward until they entered a vast cavern, whose walls and ceiling were lost in the darkness. A darkness which was punctured by dim lights off in the distance. As they walked, Askr suddenly became aware that they were traveling on a cobble-stoned road; and as they grew closer to them, he saw that the lights were torch-lights, situated in tall clay lamp-posts.

Though it must have been a great distance, the journey seemed to pass quickly, and Askr was surprised at how quickly they came to a bridge that spanned a mighty river. On the other side, he could see the dim outline of a grand hall. A figure appeared on the bridge and stopped them not long after they had set foot upon it.

"Stop!" the tall, stout figure barked. "Who seeks entrance to the Hall of Hel?"

"Beauteous and ravishing Moðguð," the All-Father said with a sweeping motion of his hands. "I am simply escorting this distinguished soul into the care and hospitality of your mistress."

The giantess stood up straighter. "Is this him?" she asked Oðinn, and the Hooded-One nodded in reply. "By all means then, please: enter." And with that, she stepped aside and let them continue.

When they finally stepped off of the bridge, Askr saw a monolithic hall before them. As they approached, its mighty double doors were pulled open by twin teams of pale, dark-bearded men and warm light poured out from within. Oðinn led Askr inside the great hall and the man saw fires burning in several hearths, there were mighty trestle tables laden with food, and music filled the air emanating from instruments wielded by more spirits of the Deep Earth. At the end of the great hall was a raised dais, upon which stood a throne, and seated on the throne was a young woman.

Oðinn and Askr crossed the intervening distance quickly and each knelt briefly before the seated woman. “Uncle,” the woman said, inclining her head to the All-Father. “Renowned Askr of Miðgarð.” She made a similar bow of her head to the mortal man.

“Blessed Lady Hel, I have brought your guest to your hall as agreed,” Odin said, gesturing to Askr.

“Thank you, Wise Uncle,” Hel replied. “You have my gratitude and hospitality. You will always be welcome within my realm.” She turned to Askr. “Noble Askr, First of Men, welcome to my Hall, may you find it a restful and inviting home during your stay. I apologize for the lack of guests at the present, you are the first of many to arrive.”

Askr voiced his thankfulness to the Lady, but he was still unsure of everything that was happening. He was given free-reign to wander about the hall and he took that freedom. Many days and weeks passed and Askr slowly began to acclimate to his new home. One day, he was surprised to find a gleaming shield and sword resting on one of the trestle tables, neither of which had been there before.

He asked Hel about the objects. “They are yours,” she said. “They are gifts from your family.”

“How does my family know that I am here?” he asked.

Hel smiled and gestured to a basin of water that sat on a pedestal near her throne and Askr looked down into it. In its waters, he saw a grassy field with a great mound rising up from it. “Your family found your corpse in the forest where you had died,” Hel explained. “They raised a great mound and buried you inside it, Noble Askr. They laid the shield and sword, along with other gifts, inside with you.”

“How did they end up here?”

"They are yours now," Hel replied. "If they are offered up to you as such, they will come to you no matter where your journey takes you."

More gifts came as the weeks passed: trinkets and weapons, casks of mead and plates of food. In time, a deep-hooded cloak and staff appeared for Askr, and Hel explained that the First Man had been given a job within her court. Much as the All-Father had welcomed and guided him into the Underworld, Askr would now do the same for the newly dead. Eager to see the Miðgarð once again, Askr gladly took up the mantle of ferrying souls into Hel's Hall. Descendants of his that Askr did not recognize were the first to follow him deep into the Earth, but eventually, Embla and their children joined Askr there, along with many others that the First Man had known in his mortal life.

And they feasted, and they laughed, and all was well.

In Early Days when the Worlds were young,
And the Cosmos fresh from re-shaping,
It happened to be that Three Brothers were walking
Along the sandy shore of the Miðgarð.
In the sand they foundsmooth pieces of driftwood
Washed up from 'cross the far waters.
Oðinn, the Eldest, eyed the wood purposefully,
Designs dancing through his head.

"Brothers," he said, "Let us shape new beings
"To inhabit the Worlds with us."
So, they worked the wood, sculpting form and gender;
But, the two figures lacked an inner fire.
Spirit, Oðinn gave them; sense and reason gave Hœnir;
Loki gave the boons of hale blood.
First man and woman, they were, in all the Miðgarð;
"Askr" and "Embla" they were named to be.

Long-lived they were, and many children they had;
Much like the trees they were shaped from.
But, one morning aged Askr woke with an itch to go wandr'ring

Sunna's Journey

And so he set out across the Land.
Old Asker meandered across hills, streams, and meadows
As Sunna crept slowly 'cross the sky.
Many hours passed, the old man felt quite labored;
Chest aching, breath beyond catching.

He closed his eyes briefly, his lids growing heavy;
When he opened them he was no longer alone.
A grey-hooded man with long, hoary beard
Stood leaning on a staff made of ash.
Askr leapt up in surprise, but was led to stay silent
When the man held up a calm hand.
He saluted Askr kindly, one eye staring out;
Askr realized it was the Alfoðr.

"Wise One, Mighty One, why do yougrace me with your presence?"
Stammered Askr in surprise.
To act as a guide, the Alfoðr told him,
Helping Askr reach his new home.
For the First Man had passed beyond the mortal world;
No longer would he dwell among the living.
Through the trees to a cave the Rúnatyr led him,
Descending deep into the Earth.

Their way lit by a lamp, Oðinn leading fearlessly,
Through darkened tunnels they traveled.
The dark silence was broken by a deep growl
Coming from a few steps ahead.
A massive dog was the growler, a beast Oðinn named "Garm",
Gaurdian of the Gates of the Dead.
The dead stay on one side, the living on the other,
And Garm keeping safe the Gate.

Oðinn calmed the beast with sweet honey-cakes;
They continued through the cold darkness.
On a path of cobbled clay they traversed a cavern
Heading for a Hall bathed in light.
A moat's bridge they approached and were met by a guard

A giantess marked as Moðguð.
Past her they walked, and the Hall's doors were opened
By teams of dark-bearded dvergar.

Within they did see that a great feast was laid out,
Though no guests gathered at the tables.
Across the vast Hall sitting in a throne on a dais
Was a young, but odd-looking, woman.
Beautiful she was – ravishing! - where soft flesh grew,
But half o' her was rotted away.
The duo approached the throne-mounted dais,
Oðinn greeted his niece, Lady Hella.

The Lady Hella did welcome them lavishly to her Hall,
Bidding Askr to rest and take comfort.
"This place is your new home, I pray it be comforting, though,
"You are the first of many to arrive."
And Askr took comfort, resting in Hella's care;
Weeks and months passed with haste.
He became adjusted to his new existence,
Enjoying the rest, relaxation.

Late one day, though, Askr did find a gift:
A shield, a sword, lying on a table.
Hella explained to him that they came from his family;
Such gifts would find him wherever he was.
More gifts came in the following weeks: casks of mead and plates of food,
Weapons and trinkets to wield and wear.
One day there came a staff and deep-hooded cloak;
Hella explained that he'd been given a job.

As the Alfoðr had done Askr would do now:
Guide the dead to feast in Hel's Hall.
Eager to the Miðgarð Askr took up the mantle,
He would ferry souls 'tween the Worlds.
His descendants he would meet when their final moment came,
Welcoming them like a father does his children.
Hel's Hall did fill with souls and joyous feasting,

And not one would be lonely, again.

Devotionals

While any large, group ritual can be an inspiring and moving affair, it is simple home observances, a.k.a. "hearth-practice", that forms the core of any religion, especially Paganism. What follows in this section of the book is a collection of devotional liturgies for a solitary practitioner or a small group to perform on their own time through the year.

One will probably note a difference between these devotionals and the High Day scripts (or even the Full Moon liturgies at the end of the section), as they follow a looser blót format instead of ADF's Core Order of Ritual. This is primarily because only public High Day rituals, technically, need to adhere to the Core Order of Ritual – anything else, especially personal rites at home, can be free-form and only stick to the Core Order as much as the practitioner(s) decides.

The devotionals themselves are broken down into four sub-sections:

- **Days of the Week**
- **The Three Kindreds**
- **Solar and Lunar Cycles**
- **Full Moon Rites**

Within each sub-section you will find several different liturgies giving ideas of how solitary and small-scale group workings can be done at home or with your worship-group. But, as I have often repeated in this book, these are only suggestions. Adapt or amend as you desire or take these ideas, run with them, and create your own rites.

Days of the Week

Getting into the habit of daily devotionals is good thing to start. These can be something as simple as offering a portion of a meal to one's ancestors, lighting a candle and burning incense to a patron deity, or leaving an offering outside one's home for the *Landvættir*. Or, if one prefers, they can do a slightly more formalized and structured devotional such as the ones that follow.

The days of the week provide the over-arching structure to these devotionals, where the practitioner(s) make offering specifically to the deity of each day. Anyone familiar with Norse lore should be acquainted with the fact that, in the English-speaking areas of the world, our days of the week are generally named after several of the important deities of the Germanic peoples (except for Saturday, which is named after the Roman deity, Saturn). Monday is "Moon's-Day" (or, Máni), Tuesday is "Tiw's-Day" (Tiw is an Anglo-Saxon cognate to the Old Norse Tyr), Wednesday is "Woden's-Day" (again, an Anglo-Saxon cognate to Oðinn), Thursday is "Thor's-Day", Friday is "Frigga's-Day", and Sunday is "Sun's-Day" (or, Sunna). Personally, I make offerings to the goddess Hella on Saturdays, but I will be leaving that one unaccounted for in this book to let you, the reader, decide whom you would like to honor that day (after all, I can't do all the work for you).

So, let's get to it!

Sunday

[Stand before the altar, light some incense, and say:]

Hail to all the Blessed Kindreds – Forfeður, Landvættir, and Guðir – and especially to Sunna, the Shining, Golden Light of the Heavens.

[make an offering to the Ancestors, saying:]

Mighty and Honored Forfeður, you whose blood and love flows within me, I make this offering [give offering] in love, remembrance, and honor. I pray that you bestow your wisdom, love, and blessings upon me always. *Verði það svo.*

[make an offering to the Spirits of the Land, saying:]

Noble and Myriad Vættir, you of stone and tree, of brick and beam; of the wild places and those tamed by human hands – I make this offering [give offering] in honor, friendship, and frið. May we live alongside one another in peace as neighbors always. *Verði það svo.*

[make an offering to the Deities, saying:]

Blessed and Shining Guðir, you who guide humanity and protect the wyrd of the Worlds, you who foster and reap, you who lead and teach – I make this offering [give offering] given in gratitude, honor, and admiration. I pray that you gift me with your luck, generosity, and wisdom always. *Verði það svo.*

[light a candle and make an offering to Sunna, saying:]

Shining Sunna, Golden Sunna: you of peerless speed and radiance – I remember you this day. I make this offering [give offering] in love, admiration, and gratitude, forever thankful for your light and warmth and for your golden countenance that enlivens the Miðgarð.

May your light shine bright and strong 'til Ragnarök comes, giving all things the light and heat they need to live. *Verði það svo.*

[take an omen using the runes, asking the following questions:]

- Were my offerings accepted?
- What blessing does Sunna give in return?
- What wisdom do the Kindreds offer me?

[give thanks to the Kindred and end the ritual, saying:]

Holy Ones, we have given to each other, strengthened the ties of wyrd between us, and I thank you. May you watch over me and mine, as I promise to honor and remember you all. Praise and thanks be upon you all. *Verði það svo.*

Monday

[Stand before the altar, light some incense, and say:]

Hail to all the Blessed Kindreds – Forfeður, Landvættir, and Guðir – and especially to Máni whose shining, Silver Face guards us through the dark of the night.

[make an offering to the Ancestors, saying:]

Honored and Wise Forfeður, you whose blood and love flows within me, I make this offering [give offering] in love, remembrance, and honor. I pray that your wisdom, love, and blessings be upon me always. *Verði það svo.*

[make an offering to the Spirits of the Land, saying:]

Noble and Myriad Vættir, you of stone and tree, of brick and beam; of the wild places and those tamed by human hands – I make this offering [give offering] in honor, friendship, and frið. May we live alongside one another in peace as neighbors always. *Verði það svo.*

[make an offering to the Deities, saying:]

Blessed and Shining Guðir, you who guide humanity and protect the wyrd of the Worlds, you who foster and reap, you who lead and teach – I make this offering [give offering] given in gratitude, honor, and admiration. I pray that your luck, generosity, and wisdom will be gifted to me always. *Verði það svo.*

[make an offering to Máni, saying:]

Shining One, Silver One – twin to Sunna, who reflects her glory but is no less mighty; you of shifting guises and many means, who sees all things that occur in the dark of night. I call out to you this evening and make this offering to you [give offering] in honor and gratitude. May your wisdom and protection be upon me for as long as may you evade the jaws of the tireless wolf – may that day be far off!. *Verði það svo.*

[take an omen using the runes, asking the following questions:]

- Were my offerings accepted?
- What blessing does Máni give in return?
- What wisdom do the Kindreds offer me?

[give thanks to the Kindred and end the ritual, saying:]

Holy Ones, we have given to each other, strengthened the ties of wyrd between us, and I thank you. May you watch over me and mine, as I promise to honor and remember you all. Praise and thanks be upon you all. *Verði það svo.*

Tuesday

[Stand before the altar, light some incense, and say:]

Hail to all the Blessed Kindreds – Forfeður, Landvættir, and Guðir – and especially to Honored Tyr, he who keeps his word or pays the price, and settles disputes between angry clans.

[make an offering to the Ancestors, saying:]

Honored and Wise Forfeður, you whose blood and love flows within me, I make this offering [give offering] in love, remembrance, and honor. I pray that your wisdom, love, and blessings be upon me always. *Verði það svo.*

[make an offering to the Spirits of the Land, saying:]

Noble and Myriad Vættir, you of stone and tree, of brick and beam; of the wild places and those tamed by human hands – I make this offering [give offering] in honor, friendship, and frið. May we live alongside one another in peace as neighbors always. *Verði það svo.*

[make an offering to the Deities, saying:]

Blessed and Shining Guðir, you who guide humanity and protect the wyrd of the Worlds, you who foster and reap, you who lead and teach – I make this offering [give offering] in gratitude, honor, and admiration. I pray that your luck, generosity, and wisdom will be gifted to me always. *Verði það svo.*

[make an offering to Tyr, saying:]

Mighty Tyr, one-handed god of honor, justice, and law, I call out to you this day. I pray that you find this offering that I make acceptable, [give offering] for I give it in respect, admiration, and gratitude for the example that you have set and the sacrifices that you have made on behalf of all creation. I pray that your generosity, wisdom, and resolve be gifted to me always. Praise and thanks be upon you. *Verði það svo.*

[take an omen using the runes, asking the following questions:]

- Were my offerings accepted?
- What blessing does Tyr give in return?
- What wisdom do the Kindreds offer me?

[give thanks to the Kindred and end the ritual, saying:]

Holy Ones, we have given to each other, strengthened the ties of wyrd between us, and I thank you. May you watch over me and mine, as I promise to honor and remember you all. Praise and thanks be upon you all. *Verði það svo.*

Wednesday

[Stand before the altar, light some incense, and say:]

Hail to all the Blessed Kindreds – Forfeður, Landvættir, and Guðir – and especially to Wise Oðinn: Father of All, Shaper of the Worlds, Sacrificer of self to Self.

[make an offering to the Ancestors, saying:]

Honored and Wise Forfeður, you whose blood and love flows within me, I make this offering [give offering] in love, remembrance, and honor. I pray that your wisdom, love, and blessings be upon me always. *Verði það svo.*

[make an offering to the Spirits of the Land, saying:]

Noble and Myriad Vættir, you of stone and tree, of brick and beam; of the wild places and those tamed by human hands – I make this offering [give offering] in honor, friendship, and frið. May we live alongside one another in peace as neighbors always. *Verði það svo.*

[make an offering to the Deities, saying:]

Blessed and Shining Guðir, you who guide humanity and protect the wyrd of the Worlds, you who foster and reap, you who lead and teach – I make this offering [give offering] given in gratitude, honor, and admiration. I pray that your luck, generosity, and wisdom will be gifted to me always. *Verði það svo.*

[make an offering to Oðinn, saying:]

Blessed Alfoðr, Master of the Mysteries, Wanderer and Riddler, Winner of the Sacred Mead. I call out to you this day and ask that you find this offering [give offering] acceptable, for it is given in honor, praise, and remembrance. May your wisdom, wit, and luck be gifted to me always. Praise and thanks be upon you. *Verði það svo.*

[take an omen using the runes, asking the following questions:]

- Were my offerings accepted?
- What blessing does Oðinn give in return?
- What wisdom do the Kindreds offer me?

[give thanks to the Kindred and end the ritual, saying:]

Holy Ones, we have given to each other, strengthened the ties of wyrd between us, and I thank you. May you watch over me and mine, as I promise to honor and remember you all. Praise and thanks be upon you all. Verði það svo.

Thursday

[Stand before the altar, light some incense, and say:]

Hail to all the Blessed Kindreds – Forfeður, Landvættir, and Guðir – and especially to Mighty Thor: jotun's-bane, Red-beard, protector of Guðir and humanity, son of Oðinn and Jorð.

[make an offering to the Ancestors, saying:]

Honored and Wise Forfeður, you whose blood and love flows within me, I make this offering [give offering] in love, remembrance, and honor. I pray that your wisdom, love, and blessings be upon me always. *Verði það svo.*

[make an offering to the Spirits of the Land, saying:]

Noble and Myriad Vættir, you of stone and tree, of brick and beam; of the wild places and those tamed by human hands – I make this offering [give offering] in honor, friendship, and frið. May we live alongside one another in peace as neighbors always. *Verði það svo.*

[make an offering to the Deities, saying:]

Blessed and Shining Guðir, you who guide humanity and protect the wyrd of the Worlds, you who foster and reap, you who lead and teach – I make this offering [give offering] given in gratitude, honor, and admiration. I pray that your luck, generosity, and wisdom will be gifted to me always. *Verði það svo.*

[make an offering to Thor, saying:]

You who strike with the force of the Storm, you who protect and provide, you who bless humanity with your mirth and your might: Thor, Oðinn's son, I call upon you this day. I pray you find this offering [give offering] acceptable, as I give it in gratitude and honor.

May you ever gift me with your luck, might, and benevolence. Praise and thanks be upon you, Red-beard. *Verði það svo.*

[take an omen using the runes, asking the following questions:]

- Were my offerings accepted?
- What blessing does Thor give in return?
- What wisdom do the Kindreds offer me?

[give thanks to the Kindred and end the ritual, saying:]

Holy Ones, we have given to each other, strengthened the ties of wyrd between us, and I thank you. May you watch over me and mine, as I promise to honor and remember you all. Praise and thanks be upon you al. *Verði það svo.*

Friday

[Stand before the altar, light some incense, and say:]

Hail to all the Blessed Kindreds – Forfeður, Landvættir, and Guðir – and especially to Blessed Frigga – wife of Oðinn, keeper of his halls, she who keeps the home sacred.

[make an offering to the Ancestors, saying:]

Honored and Wise Forfeður, you whose blood and love flows within me, I make this offering [give offering] in love, remembrance, and honor. I pray that your wisdom, love, and blessings be upon me always. *Verði það svo.*

[make an offering to the Spirits of the Land, saying:]

Noble and Myriad Vættir, you of stone and tree, of brick and beam; of the wild places and those tamed by human hands – I make this offering [give offering] in honor, friendship, and frið. May we live alongside one another in peace as neighbors always. *Verði það svo.*

[make an offering to the Deities, saying:]

Blessed and Shining Guðir, you who guide humanity and protect the wyrd of the Worlds, you who foster and reap, you who lead and teach – I make this offering [give offering] in gratitude, honor, and admiration. I pray that your luck, generosity, and wisdom will be gifted to me always. *Verði það svo.*

[make an offering to Frigga, saying:]

Honored Frigga: Keeper of the Keys, Noble Lady, Protectress of the Family. I call upon you this night and make this offering, [give offering] which I hope you find acceptable. I pray that you bestow your blessings of love and generosity upon me always. Praise and thanks be upon you. *Verði það svo.*

[take an omen using the runes, asking the following questions:]

- Were my offerings accepted?
- What blessing does Frigga give in return?
- What wisdom do the Kindreds offer me?

[give thanks to the Kindred and end the ritual, saying:]

Holy Ones, we have given to each other, strengthened the ties of wyrd between us, and I thank you. May you watch over me and mine, as I promise to honor and remember you all. Praise and thanks be upon you all. *Verði það svo.*

The Three Kindreds

The Kindreds themselves are of utmost importance to religious practice as it done in ADF – and, in a wider, more generalized context, Heathenry and Germanic Neo-Paganism in general. Whether you refer to these beings as "Gods" and "Not-Gods;" "Mighty Ones, Noble Ones, Shining Ones;" or "Forfeður, Vættir, and Guðir" establishing and perpetuating relationship with these spiritual entities liess at the heart of any religion rooted in Indo-European myth and ritual.

One's relationship to the Kindreds is, in my opinion, best visualized as a series of nested circles. At the center, you have either the individual worshiper or the "individual" group of worshipers. One step outward, you have the Forfeður, the spirits of your deceased Ancestors. But, "Ancestor" is more than just those of your blood-lineage (this is especially true of those who are adopted or fostered by non-blood relatives), it can apply to those people you were especially close to while they lived that *filled* a familial role in some way: friends, friends of the family (who hasn't had at least one "aunt" or "uncle" who wasn't a blood-relative that was always over for family events?), mentors, teachers, co-workers, etc. Culture heroes can also fall into this category, since some ancient peoples would trace their cultural lineage back to a famous mortal hero or a demi-god that founded their tribe or city.

In this "nested circle" framework, your Ancestors are definitely your "family" among these three classes of spiritual beings, if only because at one point in time they were your mortal family. I believe that you should give the most regular of offerings and prayers to them as well as seeking their aid in day-to-day matters in which you might need help. They are family, and most families are usually willing, if not happy, to help each other out even if relationships are somewhat dysfunctional or strained.

In the next circle outward you have the Vættir, the various spirits of place and thing and concept. If you think of the Ancestors as your spiritual "family" than the Spirits can be thought of as your spiritual "neighbors." Family will generally be amenable to you because you're family, though it's always nice to give at least as much as you take. With neighbors, though, there's less of a certainty that they will be immediately friendly and helpful. Sure, some vættir are more than happy to act like members of a spiritual "welcome wagon" and help you, but it's generally polite to build up some kind of a relationship with them before you start asking to borrow sugar or their lawn-mower or getting them to help with your garden.

Plus, some of them may be like the stereotypical "grouchy old man" who simply want *nothing* to do with you whatsoever, and if you keep pestering them with gifts they may get spiteful and mean. So, tread carefully and politely.

In the final circle you have the Guðir, the Deities. In most cases, its best to approach the deities in the same way you would civic or national leaders: don't pester them with small matters that can be taken care of on a level closer to "home."[15] Or, if you do, you'll probably just be dealing with an underling operating under that deity's auspices.[16]

With all of that said, the liturgies in this section focus on honoring and fostering a better relationship with the various Kindreds. There are four devotional rites for the Ancestors: a rite each for the "common" ancestors manifested as the **Alfar** and the **Disir**[17], a rite to the **Einherjar** (those warriors who haven fallen in battle), and a rite to (what ADF calls) the **"Ancient Wise"** – those ancestors who were goðis, gyðias, and vitkar. For the Spirits there are three liturgies: one for the Landvættir, one for the **Hausvættir**, and one for the **Dvergar**. And, finally, for the Deities we have two liturgies: a rite for the **Æsir** and a rite for the **Vanir**. Hopefully, you will find enjoyment and inspiration in all nine of them.

---

[15] Though, obviously, if you have a pre-existing relationship with a deity (or if you're simply out of options and you've scrapped the bottom of the barrel for ideas) then it'll probably be okay to go seek their help.

[16] Among the ancient Greeks, it was commonly believed that most of the time when one encountered one of the gods, that person was actually dealing with a *daimon* – a spirit associated with the particular deity who had the authority to speak and act in that deity's name. There's no reason to think that this may have been a purely Hellenic theology (though, obviously, we have little – if *any* – evidence to suppose that the Germanics believed such a thing), but even if it was, it still seems to make sense. Your mileage may vary, though.

[17] The male and female ancestral spirits, respectively. The Alfar were thought to watch over the land passed down, generation-to-generation, through their family, and were sometimes associated with the mounds found throughout Northern Europe. The Disir were thought to watch over and care for individual family members.

The Alfar

Note: For this working, you will need to gather one or two items each that are associated with or represent a deceased male ancestor of yours that you wish to honor. It is advised that it be something that you won't mind too much "losing" since you will be creating a miniature barrow to place them in (obviously, having land of some kind is necessary for this; though if one lives in an apartment, a pot of sufficient size filled with soil will work). This will be done outside (keep an eye to the weather forecast) by the barrow-to-be, with the final filling in to be done once the rite is over. Future devotionals can be done using a simple adaptation of this script that omits language referring to burying the artifacts/relics.

[Stand by the altar, in front of the open barrow, light some incense and say:]

Hail to my Blessed and Honored Forefeður! It is to you and your memory that I make offering this day.

[make an offering to Jorð, saying:]

Generous Mother, you who give us so much in life and provide us with shelter and rest in death, I remember you. Jorð, Bountiful Mother, may you find this offering acceptable, for I give it in love and honor. Praise and thanks be upon you. *Verði það svo.*

[make an offering to Oðinn, saying:]

Wise and Knowing Alfoðr, Walker of the Ways, I call upon you this day and ask that you watch, open, and ward the Gates Between the Worlds. Please, accept this offering *[make offering]* and with your magic may my words resound in the Deeps, may they ride the winds to the edges of the Miðgarð, may they arise to the Heavens. Praise and thanks be upon you, Hidden-One. *Verði það svo.*

[make a general offering to the Alfar, saying:]

Grandfathers, whose names I may not know but whose blood is my blood, whose flesh is my flesh, whose love is my love – hear me. I make this offering to you all, here at this sacred barrow: may it serve as a meeting place for us, where love, memory, and honor come together. Praise and thanks be upon you all. *Verði það svo.*

[make offerings to the specific Alfar whose relics you wish to bury, saying what words seem appropriate to you; finally, place the artifacts within the barrow and say:]

Grandfathers, I place mementos of your lives, of your love, here in this barrow – this mound of honor and memory. Know that I remember you and that I honor you here and may this barrow serve as a font of your love and wisdom. Praise, thanks, and much love upon you all. *Verði það svo.*

[take an omen using the runes, asking the following questions:]

- Were my offerings accepted?
- What blessing do the Alfar give in return?
- What more is asked of me?

[give thanks to Oðinn and Jorð, close the ways, and then end the rite by saying:]

Honored Forfeður, I thank you for blessing me with your love and wisdom this day. May you watch over me and mine, as I promise to honor and remember you all. Praise and thanks be upon you all. *Verði það svo.*

[fill in the barrow and re-lay the sod over it before you leave]*

* - Along with being a good shrine to honor the Alfar, one can additionally perform meditation upon, or next to, the mound to help commune with them.

The Disir

Note: Just as the Alfar devotional creates a shrine for regular offerings, so does this working. Find (or make) a thick, tall candle that you can situate near your hearth (whether that be an actual fireplace should you have one or perhaps atop your oven, where the "hearth-flame" burns). A small box for mementos of deceased female ancestors you wish to honor will be needed, as well, which will be placed underneath the candle – whose wax will be allowed to flow down over it over time, binding candle and box together. Again, this liturgy can be used after the initial set-up of the shrine if one simply uses only the appropriate language.

[Stand by the altar, in front of the hearth, light some incense and say:]

Hail to my Blessed and Honored Forefeður! It is to you and your memory that I make offering this day.

[make an offering to Jorð, saying:]

Generous Mother, you who give us so much in life and provide us with shelter and rest in death, I remember you. Jorð, Bountiful Mother, may you find this offering acceptable, for I give it in love and honor. Praise and thanks be upon you. Verði það svo.

[make an offering to Hella, saying:]

Blessed Lady of the Realms Below, You of the Hall in which so many of our Forfeður gather, I call upon you this day and ask that you watch, open, and ward the Gates Between the Worlds. Please, accept this offering *[make offering]* and with your magic may my words resound in the Deeps, may they ride the winds to the edges of the Miðgarð, may they arise to the Heavens. Praise and thanks be upon you, Hospitable One. *Verði það svo.*

[make a general offering to the Disir, saying:]

Grandmothers, whose names I may not know but who love, wisdom, and guidance have touched my life nonetheless: whose blood and flesh are my blood and flesh, and those whose only familial ties are those of love and care – hear me. I make this offering *[give offering]* to you all, here at this sacred shrine, where the Flame of Love and Memory burns. Praise and thanks be upon you all. *Verði það svo.*

[make offerings to the specific Disir whose relics you wish to keep in the shrine, saying what words seem appropriate to you; finally, place the artifacts within the shrine-box and say:]

Grandmothers, I place mementos of your lives, of your love, here in this shrine – this box of honor and memory. Know that I remember you and that I honor you here and may this shrine serves as a beacon of your love and wisdom. Praise, thanks, and much love upon you all. *Verði það svo.*

[take an omen using the runes, asking the following questions:]

- Were my offerings accepted?
- What blessing do the Disir give in return?
- What more is asked of me?

[give thanks to Hella and Jorð, close the gates, and then end the rite by saying:]

Honored Forfeður, I thank you for blessing me with your love and wisdom this day. May you watch over me and mine, as I promise to honor and remember you all. Praise and thanks be upon you all. *Verði það svo.*

The Einherjar

Note: This liturgy is simple, in that it does not involve assembling a shrine like the previous two. However, it does involve the use of one (or both) of the two previous altars assembled for the Alfar and Disir liturgies. The ritual takes place before your altar, but the specific offerings for the fallen warriors (especially those among your specific ancestors) will be deposited at both/either of the Alfar and/or Disir shrines.

[Stand by the altar, light some incense and say:]

Hail to the Honored and Mighty Einherjar, those who have fought and fallen, who now feast and fight in the Halls of the Æsir, practicing for that fateful day when Surt's kin rise. It is to you and your memory that I give offering this day.

[make an offering to Jorð, saying:]

Generous Mother, you who give us so much in life and provide us with shelter and rest in death, I remember you. Jorð, Bountiful Mother, may you find this offering acceptable, for I give it in love and honor. Praise and thanks be upon you. *Verði það svo.*

[make offerings to Oðinn and Freyja, saying:]

Wise One, Sigtyr, General of the Hosts of Heroes: Oðinn, I give offering to you this day. *[give offering]* Beauteous One, Battle Maiden, Great Valkyrie: Freyja, I give offering to you this day. *[give offering]* To you both I have made offerings and in return I ask that you open the Ways, that you let my words and my gifts reach those who have fallen in battle -- those whom you have taken to your honored Halls, those who will stand on the field of battle when Ragnarök comes. Praise and thanks be upon you both. *Verði það svo.*

[make a general offering to the Einherjar, saying:]

To you who fought and fell, who sacrificed your mortal lives for the sake of something greater than yourself – your Folk, your country, your gods; for peace, justice, and truth;

To you who fought to protect others, to protect yourselves, to safeguard freedom, security, and prosperity;

To you who lived by the sword and were felled by it – I make this offering. *[give offering]*

May it be acceptable and welcomed for I give it in honor, memory, and gratitude. Praise and thanks be upon you, Honored Warriors. *Verði það svo.*

[make offerings to the specific warriors that you wish to honor, saying what words seem appropriate to you; when finished, take an omen using the runes, asking the following questions:]

- Were my offerings accepted?
- What blessing do the Einherjar give in return?
- What more is asked of me?

[give thanks to Oðinn and Freyja, close the ways, and then end the rite by saying:]

Honored Warriors, I thank you for blessing me with your love, luck, and wisdom this day. May you watch over me and mine, as I promise to honor and remember you. Praise and thanks be upon you all. *Verði það svo.*

The Ancient Wise

Note: Much like the previous working for the Einherjar, this one does not require the construction of a separate shrine but makes use of either (or both) of the Alfar/Disir ones already built. However, a token will be made for the Ancient Wise – primarily by making a disc of ash wood and inscribing a bind-rune consisting of ansuz and othilaz. This disc will be rubbed with dirt from the Alfar's mound and/or have wax from the Disir's shrine dripped on it after the devotional, before being kept on the main altar.

[Stand by the altar, light some incense and say:]

Hail to the Learned and Inspiring Wise Ones: those who sacrificed and sang, those who risted and carved and stained, those who kept troth with the Kindreds. It is to you and your memory that I give offering this day.

[make an offering to Jorð, saying:]

Generous Mother, you who give us so much in life and provide us with shelter and rest in death, I remember you. Jorð, Bountiful Mother, may you find this offering acceptable, for I give it in love and honor. Praise and thanks be upon you. *Verði það svo.*

[make an offering to Oðinn, saying:]

Lord of Wisdom, Wise Teacher, Sacrificer: I call upon you this day and ask that you watch, open, and ward the Gates Between the Worlds. Please, accept this offering [make offering] and with your magic may my words resound in the Deeps, may they ride the winds to the edges of the Miðgarð, may they arise to the Heavens. Praise and thanks be upon you, Hidden-One. *Verði það svo.*

[make a general offering to the Ancient Wise, saying:]

Wise Ones and Pious Ones, Sacrificers and Sorcerers – you who kept troth and you who sang galdr, you who gave to the Kindreds and you who gave to the Folk, you who sought wisdom and you who offered its fruits. I call upon you this day and I make you this offering *[give offering]*, which I pray that you find pleasing. Praise and thanks be upon you, Honored Wise Ones. *Verði það svo.*

[make offerings to the specific Ancient Wise that you wish to honor, saying what words seem appropriate to you; when finished, take an omen using the runes, asking the following questions:]

- Were my offerings accepted?
- What blessing do the Ancient Wise give in return?
- What more is asked of me?

[give thanks to Oðinn, close the gates, and then end the rite by saying:]

Ancient Wise, I thank you for blessing me with your love, luck, and wisdom this day. May you watch over me and mine, as I promise to honor and remember you. Praise and thanks be upon you all. *Verði það svo.*

Ansuz & Othilaz bind-rune

Landvættir

Note: This devotional involves the creation of an out-door shrine for the Landvættir, reminiscent of the old stones found through Northern Europe that had small divots or "cups" worn into them. Find a medium-sized stone (at least a hand-span or two large) in your local area (e.g. backyard, parking lot, etc.) that you feel is appropriate and cover one surface (the "top") in a layer of Scupley. Shape a cup-like depression in the Sculpey and then bake it firm – though, if you can find a rock that naturally has depression like this, all the better. Place this somewhere outside where you can reasonably use it for leaving offerings to the Landvættir.

[Stand by the altar, light some incense and say:]

Hail to the Noble and Neighborly Landvættir -- those spirits of this Land who dwell in feather and fur, in shoot and stem, in stone and stream. Blessed spirits, I give you offering this day.

[make an offering to Jorð, saying:]

Generous Mother, you who give us so much in life and provide us with shelter and rest in death, I remember you. Jorð, Bountiful Mother, may you find this offering acceptable, for I give it in love and honor. Praise and thanks be upon you. *Verði það svo.*

[make an offering to Freyr, saying:]

Blessed Lord of the Alfar, Husband to the Land, Prince of Peace and Plenty; I call out to you this day and ask that you watch, open, and ward the Gates Between the Worlds. Please, accept this offering *[make offering]* and with your magic may my words resound in the Deeps, may they ride the winds to the edges of the Miðgarð, may they arise to the Heavens. Praise and thanks be upon you, Generous One. *Verði það svo.*

[make a general offering to the Landvættir, saying:]

Noble Neighbors, spirits of all kinds who bear no undeserved malice or capriciousness toward me and mine, I call out to you this day. I make this offering *[give offering]* in the spirit of frið, friendship, and honor to you all. May we live in peace with one another as good neighbors should. Praise and thanks be upon you all. *Verði það svo.*

[make offerings to any specific land-spirits that you wish to honor, saying what words seem appropriate to you; when finished, take an omen using the runes, asking the following questions:]

- Were my offerings accepted?
- What blessing do the Landvættir give in return?
- What more is asked of me?

[give thanks to Freyr, close the ways, and then end the rite by saying:]

Honored Spirits, I thank you for blessing me with your love, luck, and wisdom this day. May you watch over me and mine, as I promise to honor and remember you. Praise and thanks be upon you all. *Verði það svo.*

Húsvættir

Note: For this devotional, a small house will serve as the shrine for the húsvættir. This can be bought (if you like and can find something appropriate) or it can be made (this can be a fun family project done around Yule-time, especially if one makes it a gingerbread house). Once ready, the shrine should ideally be placed near the hearth or one's main altar, but if a certain area of the home just "seems right" then go with your instincts.

[Stand by the altar, light some incense and say:]

Blessed and Noble Húsvættir, house-mates and friends. I call upon you this day and make offering in your honor.

[make an offering to Jorð, saying:]

Generous Mother, you who give us so much in life and provide us with shelter and rest in death, I remember you. Jorð, Bountiful

Mother, may you find this offering acceptable, for I give it in love and honor. Praise and thanks be upon you. *Verði það svo.*

[make an offering to Frigga, saying:]

Blessed Frigga, Shining Mother, Goddess of the Hearth and Home; I call upon you this day and ask that you watch, open, and ward the Gates Between the Worlds. Please, accept this offering *[make offering]* and with your magic may my words resound in the Deeps, may they ride the winds to the edges of the Miðgarð, and may they arise to the Heavens. Praise and thanks be upon you, All-Mother. *Verði það svo.*

[make a general offering to the Hausvættir, saying:]

Honored Housevættir, house-mates and partners, you who help make this humble house a home and who watch over us mortal dwellers. I make offering to you this day *[give offering]* in honor and gratitude for your friendship, your service, and your generosity. May we always live amicably together – whether under this roof or any other. Praise and thanks be upon, honored and honorable vættir. *Verði það svo.*

[make offerings to any specific house-spirits that you wish to honor, saying what words seem appropriate to you; when finished, take an omen using the runes, asking the following questions:]

- Were my offerings accepted?
- What blessing do the Hausvættir give in return?
- What more is asked of me?

[give thanks to Frigga, close the gates, and then end the rite by saying:]

Blessed House-spirits, I thank you for blessing me with your love, luck, and wisdom this day. May you watch over me and mine as I promise to honor and remember you. Praise and thanks be upon you al. *Verði það svo.*

Dvergar

Note: The focal object for this devotional is small and easily made. Using something along the lines of Sculpey, craft an anvil and a hammer, affixing the hammer to the top surface of the anvil (the dvergar[18] being renowned smiths and all). On the "front" side of the anvil, inscribe the ansuz-kaunaz bind-rune seen below.

[Stand by the altar, light some incense and say:]

Honored and Renowned Dvergar, most-famous and highly-skilled smiths of the rocky earth, you who dwell and craft in the lightless underground. Blessed Crafters, it is to you that I give offering this day.

[make an offering to Jorð, saying:]

Generous Mother, you who give us so much in life and provide us with shelter and rest in death, I remember you. Jorð, Bountiful Mother, may you find this offering acceptable, for I give it in love and honor. Praise and thanks be upon you. *Verði það svo.*

[make an offering to Alvíss, saying:]

Astute and clever Alvíss, you who matched wits with the Thunderer and proved the wealth of your wisdom until Sunna's light touched you -- I call out to you this day and ask that you watch, open, and ward the Gates Between the Worlds. Please, accept this offering *[make offering]* and with your magic may my words resound in the Deeps, may they ride the winds to the edges of the Miðgarð, may they arise to the Heavens. Praise and thanks be upon you, Generous One. *Verði það svo.*

---

[18] Why the *dvergar* and not say…the *ljosalfar* or other types of spirits? The dwarves are recognizable enough that most won't be confused by honoring them. As well, there is a less of a murky nature surrounding them than the *ljosalfar* (Are they non-human spirits? Are they ancestral spirits?).

[make a general offering to the Dvergar, saying:]

Noble Crafters, clever dwellers beneath the earth, makers of the grand panoply of the Guðir: I give honor to you this day. May you find this offering that I give acceptable *[give offering]* and may your craftiness and invention be tools in my hands with which to shape my life. Praise and thanks be upon you, honored and honorable dvergar. *Verði það svo.*

[make offerings to any specific house-spirits that you wish to honor, saying what words seem appropriate to you; when finished, take an omen using the runes, asking the following questions:]

- Were my offerings accepted?
- What blessing do the Dvergar give in return?
- What more is asked of me?

[give thanks to Alvíss, close the ways, and then end the rite by saying:]

Honored Dvergar, I thank you for blessing me with your love, luck, and wisdom this day. May you watch over me and mine, as I promise to honor and remember you. Praise and thanks be upon you all. *Verði það svo.*

Ansuz & Kaunaz bind-rune

Æsir

Note: The only thing needed is an icon (or more) of any of the Æsir with whom you feel a connection or are interested in sparking a relationship.

[Stand by the altar, light some incense and say:]

Honored and Mighty Æsir, you who dwell in Asgarð, who shaped the Cosmos and Humankind both, you who strive to maintain the Wyrd of All. It is to you all that I give offering this day.

[make an offering to Jorð, saying:]

Generous Mother, you who give us so much in life and provide us with shelter and rest in death, I remember you. Jorð, Bountiful Mother, may you find this offering acceptable, for it is given in love and honor. Praise and thanks be upon you. *Verði það svo.*

[make an offering to Oðinn, saying:]

Wisest of the Æsir, Sacrificer and Shaper, I call out to you this day. Please, accept this offering *[make offering]* and with your magic may my words resound in the Deeps, may they ride the winds to the edges of the Miðgarð, may they arise to the Heavens. Praise and thanks be upon you, Hidden-One. *Verði það svo.*

[make a general offering to the Æsir, saying:]

Blessed Ones, Shining Ones, leaders and guardians of Humanity, you who tend to the Gardens of Men and Gods. I give praise and offering to you in gratitude for all of the blessings that you have graced upon me and mine. May you find this offering that I give *[make offering]* acceptable. Praise and thanks be upon, honored and honorable guðir. *Verði það svo.*

[make offerings to any specific house-spirits that you wish to honor, saying what words seem appropriate to you; when finished, take an omen using the runes, asking the following questions:]

- Were my offerings accepted?
- What blessing do the Æsir give in return?
- What more is asked of me?

[give thanks to Oðinn, close the gates, and then end the rite by saying:]

Blessed Æsir, I thank you for blessing me with your love, luck, and wisdom this day. May you watch over me and mine, as I promise to honor and remember you. Praise and thanks be upon you all. *Verði það svo.*

Vanir

Note: The only thing needed is an icon (or more) of any of the Vanir with which you feel a connection or are interested in sparking a relationship.

[Stand by the altar, light some incense and say:]

Blessed and Generous Vanir, you who tend to the land and the sea, you who provide abundance and joy. It is to you all that I give offering this day.

[make an offering to Jorð, saying:]

Generous Mother, you who give us so much in life and provide us with shelter and rest in death, I remember you. Jorð, Bountiful Mother, may you find this offering acceptable, for it is given in love and honor. Praise and thanks be upon you. *Verði það svo.*

[make an offering to Njorð, saying:]

Wise and Skillful Njorð, Master of Noatun, Supreme Sailor, I call out to you this day. Please, accept this offering *[make offering]* and with your magic may my words resound in the Deeps, may they ride the winds to the edges of the Miðgarð, may they arise to the Heavens. Praise and thanks be upon you, Father of the Twins. *Verði það svo.*

[make a general offering to the Vanir, saying:]

Honored Vanir, Fertile Ones and Joyous Ones, Keepers of Frið and Providers of Bounty. I give praise and offering to you in gratitude for all of the blessings that you have graced upon me and mine. May you find this offering that I give *[make offering]* acceptable. Praise and thanks be upon, honored and honorable guðir. *Verði það svo.*

[make offerings to any specific house-spirits that you wish to honor, saying what words seem appropriate to you; when finished, take an omen using the runes, asking the following questions:]

- Were my offerings accepted?
- What blessing do the Vanir give in return?
- What more is asked of me?

[give thanks to Njorð, close the ways, and then end the rite by saying:]

Mighty Vanir, I thank you for blessing me with your love, luck, and wisdom this day. May you watch over me and mine, as I promise to honor and remember you. Praise and thanks be upon you all, *verði það svo.*

Solar and Lunar Devotionals

Sunna and Máni, the Sun and Moon. Though astrological systems from around the world may give much import to the wanderings of the planets, none can deny the importance that the Sun and the Moon have upon Humanity. From the very fact that the Earth would not exist without the Sun thanks to its life-giving heat and light to the tidal-generation of the Moon's orbital movements to the presence of the seasons and the psychological impact that all of those things have upon us.

Honoring the daily, monthly, and seasonal cycles of the Sun and Moon help to ground us in the world and keep us connected to its rhythms and changes. The following short devotional prayers will help you keep pace with the cycles of the Sun and the Moon throughout the year – sunrises and sunsets, equinoxes and solstices; the waxing and waning of the Moon. The following section, though contains full ritual scripts for honoring the Full Moon throughout the year, complete with workings and an accompanying narrative.

Sunna

Dawn

[Stand by the altar, light some incense and say:]

Hail to Sunna – She of golden face and hair whose countenance warms and enlivens the World. As you saddle Skinfaxi and prepare for your day's journey, may you be swift and mighty, may you evade the jaws of the hungry wolf, and may your radiance guide us toward virtue throughout the day. Praise and thanks be upon you.

Noontide

[Stand by the altar, light some incense and say:]

Hail to Sunna – the shining, golden light of the Heavens. As you reach the zenith of your day's journey, may your might and main shine forth from the roof of the world, serving as a beacon for our hearts, our minds, and our spirits. Praise and thanks be upon you.

Dusk

[Stand by the altar, light some incense and say:]

Blessed Sunna, as you seek the comfort of the horizon, may you rest your weary body, may you relax into the dark Cloak of Night, and may you rise once again in the morning. Praise and thanks be upon you.

Vernal Equinox

[Stand by the altar, light some incense and say:]

Hail to you, Blessed Sunna! On this day your golden face returns to the frozen World, warming and enlivening it as Spring is born. May your heat and light wax and bring forth new life in the wake of Winter's desolation. Praise and thanks be upon you, Sunna. May you never leave us in darkness.

Summer Solstice

[Stand by the altar, light some incense and say:]

Hail to you, Radiant Sunna! On this day, as you ascend to the zenith of your might and main, you shine brightly down upon us. We celebrate the blessings that you selflessly give to us, day in and day out, throughout the year. May your light never be extinguished, may Sköll never taste your flesh, may your heat keep us warm in the freezing dark. Praise and thanks be upon you, Sunna. May you never leave us in darkness.

Autumnal Equinox

[Stand by the altar, light some incense and say:]

Hail to you, Rosy Sunna! On this day, your golden face sinks toward the horizon during the Dusk of the Year. The coming nights will be longer, darker, and colder – but each morning will find us ever-more joyful to see your golden face rising in the East. May we not be parted from you for too long, Shining One. Praise and thanks be upon you, Sunna. May you never leave us in darkness.

Winter Solstice

[Stand by the altar, light some incense and say:]

Hail to you, Mighty Sunna! On this day, your light is fleeting and ice covers the face of the World. We take shelter from the howling wind and hold the Vigil of the Longest Night, making offerings to the Furious Host to pass us by. But your light gives us hope of the coming of Spring, the return of light and life to the World. Praise and thanks be upon you, Sunna. May you never leave us in darkness for too long.

Máni

New Moon

[Stand by the altar, light some incense and say:]

Blessed Máni, though your face is hidden your presence is still felt this night. Hati cannot find you, though he knows that you are still here. Please, Blessed Máni, leave us not in darkness and let your silver face return to guide us safely through the night. Praise and thanks be upon you, Hidden One.

Waxing Moon

[Stand by the altar, light some incense and say:]

Honored Máni, the silver sliver of your face shines radiant among the mantle of the stars. You return to us from your monthly seclusion, your light, might, and main growing with every passing night. Máni, we ask that you guide us safely through the night, watching over us with your shining visage. Praise and thanks be upon you, Silv'ry One.

Full Moon

[Stand by the altar, light some incense and say:]

Shining Máni, your face radiates silvery and bright in the dark night, effulgent and mighty. Hati dares not run you down, in fear of you laying him low at the apex of your might and main. Your silver light shines down upon us like a heavenly beacon, guiding us safely through the night. Praise and thanks be upon you, Shining One.

Waning Moon

[Stand by the altar, light some incense and say:]

Blessed Máni, you of shifting guises and swift travel – Hati grows close now. His teeth seek your flesh, and so you must flee, you must hide. There is no honor lost, it is not your wyrd to stand and fight. As your light lessens, guide us safely through the dark half of rht month, until we can see your shining face once more. Praise and thanks be upon you, Swift One.

The Full Moon

Just as Sunna has a short-term and a long-term cycle – the daily cycle of rising and setting and that of the solstices and equinoxes - so does Máni. We have covered the monthly cycles of the waxing and waning Moon, so now we look toward a more yearly span. In ADF, there are several Groves and many members who honor the "Sixth Night" of the Moon, which according to Pliny the Elder and Tacitus was an auspicious time among the Celtic peoples just after the New Moon. Now, while there's no evidence (at least, none known to this author) that the Germanics counted the Sixth Night as special, we do know that each moon was given a colloquial name, so it obvious that reckoning time by the yearly cycles of Máni was important.

To that end, the following is a year-long series of rituals to be performed on one of the three nights of the Full Moon. Much like with the High Day rituals, each of these liturgical scripts is accompanied by a working and a section of poem. Performed over the course of the year, the poems tell a single, unified story[19] which mirror the ritual working at each step. The intent is to create a consistent narrative thread – both in thought and action – throughout the year to help give meaning while also re-connecting the ritualist and/or the Grove with the Kindreds. The idea behind this particular set of liturgies was two-fold: 1) to give an over-arching mythic narrative to run as a connecting thread from month-to-month, and 2) to try turning these individual rituals into steps in one extended, year-long ritual. Hence, you'll notice some artistic or liturgical licenses being taken here and there in the workings (e.g. – the working for January is inspired by the Roman festival of the *Terminalia*, etc.), but again – as has been noted several times thus far – this book is about ideas. If you don't particularly like one or any of the workings or rituals, please amend and invent as you see fit.

It should also be noted that at least a third of the workings include journeying and trance-induction of some kind. If you have never done this before, it is highly suggested that you practice (either solo or in a group) in the months prior to the first of the journey-work

[19] The collected text of which will be found at the end of this section.

– Ian Corrigan's *Sacred Fire, Holy Well* is recommended for some basic exercises, though there are plenty of other good books on trance-induction and journeying on the market.

January

The year is fresh and it is a time of new beginnings, resolutions are made and boundaries are set (even if only mentally) separating the new year from the previous one. A fresh re-birth where anything is possible.

Working

The working for this moon is one of establishing boundaries, either physical or metaphorical. Physical, if one is working alone or at their hearth-shrine or if their group has physical land of its own upon which to worship; metaphorical for pretty much any other situation, especially if one if working in a group that does not have its own land and thus must be a bit less literal in the kind of boundary that it is establishing.

Either way, though, all one really needs to perform this working is some incense, some water, and suitable offerings for the *vættir*. If one is blessing and marking the boundaries of one's land (whether that be the home or the temple), it would be best to make offerings to the spirits that one knows they will like. Should one not know what the spirits like, such gifts as honey, milk, bread, and butter are good, traditional main-stays (note to Americans and other non-Europeans: it's also not a bad idea to research what the native cultures of your area historically offered – in example: tobacco here in the Eastern and Mid-West parts of the U.S. – as the local spirits will no doubt appreciate those non-Eurocentric gifts, as well). One will want to have on hand as much incense and water as one thinks will be needed to mark the boundaries – larger properties needing a larger amount of both, obviously.

For those groups without land of their own but who still want to mark off a "boundary", this working is still viable: simply make a metaphorical boundary between yourselves and the larger community. This is not to say that you should become snobs or form an insular clique, but there's nothing wrong with adapting the working for this moon to reinforce group-identity. Simply make offerings to the spirits of your local land and community, then cense and asperse your group (amending the *galdr* accordingly to focus on your group of people, as opposed to a plot of land).

Script

Processional

[Insert song/chant here]

Outdweller Entreaty

To all those whose voices do not harmonize with our own, whose purposes may be cross with ours, who may seek to harm and harrow with no legitimate grievance, accept this token of treaty and leave our working be. *[give offering]* Blessed Disir, noble women of our lineages, protectresses and grand-mothers, we ask that you stand watch over this space and make sure that the treaty is upheld. *[give offering]* Praise and thanks be upon on you all. *Verði það svo.*

Purification

[cense and asperse the Folk]

Opening Statement

[ring bells three times to signal the beginning of the rite]

We are gathered here this night to celebrate the fullness of Máni's might and main, to re-connect to the cycles of the Miðgarð, and to give worship to the Kindreds. Tonight, we hallow our borders – marking off that which we consider sacred and special from the profane and commonplace. So let us join together as one folk to make our offerings in joy and reverence.

Opening Prayer

The skull of Mighty Ymir stretches out above us.
The bones of Mighty Ymir support the land about us.
The blood of Mighty Ymir flows under and around us.
All things are of His flesh,

Our wyrds woven together,
May we pray with a good fire.

Inspiration

Noble Skaði: Mistress of the Wastes, Huntress of the Wilds, Wanderer of the Borderlands – we call to you this night. Impart your inspiration, help us to know that which should be within our borders and that which should wander freely outside them. Accept this offering given in gratitude and honor, *[give offering]* and share the warmth and light of our fire this eve. Praise and thanks be upon you.

Honoring the Earth Mother

The Children of the Earth call out to Blessed Jorð – Birther of Storms, Consort of the Shaper, Mother of All. We who walk upon you, who take sustenance from you, who find comfort and rest within your bosom, remember you this day. *[give offering]* May you find this offering acceptable, for it is given in love and gratitude. Earth Mother, accept this offering!

(Re)Creating the Cosmos

In the primal times, the Great Rimthurs was slain and quartered by the Sons of Búri: his Skull became the Sky, his Blood became the Sea, his Body became the Land. And from his Flesh grew a Great Tree, which connected all of the Worlds. May we recreate that Holy Sacrifice this day as we emulate the ordering of the worlds.

[hallow the Hallows by censing and aspersing them]

Grove Attunement

[perform the Two Powers meditation]

We are shaped from driftwood at the Shore of the Worlds,
Grown from the Land,
Washed in the Sea,
Dried by the Sky.

We are tied together by the gifts of the Three Brothers,
By the weavings of the Nornir.
May we be just and true to each other.
May our worship be pious and pure.
Verði það svo.

The Gates

See now in your mind's eye the tree-line of a vast and ancient forest. Within the deep shadows of the trees, a figure moves about. Tall and lean, the man's movements have a wolfish quality to them: efficient, silent, watchful. When he steps through the intermittent spots of light slashed through the darkness of the undergrowth – where the movements of small animals are evident as they rustle through the bushes and fallen leaves – you can see that the man is dressed in a ranger's raiment. Ever silent he stalks the boundaries, keeping his watchful eyes on the darkness and the chaos that lies beyond the orderly world.

This is Viðarr - son of Oðinn and last avenger of his father – and we call upon him now: Silent Viðarr, border-walker and guardian of the farthest edges of the Cosmos, we call out you and ask that you open the Gates for us. We come in frið and friendship, and seek to commune with the Kindreds. Accept this offering and join your powers with ours, Wordless Strider of the Bawn, as we open the Gates Between the Worlds.

[give offering and open the Gates: pull the Two Powers into your hands, feeling the fire and water mix, and draw a clockwise triangle over the Well, saying:]

May this well be the Triple Well.

[draw a triangle over the Fire, saying:]

May this fire be Bifrost's undying flame.

[draw a triangle over the Tree, saying:]

May this tree be mighty Yggdrasil, rising high and low before me.

[see the three triangles – water, fire, and growing wood – hang before in the air and then come together in a valknot, while declaring:]

Latið opna hliðin! Let the Gates be opened!

Forfeður Offering

Blessed Forfeður, you who came before us, you who bore us, you who helped to shape the path that lies ahead. Ancient Wise; Honored Einherjar; You Countless Masses who toiled in obscurity, but upon whose backs our society is built. Meet us at the boundaries. Join us at our Sacred Hearth and be warmed by our good fire. Aid us and guide us as we walk the Elder Ways. Forfeður, accept this offering! *[give offering]*

Landvættir Offering

Noble Vættir, you who inhabit this Land, who lurk in stone and tree and river. Those of the primal wilds, those of the tilled and planted field, those of cobbled stones and bricked-walls: hear our call. May you join us by our fire, may you share your bounties with us as we share ours with you. Meet us at the boundaries, give your ægis that this place be made sacred and special. Join us at our Sacred Hearth and be warmed by our good fire. Aid us and guide us as we walk the Elder Ways. Blessed Vættir, accept this offering! *[give offering]*

Guðir Offering

Shining Guðir, you who shaped the Cosmos, you who guard and guide the World's wyrd, you who teach us and bless us with bounty. May your radiance light our hall, may your warmth stoke our fire, and may your presence alongside us this evening make the Long Night that much more pleasant. Meet us at the boundaries. Join us at our Sacred Hearth and be warmed by our good fire. Aid us and guide us as we walk the Elder Ways. Shining Guðir, accept this offering! *[give offering]*

Key Offering

We now recite a portion of the Lay of Stigr, before we make offerings to Blessed Máni:

The Land was cold and the wind blew hard
so it always was around the new year's birth.
But, beginnings are harsh - fruit is born slowly –
Whether from the Land or Man's beating heart.

On a grand farmstead far into the country,
dwelled the household of Aki - an honorable folk
well-known through the Land for their wisdom and wealth,
and their willingness to share with those in need.

A celebration was being held to bless the land
and mark the boundaries of Aki's fields.
The folk of the region came for the festivities
And to help with the hallowing of the land.

The borders were walked, blessed with incense and water;
offerings were left for the spirits of the land.
Blessings and gifts would yield a good bounty
bringing prosperity and weal to who worked it.

After the blessings and gifts were given,
the Folk retired forwith to Aki's stead.
Food was laid out and drink were ready,
music was made for the Folk to be merry.

Among the revelers was Aki's son, Stigr,
first-born of his children and formidable of mind.
He mingled with the Folk as a good host should,
dancing and singing, and drinking with the men.

A young woman caught his eye, fair and comely,
a far-traveled guest whose bane was given as 'Eydís.'
Together they talked, together they ate,

together they drank   and danced merrily.

'Come with me,' she said,   'to my far kingdom.
    'Fortune and fame you'll find.'
As much as he desired it,   Stigr had to decline:
    'My father 'n' folk need me here.'

Shyly, they parted,   she told him to think on it:
come morning's light, the offer would be made, again.
And the feasting continued   far into the night.
Drunk 'n' sleepy was Stigr   when he stumbled to bed.

Blessed Máni, Silv'ry Eye of the Heavens, Brother to the Golden One, and Guide of Humanity through the Dark Night, we honor you this eve'. May your blessings of illumination and guidance be with us through the coming weeks until your face shines bright and full once more. Honored Máni, accept our offerings!

Omen

[make an offering to the Norns, saying:]

Wise Sisters, Tenders of the Great Tree, Weavers of That-Which-Is and That-Which-Is-Becoming. Accept this offering, please, and let me peer into your Sacred Well.

[take the omens, preferably with runes]

The seer for this rite will ask four questions:

- Have our offerings been accepted?
- What do the Forfeður give in return?
- What do the Vættir give in return?
- What do the Guðir give in return?

Calling for, Hallowing, and Affirmation of the Blessings

Holy Ones, we have given in friendship and love, so that you might give in return. Kindreds, we ask that you give us the Blessed

Waters: the Waters of Wyrd, the Waters of Wisdom, the Waters of Life!

Mighty Ones, give us the Waters!

Noble Ones, give us the Waters!

Shining Ones, give us the Waters!

[charge the Waters by intoning the rune associated with the specific Kindred during their part of the call-and-response, while pushing energy into the pitcher; when Waters are charged, hold them up to the congregation]

Sjáið vatn lífsins!

Children of the Earth, before you is the holy cup. Do you wish to share in these blessings?

All: We do!

Then, as the waters are poured out, know that they hold blessings for you and this grove and this community. Work well with these blessings, Children of the Earth.

[pass out the Waters to the Folk; a portion of the Waters is poured into the Blessing Bowl for the working]

Working

[stand over the bowl of water and the incense to be used, drawing the Two Powers into you and then shunting them down into the water and incense while saying:]

Noble Máni,
May your might and main fill these vessels of blessing,
Sanctifying their contents for the work ahead.
Verði það svo.

[take up the bowls and walk the boundary of the land to be blessed, aspersing and censing as you go, while speaking this galdr:]

Let this Land be set aside,
Made sacred and holy
For twelve more turnings
Of Máni's Bright Face.

[repeat this galdr until you are finished censing and aspersing; when finished, return to the altar]

Thanking

[thank the assembled Kindreds in reverse order: Deities, Land-Spirits, and Ancestors]

Closing the Gates

Silent Warder, Sojourning Ranger, Blessed Viðarr: we call out to you once more. Give us the power your vigilant attention, give us your power to demarcate order from chaos. Give us your authority to close the Gates Between the Worlds.

[give an offering and close the Gates: draw the Two Powers back into your hands, feeling the water and fire turn to ice within you, drawing a counter-clockwise triangle over the Tree, saying:]

May this Tree be just a tree.

[draw a triangle over the Fire, saying:]

May this Fire be just flame.

[draw a triangle over the Well, saying:]

May this Well be just water.

[as you draw the triangles, see the them form from ice, hanging in the air by the Hallows; declare:]

Latið loka hliðunum! Let the Gates be Closed!

[clap your hands firmly together and see the icy triangles shatter, the cosmic powers keeping the Gates open dispersing; and say:]

Honored Viðarr, we thank you.

Thanking Inspiration

Blessed Skaði – strident and far-traveling huntress: we thank you.

Thanking the Earth Mother

Jorð, beauteous and bountiful mother, we thank you.

Closing the Rite

Go now, Children of Earth, in peace with the blessings of the Kindred and a Fire in your Heart. This rite is ended.

February

In temperate, Northern climes, February is usually one of the coldest months of the year, if only because one is generally quite tired of winter by that point. Depending on where you live, it may have been snowing for three or four months (maybe more) by then and the desire for something other than freezing cold and featureless blankets of snow covering everything can inspire a restless kind of cabin fever.

At this time especially, an outer and inner purification can help.

Working

The working for this moon will require only one additional ritual item: a hammer. Generally, a sledge of some (whether big or small) kind fits the archetypal imagery best, since the idea is to evoke the association with Thor's hammer, Mjölnir, and a claw-hammer would just seem odd.

Much like with the working for January, this one may need alteration depending on your circumstances. Don't have common, sacred land that you would like to bless? Then just bless the Folk in your group (again, like working for the previous Full Moon).

Script

Processional

[Insert song/chant here]

Outdweller Entreaty

To all those whose voices do not harmonize with our own, whose purposes may be cross with ours, who may seek to harm and harrow with no legitimate grievance, accept this token of treaty and leave our working be. *[give offering]* Blessed Disir, noble women of our lineages, protectresses and grand-mothers, we ask that you stand watch over this space and make sure that the treaty is upheld. *[give offering]* Praise and thanks be upon on you all. *Verði það svo.*

Purification

[cense and asperse the Folk]

Opening Statement

[ring bells three times to signal beginning of the rite]

We are gathered here this night to celebrate the fullness of Máni's might and main, to re-connect to the cycles of the Miðgarð, and to give worship to the Kindreds. Tonight we seek to purify ourselves and our sacred space, banishing all those forces that would seek to harm us – whether intentionally or not. So let us join together as one folk to make our offerings in joy and reverence.

Opening Prayer

The skull of Mighty Ymir stretches out above us.
The bones of Mighty Ymir support the land about us.
The blood of Mighty Ymir flows under and around us.
All things are of His flesh,

Our wyrds woven together,
May we pray with a good fire.

Inspiration

Mighty Thor, you who bless and protect, you who hallow and keep safe, we call out to you. Please stand with us with us this day as we invite the Kindreds in frið and kinship. Accept this offering given in gratitude and honor, *[give offering]* and share with us your might and main to protect against wild forces. Praise and thanks be upon you.

Honoring the Earth Mother

The Children of the Earth call out to Blessed Jorð – Birther of Storms, Consort of the Shaper, Mother of All. We who walk upon you, who take sustenance from you, who find comfort and rest within your bosom, remember you this day. *[give offering]* May you find this offering acceptable, for it is given in love and gratitude. Earth Mother, accept this offering!

(Re)Creating the Cosmos

In the primal times, the Great Rimthurs was slain and quartered by the Sons of Búri: his Skull became the Sky, his Blood became the Sea, his Body became the Land. And from his Flesh grew a Great Tree, which connected all of the Worlds. May we recreate that Holy Sacrifice this day as we emulate the ordering of the worlds.

[hallow the Hallows by censing and aspersing them]

Grove Attunement

[perform the Two Powers meditation]

We are shaped from driftwood at the Shore of the Worlds,
Grown from the Land,
Washed in the Sea,
Dried by the Sky.
We are tied together by the gifts of the Three Brothers,

By the weavings of the Nornir.
May we be just and true to each other.
May our worship be pious and pure.
Verði það svo.

The Gates

See now in your mind's eye the mighty ramparts of a great, walled city. Made of cyclopean blocks of granite, the wall is strong and tall, capable of rebuffing any host who might dare to breach it. But, along the ramparts walks the figure of a man, his gaze ever outward beyond the city's bounds. He is tall and of a noble bearing, with long, white hair that resembles the foam of the sea in its color and the way it moves; his skin is white, as well, pale like alabaster and one could almost mistake him for an albino.

He wears the raiment of a guardsman and carries with him two horns: one in his hand and worn from use, the other slung by his side and pristine as it awaits its purpose. The man squints towards the horizon – where he sees figures, small as ants at that distance – moving toward the city. He cocks an ear toward them, nods satisfactorily after a moment, and peals out a call on his weathered horn.

The gates of this great city open and close upon the signal of this man – this noble gatekeeper and vigilant watchman – known as Heimdall.

We call upon him now: Noble Heimdall, Eagle-Eye, Blower of the Gjallarhorn, we call out to you and ask that you open the Gates for us. We come in frið and friendship, and seek to commune with the Kindreds. Accept this offering and join your powers with ours, Vigilant Watchman of the Gods, as we open the Gates Between the Worlds.

[give offering and open the Gates: pull the Two Powers into your hands, feeling the fire and water mix, and draw a clockwise triangle over the Well, saying:]

May this well be the Triple Well.

[draw a triangle over the Fire, saying:]

May this fire be Bifrost's undying flame.

[draw a triangle over the Tree, saying:]

May this tree be mighty Yggdrasil, rising high and low before me.

[see the three triangles – water, fire, and growing wood – hang before in the air and then come together in a valknot, while declaring:]

Latið opna hliðin! Let the Gates be opened!

Forfeður Offering

Blessed Forfeður, you who came before us, you who bore us, you who helped to shape the path that lies ahead. Ancient Wise; Honored Einherjar; You Countless Masses who toiled in obscurity, but upon whose backs our society is built. Meet us at the boundaries. Join us at our Sacred Hearth and be warmed by our good fire. Aid us and guide us as we walk the Elder Ways. Forfeður, accept this offering! *[give offering]*

Landvættir Offering

Noble Vættir, you who inhabit this Land, who lurk in stone and tree and river. Those of the primal wilds, those of the tilled and planted field, those of cobbled stones and bricked-walls: hear our call. May you join us by our fire, may you share your bounties with us as we share ours with you. Meet us at the boundaries. Join us at our Sacred Hearth and be warmed by our good fire. Aid us and guide us as we walk the Elder Ways. Blessed Vættir, accept this offering! *[give offering]*

Guðir Offering

Shining Guðir, you who shaped the Cosmos, you who guard and guide the World's wyrd, you who teach us and bless us with bounty. May your radiance light our hall, may your warmth stoke our fire, and may your presence alongside us this evening make the Long Night that much more pleasant. Meet us at the boundaries. Join us at our Sacred Hearth and be warmed by our good fire. Aid us and guide us as we walk the Elder Ways. Shining Guðir, accept this offering! *[give offering]*

Key Offering

We now recite a portion of the Lay of Stigr, before we make offerings to Blessed Máni:

In morning's light Eydís made her offer once more;
but, again, Stigr answered 'No.'
And so she traveled far from Aki's stead,
with Stigr regretting his responsibilities.

Swiftly passed the weeks as Stigr worked the farmstead,
helping his father and his folk.
The days grew longer by little increments,
the Sun's light lifting Stigr's spirits some.

But word soon came of neighbors being harried
by bandits fierce and fearsome.
Sweeping in from the mountains, making trouble,
causing worry and woe for the Folk.

Barbarous men they were, brash and angry,
itching for a fight and impudent.
Fields they burned and farmsteads they razed,
seeking gold and glory.

Stigr rode out to face them, when they neared his stead.
His bearing courageous and his mind cunning,
for the bandits outnumbered him fourteen to one.

His wits he would need	to win this battle.

In deep-hooded cloak with spear in hand
he met them	at the cross-roads.
They heckled and threatened, the harrowers did,
seeing him as easy game	to be grabbed.

In a flash	the spear flew,
striking the leader	from his steed;
from deep in his hood,	one eye hidden from sight,
Stigr growled a warning	to the warriors.

Fearing the Alfoðr,	the bandits all fled,
leaving their bloody, fallen	leader to die.
Retrieving the spear, Stigr	spoke o the bandit,
forcing an oath to leave	he lands 'n' folk alone.

Riding home astride	his stout, strong horse,
Stigr couldn't fight	the feeling of pride.
It was then that he sighted	a strange, hobbling woman
forcing herself to cross	the fields.

Blessed Máni, Silv'ry Eye of the Heavens, Brother to the Golden One, and Guide of Humanity through the Dark Night, we honor you this eve'. May your blessings of illumination and guidance be with us through the coming weeks until your face shines bright and full once more. Honored Máni, accept our offerings!

Omen

[make an offering to the Norns, saying:]

Wise Sisters, Tenders of the Great Tree, Weavers of That-Which-Is and That-Which-Is-Becoming. Accept this offering, please, and let me peer into your Sacred Well.

[take the omens, preferably with runes]

The seer for this rite will ask four questions:

- Have our offerings been accepted?
- What do the Forfeður give in return?
- What do the Vættir give in return?
- What do the Guðir give in return?

Calling for, Hallowing, and Affirmation of the Blessings

Holy Ones, we have given in friendship and love, so that you might give in return. Kindreds, we ask that you give us the Blessed Waters: the Waters of Wyrd, the Waters of Wisdom, the Waters of Life!

Mighty Ones, give us the Waters!

Noble Ones, give us the Waters!

Shining Ones, give us the Waters!

[charge the Waters by intoning the rune associated with the specific Kindred during their part of the call-and-response, while pushing energy into the pitcher; when Waters are charged, hold them up to the congregation]

Sjáið vatn lífsins!

Children of the Earth, before you is the holy cup. Do you wish to share in these blessings?

All: We do!

Then, as the waters are poured out, know that they hold blessings for you and this grove and this community. Work well with these blessings, Children of the Earth.

[pass out the Waters to the Folk; a portion of the Waters is poured into the Blessing Bowl for the working]

Working

[take up the hammer and walk to each of the four directions – starting in the east and turning clockwise - in the space to be purified, hold it up before you, saying each time:]

By the might and main of divine Mjölnir,
Fashioned by the crafty dvergar
And wielded by the noble Æsir,
May this space be cleansed and hallowed.

[return to the altar and hold the hammer up, saying:]

With the blessings of Thor and
Austri, Suðri, Vestri, and Norðri –
The dvergar of the four directions –
May this place be safe and holy
For twelve more turnings
Of Máni's shining face.
Verði það svo.

[pull the Two Powers into you and guide their energy into the hammer, filling it until it feels "full", then direct the energy out in your mind's eye to the boundaries of the space, the energy arcing out like lightning from the hammer's head; keep this visualization going for a few breaths or until it feels right to stop, then set the hammer back down upon the altar, and say:]

Let no ill will, nor capricious or malevolent being, enter this space while this blessing remains. *Verði það svo.*

Thanking

[thank the assembled Kindreds in reverse order: Deities, Land-Spirits, and Ancestors]

Closing the Gates

Noble Watchmen, Guardian upon the Walls of Asgarð, Vigilant Heimdall: we call out to you once more. Give us the power of your unrivalled sight, give us the range of your inescapable hearing. Give us your authority to close the Gates Between the Worlds.

[give an offering and close the Gates: draw the Two Powers back into your hands, feeling the water and fire turn to ice within you, drawing a counter-clockwise triangle over the Tree, saying:]

May this Tree be just a tree.

[draw a triangle over the Fire, saying:]

May this Fire be just flame.

[draw a triangle over the Well, saying:]

May this Well be just water.

[as you draw the triangles, see the them form from ice, hanging in the air by the Hallows; declare:]

Latið loka hliðunum! Let the Gates be Closed!

[clap your hands firmly together and see the icy triangles shatter, the cosmic powers keeping the Gates open dispersing; and say:]

Vigilant Heimdall, we thank you.

Thanking Inspiration

Deep-thinker, Jotun's Bane, Noble Thor: we thank you for you aid this evening.

Thanking the Earth Mother

Jorð, beauteous and bountiful mother, we thank you.

Closing the Rite

Go now, Children of Earth, in peace with the blessings of the Kindred and a Fire in your Heart. This rite is ended.

March

With the coming of March, the snows slowly begin to melt and the earth softens. It is not yet spring, but winter's grip upon the world is weakening as the Vernal Equinox draws ever nearer. And at this time, we remember the promise of bounty that the Land gives to us.

Working

This moon's working consists of consecrating and making offerings to a physical representation of the Earth Mother, in general, and the local Land, in particular.

If this is your first time performing this working, you'll need to make the representation first. The core ingredient(s) of this representation will be earth and stones from the land you live on (note: this does not necessarily have to be from the place where your house/apartment/etc. is located, but from anywhere in your city or surrounding countryside that feels appropriate is fine), the rest of the representation is best constructed from a polymer clay (like Scupley) which can be bought at any number of craft stores or supermarkets. If one is practiced in working with *actual* clay, you may want to use that if you so desire; but something easy to work with and fire (e.g. – with a standard kitchen oven) is recommended.

When procuring the earth and rocks, you should make an offering of milk or beer or anything else that feels like an appropriate offering for the Earth Mother (whether as a universal concept or the local manifestation of the Land) and say a short prayer of thanks (divining whether the exchange is accepted is a good idea, as well). Then, take a small amount of dirt and nine stones – how big those stones are depend on how big you plan to make your representation. The actual form of the representation depends on you – the easiest forms could be a simple disk with a pocket for the dirt and stones or a quasi-humanoid idol (think "Venus of Willendorf") with the dirt and stones worked into the body and/or appendages. The only thing that is truly required is the inscribing of the bind-rune below upon the surface of the representation.

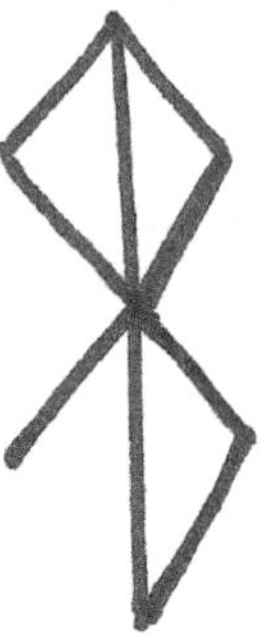

Berkano-Othilaz-Sowilo

While inscribing the bind-rune, you'll want to center yourself first and sing the seed-syllables of the three runes ("Buhh-Ohh-Suhh") as you send the energy of the Two Powers down into it via your rister/knife. Once the representation is fired and ready to go, you can feel free to decorate it in any way that feels appropriate or keep it simple and blank (aside from the bind-rune, that is). The script will provide what to do with the representation in ritual, but prior to and after ritual for the three nights of the Full Moon, make sure that representation is exposed to the light of the Moon – either by sitting at a window or outside under the open sky.

The working will also include a journey of short to moderate length, where the lead ritualist will guide the participants to a meeting with the Earth Mother. Should you be working alone or in a small group, it may be necessary to either memorize the script (and amend the language where necessary) prior to the ritual or have a recording of it that can be played, so that the lead ritualist can participate, as well. Whether in a group or solo, having something some thing on hand to record possible messages with will be useful; though pen and paper will suffice, some form of audio recording (tape, digital recorder, etc.) will be ideal.

Note: for those who might end up moving (to another city, state, country, etc.) at some point after having made this representation, it is recommended that you make a new one once you are settled in your new area – especially if you associated the previous one with the specific, local manifestation of the Land you used to live in. The old one can still be kept and used, especially if you would like to maintain ties to the spirits of the Land you used to live upon, but it would be best to make a new representation of the Land/Earth Mother when settling in a new area.

Script

Processional

[Insert song/chant here]

Outdweller Entreaty

To all those whose voices do not harmonize with our own, whose purposes may be cross with ours, who may seek to harm and harrow with no legitimate grievance, accept this token of treaty and leave our working be. *[give offering]* Blessed Disir, noble women of our lineages, protectresses and grand-mothers, we ask that you stand watch over this space and make sure that the treaty is upheld. *[give offering]* Praise and thanks be upon on you all. *Verði það svo.*

Purification

[cense and asperse the Folk]

Opening Statement

[ring bells three times to signal beginning of the rite]

We are gathered here this night to celebrate the fullness of Máni's might and main, to re-connect to the cycles of the Miðgarð, and to give worship to the Kindreds. Tonight we seek a connection with the Earth Mother, she who bears, sustains, and comforts us. So let us join together as one folk to make our offerings in joy and reverence.

Opening Prayer

The skull of Mighty Ymir stretches out above us.
The bones of Mighty Ymir support the land about us.
The blood of Mighty Ymir flows under and around us.
All things are of His flesh,

Our wyrds woven together,
May we pray with a good fire.

Inspiration

Blessed Gefjon, blesser of the land, sower of seeds, giver of bounties. You who know the Land so, we call out to you. Please stand with us with us this day as we invite the Kindreds in frið and kinship. Accept this offering given in gratitude and honor, *[give offering]* and share with us your ability to love and work the Land. Praise and thanks be upon you.

Honoring the Earth Mother

The Children of the Earth call out to Blessed Jorð – Birther of Storms, Consort of the Shaper, Mother of All. We who walk upon you, who take sustenance from you, who find comfort and rest within your bosom, remember you this day. *[give offering]* May you find this offering acceptable, for it is given in love and gratitude. Earth Mother, accept this offering!

(Re)Creating the Cosmos

In the primal times, the Great Rimthurs was slain and quartered by the Sons of Búri: his Skull became the Sky, his Blood became the Sea, his Body became the Land. And from his Flesh grew a Great Tree, which connected all of the Worlds. May we recreate that Holy Sacrifice this day as we emulate the ordering of the worlds.

[hallow the Hallows by censing and aspersing them]

Grove Attunement

[perform the Two Powers meditation]

We are shaped from driftwood at the Shore of the Worlds,
Grown from the Land,
Washed in the Sea,
Dried by the Sky.

We are tied together by the gifts of the Three Brothers,
By the weavings of the Nornir.
May we be just and true to each other.
May our worship be pious and pure.
Verði það svo.

The Gates

See now in your mind's eye a vast field of ripening grain, and walking through it a young, voluptuous woman with golden brown hair. She walks with a short metal staff and a hand-sickle slung from her belt, her hands covered by cat-skin gloves. Cheerful and rosy-cheeked, her throat is encircled by a thick necklace made of gold and silver and bits of amber. This beauteous woman is Freyja – the Lovely Lady, Vanadís, and a Chooser of the Battle-Slain.

Blessed Lady, we call out to you today – you of Glittering Gold and Rich Amber, of the Shield and Sword, of the Fruitful Field, you who know the secret ways of the Worlds. We pray that you accept this offering *[make offering]* and in return join your power with ours as we open the Gates Between the Worlds.

[give offering and open the Gates: pull the Two Powers into your hands, feeling the fire and water mix, and draw a clockwise triangle over the Well, saying:]

May this well be the Triple Well.

[draw a triangle over the Fire, saying:]

May this fire be Bifrost's undying flame.

[draw a triangle over the Tree, saying:]

May this tree be mighty Yggdrasil, rising high and low before me.

[see the three triangles – water, fire, and growing wood – hang before in the air and then come together in a valknot, while declaring:]

Latið opna hliðin! Let the Gates be opened!

Forfeður Offering

Blessed Forfeður, you who came before us, you who bore us, you who helped to shape the path that lies ahead. Ancient Wise; Honored Einherjar; You Countless Masses who toiled in obscurity, but upon whose backs our society is built. Meet us at the boundaries. Join us at our Sacred Hearth and be warmed by our good fire. Aid us and guide us as we walk the Elder Ways. Forfeður, accept this offering! *[give offering]*

Landvættir Offering

Noble Vættir, you who inhabit this Land, who lurk in stone and tree and river. Those of the primal wilds, those of the tilled and planted field, those of cobbled stones and bricked-walls: hear our call. May you join us by our fire, may you share your bounties with us as we share ours with you. Meet us at the boundaries. Join us at our Sacred Hearth and be warmed by our good fire. Aid us and guide us as we walk the Elder Ways. Blessed Vættir, accept this offering! *[give offering]*

Guðir Offering

Shining Guðir, you who shaped the Cosmos, you who guard and guide the World's wyrd, you who teach us and bless us with bounty. May your radiance light our hall, may your warmth stoke our fire, and may your presence alongside us this evening make the Long Night that much more pleasant. Meet us at the boundaries. Join us at our Sacred Hearth and be warmed by our good fire. Aid us and guide us as we walk the Elder Ways. Shining Guðir, accept this offering! *[give offering]*

Key Offering

We now recite a portion of the Lay of Stigr, before we make offerings to Blessed Máni:

Stigr hailed the woman and asked if she were well.
Her foot she'd hurt, she answered in response.
Her ankle twisted from falling a gopher hole,
and now she limped lamely on her way home.

The young man was moved
and sympathy forced him from his mount.
He examined the woman, eyeing her ankle,
before offering her a ride back to his stead.

Onto the horse he helped her, gently,
Walking alongside all the way home.
As they traveled, they talked
and Stigr learned about the stranger.

She was a mother and a grandmother,
and she lived not far from there.
On the Land her Folk had lived
from time out of mind, forever it had seemed.

Arriving at the stead, his folk all gathered 'round
they helped the woman with her ankle;
mending and healing, making it better,
and she thanked them for their aid.

'Why are you here? You should be out adventuring,'
she said to Stigr.
'My family,' he said. 'They need me here.
'I dare not disappoint them.'

She produced an amulet and pressed it in his hands,
stating that it was a gift for Stigr's help.
She urged him to follow his heart's desire;
without him, his family would fare fine.

'Go on,' she told him. 'Go find Eydís.
'Go find your heart's fulfillment.'
Stigr was shocked: how did she know of Eydís?

Who was this woman before him?

With that, the woman left leaving Stigr alone
with her amulet and his confusion.
In the next dawn's light he left,
setting out to find his fortune and his lady.

Blessed Máni, Silv'ry Eye of the Heavens, Brother to the Golden One, and Guide of Humanity through the Dark Night, we honor you this eve'. May your blessings of illumination and guidance be with us through the coming weeks until your face shines bright and full once more. Honored Máni, accept our offerings!

Omen

[make an offering to the Norns, saying:]

Wise Sisters, Tenders of the Great Tree, Weavers of That-Which-Is and That-Which-Is-Becoming. Accept this offering, please, and let me peer into your Sacred Well.

[take the omens, preferably with runes]

The seer for this rite will ask four questions:

- Have our offerings been accepted?
- What do the Forfeður give in return?
- What do the Vættir give in return?
- What do the Guðir give in return?

Calling for, Hallowing, and Affirmation of the Blessings

Holy Ones, we have given in friendship and love, so that you might give in return. Kindreds, we ask that you give us the Blessed Waters: the Waters of Wyrd, the Waters of Wisdom, the Waters of Life!

Mighty Ones, give us the Waters!

Noble Ones, give us the Waters!

Shining Ones, give us the Waters!

[charge the Waters by intoning the rune associated with the specific Kindred during their part of the call-and-response, while pushing energy into the pitcher; when Waters are charged, hold them up to the congregation]

Sjáið vatn lífsins!

Children of the Earth, before you is the holy cup. Do you wish to share in these blessings?

All: We do!

Then, as the waters are poured out, know that they hold blessings for you and this grove and this community. Work well with these blessings, Children of the Earth.

[pass out the Waters to the Folk]

Working

[make sure the Earth Mother representation is seated in a visible place on the altar and let the assembled folk settle into a comfortable position – whether sitting, reclined, or prone on the floor; the lead ritualist will now guide the folk through a journey to meet with the Earth Mother, saying:]

Take a moment to relax and get comfortable, closing your eyes and breathing slowly and deeply. [pause for an appropriate amount of time, then:] See yourselves surrounded by the Mists of Magic, those Mists that lie Between the Worlds, see the others here with you through the Mists. Move forward through the Mists until you find yourselves on the grounds outside this room, the Mists floating gently just barely above the earth.

The Mists coalesce briefly in front of the group, building up and forming the shape of a woman. The Mists solidify and the woman takes a step toward you, smiling. This is the Earth Mother. One by one, approach her – introduce yourself and ask if there is anything that she wishes to impart to you in particular or to the group in general. [pause here and give the participants a few silent minutes to interact with the Earth Mother; if any of them voice a message for the group from her, record it; when ready, continue by saying:] Say good-bye to the Earth Mother now, and watch her disappear back into the Mists. Each of you now will turn back toward the Mists from which you emerged and re-enter them. Walk until you find the still form of your physical body within the Mists and merge with it.

Take a few deep breaths and come back into the room, into your physical body. Stand up and stretch if need be.

[the lead ritualist will make an offering to the representation of the Earth Mother, saying:]

Blessed Mother, you from whose womb we all emerge, you who sustain and comfort us, we make you this offering and pray your blessings will be upon for another twelve turnings of Máni's face.

Thanking

[thank the assembled Kindreds in reverse order: Deities, Land-Spirits, and Ancestors]

Closing the Gates

Blessed Lady, Holy Twin of the Vanir, Giver of Prosperity, we call upon you once again ask that you join your magic with ours so that we might close the Gates Between the Worlds.

[give an offering and close the Gates: draw the Two Powers back into your hands, feeling the water and fire turn to ice within you, drawing a counter-clockwise triangle over the Tree, saying:]

May this Tree be just a tree.

[draw a triangle over the Fire, saying:]

May this Fire be just flame.

[draw a triangle over the Well, saying:]

May this Well be just water.

[as you draw the triangles, see the them form from ice, hanging in the air by the Hallows; declare:]

Latið loka hliðunum! Let the Gates be Closed!

[clap your hands firmly together and see the icy triangles shatter, the cosmic powers keeping the Gates open dispersing; and say:]

Blessed Freyja, we thank you.

Thanking Inspiration

Blessed Gefjon, Tender of the Earth, She of the Plow, Planter of Bounty: we thank you.

Thanking the Earth Mother

Jorð, beauteous and bountiful mother, we thank you.

Closing the Rite

Go now, Children of Earth, in peace with the blessings of the Kindred and a Fire in your Heart. This rite is ended.

April

This is traditionally the time when the year is either on the cusp of the Vernal Equinox or has just passed it, heralding the arrival of Spring and the end of Winter. The world gets warmer – and wetter, of course – and it becomes more comfortable to go out wandering for longer periods of time.

During this month, we honor the Gatekeeper – who knows the Ways and guards them – and the orienting influence given to us, in this world and the Otherworld.

Working

Much like the working for March, this working involves some journeying and some creation – however, you'll be doing both at the same time. For this working, the Gatekeeper will be invoked just prior to the beginning of the journey, to help guide and protect the participants as they work to create a collaborative "Inner Grove"[20] or

[20] Shamelessly co-opted from Ian Corrigan: *cite SF, HW*

"Inner Homestead" from which further journeys can be launched – especially over the next three workings.

While doing the journeying, the participants will need to carefully balance their frame of mind as they will be asked to report back what they observe and experience (again, an audio recorder of some kind is ideal) so that the shape of the Grove/Homestead can be moderately concretized within the mind's of the participants. Should you be working alone or in a small group, it may again be necessary to either memorize the script prior to the ritual or have a recording of it that can be played, so that the lead ritualist can participate, as well.

Why do this now instead of during the previous working? The last working was about getting in touch with the Earth Mother, whereas this one is about getting to know the "Gatekeeper" (who may manifest as a specific deity for you or your group, or be a slightly more ambiguous individual with no set, lore-based identity – though Oðinn is called as the "Gatekeeper" for this ritual, he need not be the one who shows up during the working) and thus the "mapping out" of a space in the Otherworld for you and your group to journey forth from seems appropriate. Of course, if this working is performed more than once, you will have to tweak it some – though, that will be left up to you, as it should be something that evolves naturally as you (and your group) work with the Gatekeeper over time.

Script

Processional

[Insert song/chant here]

Outdweller Entreaty

To all those whose voices do not harmonize with our own, whose purposes may be cross with ours, who may seek to harm and harrow with no legitimate grievance, accept this token of treaty and leave our working be. *[give offering]* Blessed Disir, noble women of our lineages, protectresses and grand-mothers, we ask that you stand watch over this space and make sure that the treaty is upheld. *[give offering]* Praise and thanks be upon on you all, verði það svo.

Purification

[cense and asperse the Folk]

Opening Statement

[ring bells three times to signal beginning of the rite]

We are gathered here this night to celebrate the fullness of Máni's might and main, to re-connect to the cycles of the Miðgarð, and to give worship to the Kindreds. Tonight we seek a meeting with the Gatekeeper, one who will lead us into the Otherworld and help us establish a safe refuge there. So let us join together as one folk to make our offerings in joy and reverence.

Opening Prayer

The skull of Mighty Ymir stretches out above us.
The bones of Mighty Ymir support the land about us.
The blood of Mighty Ymir flows under and around us.
All things are of His flesh,

Our wyrds woven together,
May we pray with a good fire.

Inspiration

Blessed Sága, Mistress of the Sunken Benches, weaver of stories and chanter of tales, we call out to you. Please stand with us with us this day as we invite the Kindreds in frið and kinship. Accept this offering given in gratitude and honor, *[give offering]* and share with us your ability to enthrall an audience this day. Praise and thanks be upon you.

Honoring the Earth Mother

The Children of the Earth call out to Blessed Jorð – Birther of Storms, Consort of the Shaper, Mother of All. We who walk upon you, who take sustenance from you, who find comfort and rest within your bosom, remember you this day. *[give offering]* May you find this offering acceptable, for it is given in love and gratitude. Earth Mother, accept this offering!

(Re)Creating the Cosmos

In the primal times, the Great Rimthurs was slain and quartered by the Sons of Búri: his Skull became the Sky, his Blood became the Sea, his Body became the Land. And from his Flesh grew a Great Tree, which connected all of the Worlds. May we recreate that Holy Sacrifice this day as we emulate the ordering of the worlds.

[hallow the Hallows by censing and aspersing them]

Grove Attunement

[perform the Two Powers meditation]

We are shaped from driftwood at the Shore of the Worlds,
Grown from the Land,
Washed in the Sea,
Dried by the Sky.

We are tied together by the gifts of the Three Brothers,
By the weavings of the Nornir.
May we be just and true to each other.
May our worship be pious and pure.
Verði það svo.

The Gates

See now in your mind's a darkened, rain-soaked road. Rain falls and obscures your vision, the scent of hearth-fires drifts on the air. You hear the soft splashing of footsteps nearby - a dark, indistinct figure approaches on the road. The figure's form resolves into that of a man wearing a thick cloak with a deep, deep hood pulled up hiding his face from the cold. In one hand he carries a tall, thick staff, which gives off a wet clack! every time it touches the slick road.

As he grows closer, you can see within the shadow of his hood, and from within that darkness gleams one, sparkling eye. You recognize him now - the Wise Wanderer, the High One, the Hooded One, the God of the Mysteries: Oðinn.

We call upon him now: Blessed Alfoðr, Shaper of Worlds, and Counselor to those wise enough to listen; you who know all the roads and ways through-out the Worlds, we call out to you and ask a boon. Accept this offering and join your power with ours, Wisest of the Æsir, as we open the Gates Between the Worlds.

[give offering and open the Gates: pull the Two Powers into your hands, feeling the fire and water mix, and draw a clockwise triangle over the Well, saying]

May this well be the Triple Well.

[draw a triangle over the Fire, saying:]

May this fire be Bifrost's undying flame.

[draw a triangle over the Tree, saying:]

May this tree be mighty Yggdrasil, rising high and low before me.

[see the three triangles – water, fire, and growing wood – hang before in the air and then come together in a valknot, while declaring:]

Latið opna hliðin! Let the Gates be opened!

Forfeður Offering

Blessed Forfeður, you who came before us, you who bore us, you who helped to shape the path that lies ahead. Ancient Wise; Honored Einherjar; You Countless Masses who toiled in obscurity, but upon whose backs our society is built. Meet us at the boundaries. Join us at our Sacred Hearth and be warmed by our good fire. Aid us and guide us as we walk the Elder Ways. Forfeður, accept this offering! *[give offering]*

Landvættir Offering

Noble Vættir, you who inhabit this Land, who lurk in stone and tree and river. Those of the primal wilds, those of the tilled and planted field, those of cobbled stones and bricked-walls: hear our call. May you join us by our fire, may you share your bounties with us as we share ours with you. Meet us at the boundaries. Join us at our Sacred Hearth and be warmed by our good fire. Aid us and guide us as we walk the Elder Ways. Blessed Vættir, accept this offering! *[give offering]*

Guðir Offering

Shining Guðir, you who shaped the Cosmos, you who guard and guide the World's wyrd, you who teach us and bless us with bounty. May your radiance light our hall, may your warmth stoke our fire, and may your presence alongside us this evening make the Long Night that much more pleasant. Meet us at the boundaries. Join us at our Sacred Hearth and be warmed by our good fire. Aid us and guide us as we walk the Elder Ways. Shining Guðir, accept this offering! *[give offering]*

Key Offering

We now recite a portion of the Lay of Stigr, before we make offerings to Blessed Máni:

Several days passed as Stigr did travel
out from the lands of his Folk.
Strange were the lands into which he'd strayed,
following in the wake of the woman, Eydís.

Unknown forests and unknown rivers,
fields and groves that were foreign to him.
It did not take long for him to lose the trail,
not a soul there was from whom to seek guidance.

At night he would hear whispering voices
flitting among the trees of the darkened forests.
On the following morn' he'd find himself confused
unsure of where he'd woken.

More days passed and Stigr pressed on,
catching glimpses of figures from the corners of his eyes.
In the night he saw spirits among the trees,
giggling and mocking as they made him lose his way.

They taunted and teased him and turned him about,
delighting in his helpless, directionless wandering.
One night he stood watch and waited for the spirits,
seeking a way to stop their maliciousness.

Pretending to sleep he waited the spirits out,
then followed them back through the forest.
They led him to a cave - their home, their lair –
within which he found a cage 'n' wizened prisoner.

The old man told him how to banish the spirits,
his own magic bound while he was imprisoned.
Chanting the galdr given to him

Stigr scattered the spirits on the wind.

Freed from the cage the old fellow was grateful
and promised two boons to be paid in return.
Stigr simply asked the wise, old stranger
how he could find Eydís' home.

Smiling, the old man made Stigr a map
showing him which way to travel.
Grateful and elated Stigr bid farewell to the elder
and continued on his course to find Eydís.

Blessed Máni, Silv'ry Eye of the Heavens, Brother to the Golden One, and Guide of Humanity through the Dark Night, we honor you this eve'. May your blessings of illumination and guidance be with us through the coming weeks until your face shines bright and full once more. Honored Máni, accept our offerings!

Omen

[make an offering to the Norns, saying:]

Wise Sisters, Tenders of the Great Tree, Weavers of That-Which-Is and That-Which-Is-Becoming. Accept this offering, please, and let me peer into your Sacred Well.

[Take the omens, preferably with runes]

The seer for this rite will ask four questions:

- Have our offerings been accepted?
- What do the Forfeður give in return?
- What do the Vættir give in return?
- What do the Guðir give in return?

Calling for, Hallowing, and Affirmation of the Blessings

Holy Ones, we have given in friendship and love, so that you might give in return. Kindreds, we ask that you give us the Blessed

Waters: the Waters of Wyrd, the Waters of Wisdom, the Waters of Life!

Mighty Ones, give us the Waters!

Noble Ones, give us the Waters!

Shining Ones, give us the Waters!

[charge the Waters by intoning the rune associated with the specific Kindred during their part of the call-and-response, while pushing energy into the pitcher; when Waters are charged, hold them up to the congregation]

Sjáið vatn lífsins!

Children of the Earth, before you is the holy cup. Do you wish to share in these blessings?

All: We do!

Then, as the waters are poured out, know that they hold blessings for you and this grove and this community. Work well with these blessings, Children of the Earth.

[pass out the Waters to the Folk]

Working

We now call upon the Keeper of Gates, the Wanderer of the Ways, to join us this night and aid us in shaping a home in the Otherworlds.

[let the assembled folk settle into a comfortable position – whether sitting, reclined, or prone on the floor; the lead ritualist will now guide the folk through a journey to meet with the Gatekeeper, saying:]

Take a moment to relax and get comfortable, closing your eyes and breathing slowly and deeply. *[pause for an appropriate amount of time, then:]* See yourselves surrounded by the Mists of Magic, those Mists that lie Between the Worlds, see the others here with you through the Mists. Move forward through the Mists until you find yourselves on the grounds outside this room, the Mists floating gently just barely above the earth.

From the shadows and the Mists that ring the periphery of the area you hear a figure a approaching before you can even see a silhouette, but as they come closer you can begin to make out their form. *[the lead ritualist can pause at this point, if they desire, and let the participants describe the Gatekeeper or wait until after the journey/ritual is finished to compare experiences]* Greet the Gatekeeper and after a moment he will guide you – as a group – toward the Mists, through which you can see the vague silhouettes of trees and other flora. The Mists slowly coalesce into a forest *[note: for those living in non-temperate, forested areas, changing these descriptions to match your home territory a bit better is advisable]* through which the Gatekeeper guides the group along a long unused and overgrown track through the undergrowth.

Eventually, you all will emerge into a large clearing, the Full Moon and the vast panoply of stars visible overhead. Take a few moments to explore, to converse with the Gatekeeper…

[Let no more than 5 minutes go by before continuing]

The Gatekeeper now gathers you all together, guiding you back out into the forest, out along the track that you journeyed in on. The Gatekeeper leads you through the night-darkened woods until you arrive back at the grounds outside this room. Bid your farewells to the Gatekeeper – who tells you all that now you can find the clearing on you own – before they turn and disappear back into the Mists.

Turn back toward the Mists that you initially emerged from, enter them, and walk until you find the still form of your physical body within the Mists and merge with it.

Take a few deep breaths and come back into the room, into your physical body. Stand up and stretch if need be.

[all participants should take moment or two to stretch and ground themselves, before the ritualist who initially invoked the Gatekeeper at the beginning of the ritual makes one more offering, saying:]

Wise one, cunning one, blessed guide – Gatekeeper, accept this offering given in gratitude and honor.

Thanking

[thank the assembled Kindreds in reverse order: Deities, Land-Spirits, and Ancestors]

Closing the Gates

Blessed Alfoðr, Sacrificer of Self, Knower of the Mysteries, Wise Wanderer: we call upon you once more and ask that you join your power with ours in order to close the Gates Between the Worlds.

[give an offering and close the Gates: draw the Two Powers back into your hands, feeling the water and fire turn to ice within you, drawing a counter-clockwise triangle over the Tree, saying:]

May this Tree be just a tree.

[draw a triangle over the Fire, saying:]

May this Fire be just flame.

[draw a triangle over the Well, saying:]

May this Well be just water.

[as you draw the triangles, see the them form from ice, hanging in the air by the Hallows; declare:]

Latið loka hliðunum! Let the Gates be Closed!

[clap your hands firmly together and see the icy triangles shatter, the cosmic powers keeping the Gates open dispersing; and say:]

Noble Oðinn, we thank you.

Thanking Inspiration

Soul-stirring, story-weaving, audience-enchanting Sága: we thank you.

Thanking the Earth Mother

Jorð, beauteous and bountiful mother, we thank you.

Closing the Rite

Go now, Children of Earth, in peace with the blessings of the Kindred and a Fire in your Heart. This rite is ended.

May

With the arrival of May – and both its proverbial flowers and warmth – one can't help but be inspired by the effulgent blossoming of Spring in full force. And so, during this Moon, we seek to strengthen and anchor the forces of inspiration in our lives for the coming year.

Working

This month's working is a small breather in between the journey work of the previous two months and the journey work of the following three (I would suggest taking time this month to continue practicing basic trance induction exercises during the down-time) and the prep-work for it isn't that difficult.

This month we will be fashioning a talisman to attract and focus the forces of inspiration. I suggest a small, wooden disk (the type which can be found in generally any craft or hobby store) as the base medium for the talisman, though should another medium present itself to you or strike your fancy and is capable of having runes carved into it, by all means use it. That being said: runes. The base medium of the talisman will have a bind-rune carved it and also a hole drilled through for a chain or a thong or a piece of string threaded through – so, it should be large enough and malleable enough for the bind-rune and the hole to fit comfortably on it.

The bind-rune itself is a combination of *Ansuz*, *Sowilo*, and *Jera*:

Ansuz-Sowilo-Jera bind-rune

As you rist it into the surface of the talisman, sing the rune names or their seed syllables ("Ah", "So", "Ja"[21]) while charging the bind-rune with the Two Powers. Just like with the Earth Mother representation you will want to let the talisman bathe in the light of the Full Moon during its three-night span.

[21] "Yah" like the German word for "yes".

Script

Processional

[Insert song/chant here]

Outdweller Entreaty

To all those whose voices do not harmonize with our own, whose purposes may be cross with ours, who may seek to harm and harrow with no legitimate grievance, accept this token of treaty and leave our working be. *[give offering]* Blessed Disir, noble women of our lineages, protectresses and grand-mothers, we ask that you stand watch over this space and make sure that the treaty is upheld. *[give offering]* Praise and thanks be upon on you all. *Verði það svo.*

Purification

[cense and asperse the Folk]

Opening Statement

[ring bells three times to signal beginning of the rite]

We are gathered here this night to celebrate the fullness of Máni's might and main, to re-connect to the cycles of the Miðgarð, and to give worship to the Kindreds. Tonight we seek the presence of Inspiration in our lives. So let us join together as one folk to make our offerings in joy and reverence.

Opening Prayer

The skull of Mighty Ymir stretches out above us.
The bones of Mighty Ymir support the land about us.
The blood of Mighty Ymir flows under and around us.
All things are of His flesh,
Our wyrds woven together,

May we pray with a good fire.

Inspiration

Blessed Kvasir, born of the Peace of the Guðir, you whose blood is the Mead of Inspiration, we call out to you this day. Please, stand with us as we invite the Kindreds in frið and kinship. Accept this offering given in gratitude and honor, *[give offering]* and bless our speech actions with your intoxicating inspiration. Praise and thanks be upon you.

Honoring the Earth Mother

The Children of the Earth call out to Blessed Jorð - Birther of Storms, Consort of the Shaper, Mother of All. We who walk upon you, who take sustenance from you, who find comfort and rest within your bosom, remember you this day. *[give offering]* May you find this offering acceptable, for it is given in love and gratitude. Earth Mother, accept this offering!

(Re)Creating the Cosmos

In the primal times, the Great Rimthurs was slain and quartered by the Sons of Búri: his Skull became the Sky, his Blood became the Sea, his Body became the Land. And from his Flesh grew a Great Tree, which connected all of the Worlds. May we recreate that Holy Sacrifice this day as we emulate the ordering of the worlds.

[hallow the Hallows while the Folk sing the "Portal Song"]

Grove Attunement

[perform the Two Powers meditation]

We are shaped from driftwood at the Shore of the Worlds,
Grown from the Land,
Washed in the Sea,
Dried by the Sky.
We are tied together by the gifts of the Three Brothers,

By the weavings of the Nornir.
May we be just and true to each other.
May our worship be pious and pure.
Verði það svo.

The Gates

See now your mind's eye the hearth- and candle-lit interior of a long, wooden hall. Near the stone hearth sits a man with a string-instrument in his hands that seems at one moment to be a mandolin, at another a guitar or a small harp or a lyre – constantly shifting as you watch. He sings and waxes poetic, his voice at times soothing and at others rousing, but always is his voice pleasant, his performance and bearing eloquent and entertaining.

This is Bragi, the greatest of skalds, the most divine performer of the Æsir, who delights the Guðir themselves with wit, wisdom, and wily turns of phrase. We call out to him now: Blessed Bragi, silver-tongued skald of the Halls of Asgarð, we ask of you a boon – join your magic with ours, sing and charm and inspire the very Nine Worlds themselves to open to us, as we open the Gates Between the Worlds.

[give offering and open the Gates: pull the Two Powers into your hands, feeling the fire and water mix, and draw a clockwise triangle over the Well, saying:]

May this well be the Triple Well.

[draw a triangle over the Fire, saying:]

May this fire be Bifrost's undying flame.

[draw a triangle over the Tree, saying:]

May this tree be mighty Yggdrasil, rising high and low before me.

[see the three triangles – water, fire, and growing wood – hang before in the air and then come together in a valknot, while declaring:]

Latið opna hliðin! Let the Gates be opened!

Forfeður Offering

Blessed Forfeður, you who came before us, you who bore us, you who helped to shape the path that lies ahead. Ancient Wise; Honored Einherjar; You Countless Masses who toiled in obscurity, but upon whose backs our society is built. Meet us at the boundaries. Join us at our Sacred Hearth and be warmed by our good fire. Aid us and guide us as we walk the Elder Ways. Forfeður, accept this offering! *[give offering]*

Landvættir Offering

Noble Vættir, you who inhabit this Land, who lurk in stone and tree and river. Those of the primal wilds, those of the tilled and planted field, those of cobbled stones and bricked-walls: hear our call. May you join us by our fire, may you share your bounties with us as we share ours with you. Meet us at the boundaries. Join us at our Sacred Hearth and be warmed by our good fire. Aid us and guide us as we walk the Elder Ways. Blessed Vættir, accept this offering! *[give offering]*

Guðir Offering

Shining Guðir, you who shaped the Cosmos, you who guard and guide the World's wyrd, you who teach us and bless us with bounty. May your radiance light our hall, may your warmth stoke our fire, and may your presence alongside us this evening make the Long Night that much more pleasant. Meet us at the boundaries. Join us at our Sacred Hearth and be warmed by our good fire. Aid us and guide us as we walk the Elder Ways. Shining Guðir, accept this offering! *[give offering]*

Key Offering

We now recite a portion of the Lay of Stigr, before we make offerings to Blessed Máni:

With the aid of the map   Stigr made good time
traveling through   the murky forests.
With the mischievous spirits   harassing him no more,
he found navigation   fairly easy.

A day and a night passed,   and Stigr found himself
not far from where the old man
had marked   on the map
where his destination   would be.

At dusk   he bedded down
'mong the roots   of a mighty tree,
but his rest   was ripped from him
by the approach of   bold, angry spirits.

Brothers they were   to the spirits he'd banished
and wrathful they were   with Stigr.
They hounded him   through the trees,
running him ragged   as he fled.

They captured Stigr   'neath a craggy mount
and dragged him   by his heels
to an ancient well   dug deep within
the rock of that   deep-rooted mountain.

They cursed him   and crowed at him
and tossed him deep   into that treach'rous well.
Stigr fell swiftly,   swimming through the darkness
'til he landed in a   lump at the bottom.

There he languished, how long he knew not –
maybe hours, maybe days,
the darkness was   too deep to tell.
He prayed for help,   for deliverance.

He sunk into slumber and when he surfaced
moonlight shone, silv'ry,   on a sinuous crack in the stone.
Inspired and elated   he worked industriously,

breaking through the wall   to an old, worn tunnel.

The tunnel wound lazily   through the lightless earth,
though strange mushrooms   glowed strikingly on the walls.
Daylight, eventually, dazzled Stigr's eyes
as he emerged, safely 'n' suddenly, in a new land.

Blessed Máni, Silv'ry Eye of the Heavens, Brother to the Golden One, and Guide of Humanity through the Dark Night, we honor you this eve'. May your blessings of illumination and guidance be with us through the coming weeks until your face shines bright and full once more. Honored Máni, accept our offerings!"

Omen

[make an offering to the Norns, saying:]

Wise Sisters, Tenders of the Great Tree, Weavers of That-Which-Is and That-Which-Is-Becoming. Accept this offering, please, and let me peer into your Sacred Well.

[take the omens, preferably with runes]

The seer for this rite will ask four questions:

- Have our offerings been accepted?
- What do the Forfeður give in return?
- What do the Vættir give in return?
- What do the Guðir give in return?

Calling for, Hallowing, and Affirmation of the Blessings

Holy Ones, we have given in friendship and love, so that you might give in return. Kindreds, we ask that you give us the Blessed Waters: the Waters of Wyrd, the Waters of Wisdom, the Waters of Life!

Mighty Ones, give us the Waters!

Noble Ones, give us the Waters!

Shining Ones, give us the Waters!

[charge the Waters by intoning the rune associated with the specific Kindred during their part of the call-and-response, while pushing energy into the pitcher; when Waters are charged, hold them up to the congregation]

Sjáið vatn lífsins!

Children of the Earth, before you is the holy cup. Do you wish to share in these blessings?

All: We do!

Then, as the waters are poured out, know that they hold blessings for you and this grove and this community. Work well with these blessings, Children of the Earth.

[pass out the Waters to the Folk and save a bit for the working.]

Working

[the group's individual talismans should have been placed together upon the altar prior to the beginning of the rite; now the lead ritualist shall stand over them and asperse them with the Waters, while saying:]

May the Light of Máni and the Blessings of the Kindreds infuse these talismans holy main, empowering them to serve as beacons for inspiration – in all it myriad aspects and forms – in our lives.

May Inspiration fill our heads with wisdom and silver our tongues; *[inscribe Ansuz in the air over the talismans]*
May Inspiration guide us and ours to victory and light; *[inscribe Sowilo in the air]*
May Inspiration fill our hearts, our minds, and our hands with bounty. *[inscribe Jera in the air]*

Verði það svo!

[the lead ritualist will hand out the talismans to the participants, saying the following as they don them:]

May the Inspiration of the Kindreds be with you, in you, flowing through you as you act and speak. *Verði það svo*

Thanking

[thank the assembled Kindreds in reverse order: Deities, Land-Spirits, and Ancestors]

Closing the Gates

Blessed Bragi, Poet of Poets, Skald of Skalds, we call upon you and ask that you join your magic with ours one last time as we close the Gates between the Worlds.

[give an offering and close the Gates: draw the Two Powers back into your hands, feeling the water and fire turn to ice within you, drawing a counter-clockwise triangle over the Tree, saying:]

May this Tree be just a tree.

[draw a triangle over the Fire, saying:]

May this Fire be just flame.

[draw a triangle over the Well, saying:]

May this Well be just water.

[as you draw the triangles, see the them form from ice, hanging in the air by the Hallows; declare:]

Latið loka hliðunum! Let the Gates be Closed!

[Clap your hands firmly together and see the icy triangles shatter, the cosmic powers keeping the Gates open dispersing; and then say:]

Noble Bragi, we thank you.

Thanking Inspiration

Intoxicating and inspiring Kvasir, we thank you.

Thanking the Earth Mother

Jorð, beauteous and bountiful mother, we thank you.

Closing the Rite

Go now, Children of Earth, in peace with the blessings of the Kindred and a Fire in your Heart. This rite is ended.

June

As Sunna makes for her yearly zenith at the equinox, the days become their longest and hottest, and there is little doubt that Summer is in full swing. It is during this time of the year's greatest light, warmth, and life that we should stop for a moment and appreciate life by pausing to remember and meditate upon the dead.

Working

Again, this working is primarily a group journey. However, unlike the March and April workings, the focus of this one is much more personal as opposed to group-oriented. Once again, the lead ritualist will guide the group through the Mists and into the group's Inner Grove. There they will meet with the Ancestors.

While it's very likely to experience a contact with one's blood relations, the Ancestors are not relegated solely to genetics. Adopted relatives, friends, mentors, even culture heroes are likely to present themselves – and since we all know that blood-relations can sometimes be dysfunctional and one might not *want* to interact with them even in this way, it may be advisable to let the participants know that it's okay to seek interaction with any of the non-blood "family" already mentioned.

Script

Processional

[Insert song/chant here]

Outdweller Entreaty

To all those whose voices do not harmonize with our own, whose purposes may be cross with ours, who may seek to harm and harrow with no legitimate grievance, accept this token of treaty and leave our working be. *[give offering]* Blessed Disir, noble women of our lineages, protectresses and grand-mothers, we ask that you stand watch over this space and make sure that the treaty is upheld. *[give offering]* Praise and thanks be upon on you all. *Verði það svo.*

Purification

[cense and asperse the Folk]

Opening Statement

[ring bells three times to signal beginning of the rite]

We are gathered here this night to celebrate the fullness of Máni's might and main, to re-connect to the cycles of the Miðgarð, and to give worship to the Kindreds. Tonight we seek a connection with the Honored Dead, those whose blood and love flow within us. So let us join together as one folk to make our offerings in joy and reverence.

Opening Prayer

The skull of Mighty Ymir stretches out above us.
The bones of Mighty Ymir support the land about us.
The blood of Mighty Ymir flows under and around us.
All things are of His flesh,

Our wyrds woven together,
May we pray with a good fire.

Inspiration

Noble Askr, Progenitor of Humanity, Husband to the Elm, First Ancestor, we call out to you. Please stand with us this day as we invite the Kindreds in frið and kinship. Accept this offering given in gratitude and honor, *[give offering]* and share your love, your luck, your blessing, and your insight into the mortal condition with us. Praise and thanks be upon you.

Honoring the Earth Mother

The Children of the Earth call out to Blessed Jorð – Birther of Storms, Consort of the Shaper, Mother of All. We who walk upon you, who take sustenance from you, who find comfort and rest within your bosom, remember you this day. *[give offering]* May you find this offering acceptable, for it is given in love and gratitude. Earth Mother, accept this offering!

(Re)Creating the Cosmos

In the primal times, the Great Rimthurs was slain and quartered by the Sons of Búri: his Skull became the Sky, his Blood became the Sea, his Body became the Land. And from his Flesh grew a Great Tree, which connected all of the Worlds. May we recreate that Holy Sacrifice this day as we emulate the ordering of the worlds.

[hallow the Hallows by censing and aspersing them]

Grove Attunement

[perform the Two Powers meditation]

We are shaped from driftwood at the Shore of the Worlds,
Grown from the Land,
Washed in the Sea,
Dried by the Sky.

We are tied together by the gifts of the Three Brothers,
By the weavings of the Nornir.
May we be just and true to each other.
May our worship be pious and pure.
Verði það svo.

The Gates

See now in your mind's eye a darkened bridge, lit only by a handful of torches along its length. Though the torches light the bridge surface, they do little to enlighten the impenetrable darkness beyond the bridge. A silhouetted figure comes into view amidst the bridge's length: tall, stout and firm like a mountain, and undeniably feminine. This is Moðguð, Hel's sentry-giantess and guardian of the bridge that leads to Hel's Hall.

We call upon her now: Honored Moðguð, Bridge-Watcher, Keeper of the Gate of Hel, we call out to you and ask that you open the Gates for us. We come in frið and friendship and seek to commune with the Kindreds – especially the Might Dead. Accept this offering and join your power with ours, Oh Mighty Guardian of the Underworld, as we open the Gates Between the Worlds.

[give offering and open the Gates: pull the Two Powers into your hands, feeling the fire and water mix, and draw a clockwise triangle over the Well, saying:]

May this well be the Triple Well.

[draw a triangle over the Fire, saying:]

May this fire be Bifrost's undying flame.

[draw a triangle over the Tree, saying:]

May this tree be mighty Yggdrasil, rising high and low before me.

[see the three triangles – water, fire, and growing wood – hang before in the air and then come together in a valknot, while declaring:]

Latið opna hliðin! Let the Gates be opened!

Forfeður Offering

Blessed Forfeður, you who came before us, you who bore us, you who helped to shape the path that lies ahead. Ancient Wise; Honored Einherjar; You Countless Masses who toiled in obscurity, but upon whose backs our society is built. Meet us at the boundaries. Join us at our Sacred Hearth and be warmed by our good fire. Aid us and guide us as we walk the Elder Ways. Forfeður, accept this offering! *[give offering]*

Landvættir Offering

Noble Vættir, you who inhabit this Land, who lurk in stone and tree and river. Those of the primal wilds, those of the tilled and planted field, those of cobbled stones and bricked-walls: hear our call. May you join us by our fire, may you share your bounties with us as we share ours with you. Meet us at the boundaries. Join us at our Sacred Hearth and be warmed by our good fire. Aid us and guide us as we walk the Elder Ways. Blessed Vættir, accept this offering!

Guðir Offering

Shining Guðir, you who shaped the Cosmos, you who guard and guide the World's wyrd, you who teach us and bless us with bounty. May your radiance light our hall, may your warmth stoke our fire, and may your presence alongside us this evening make the Long Night that much more pleasant. Meet us at the boundaries. Join us at our Sacred Hearth and be warmed by our good fire. Aid us and guide us as we walk the Elder Ways. Shining Guðir, accept this offering!

Key Offering

We now recite a portion of the Lay of Stigr, before we make offerings to Blessed Máni:

Stigr slowly wanderedthrough woods and fields,
inexplicably unnervedby this unknown land.
Whispers haunted him and flashes of motion weaved through the trees
though he never saw a single person.

Night came and Stigr nestled in some tree roots,
slipping quickly into a sound sleep.
He was startled awake'neath a star-strewn sky
faced with the visage of a barely visible man.

The geist was quite maddened as it got closer to Stigr,
its eyes full of fury and a pale, cold fire.
Stigr scrambled to his feet 'n' staggered into the night,
fleeing from the shadewith fear-frozen blood.

He stumbled 'cross a farm, far from the woods,
and found it inhabited by folk living 'n' kind.
The land, they warned, was haunted by the dead:
restless and angry they all sought revenge.

The problem they knew, lay deep in the woods:
a monument desecrated by mortal hands.
Water from a holy well and the fruits of honey, bottled,
he'd need for the necessary cleansing.

Mead they gave him, to help his noble quest,
and told him where a sacred well sat
nestled stout and ancient 'neath a hoary Ash.
Stigr did set out, fearing the roaming dead.

He found the Ash and the well that fed it,
and filled his skin though his nerves were skittish.
Through the wood he traveled with hase
seeking the monument that moved the dead so.

Stigr braved the wilds and the winding paths,
dodged the draugar and the dreadful geists,

ventured forth through   the dark, dread forest
and made it   to the unclean monument.

He washed it   with the holy water
and poured mead   to the many gods.
The darkness lifted   and the dead grew quiet,
and the land seemed   to lay peaceful.

Blessed Máni, Silv'ry Eye of the Heavens, Brother to the Golden One, and Guide of Humanity through the Dark Night, we honor you this eve'. May your blessings of illumination and guidance be with us through the coming weeks until your face shines bright and full once more. Honored Máni, accept our offerings!

Omen

[make an offering to the Norns, saying:]

Wise Sisters, Tenders of the Great Tree, Weavers of That-Which-Is and That-Which-Is-Becoming. Accept this offering, please, and let me peer into your Sacred Well.

[take the omens, preferably with runes]

The seer for this rite will ask four questions:

- Have our offerings been accepted?
- What do the Forfeður give in return?
- What do the Vættir give in return?
- What do the Guðir give in return?

Calling for, Hallowing, and Affirmation of the Blessings

Holy Ones, we have given in friendship and love, so that you might give in return. Kindreds, we ask that you give us the Blessed Waters: the Waters of Wyrd, the Waters of Wisdom, the Waters of Life!

Mighty Ones, give us the Waters!

Noble Ones, give us the Waters!

Shining Ones, give us the Waters!

[charge the Waters by intoning the rune associated with the specific Kindred during their part of the call-and-response, while pushing energy into the pitcher; when Waters are charged, hold them up to the congregation]

Sjáið vatn lífsins!

Children of the Earth, before you is the holy cup. Do you wish to share in these blessings?

All: We do!

Then, as the waters are poured out, know that they hold blessings for you and this grove and this community. Work well with these blessings, Children of the Earth.

[pass out the Waters to the Folk]

Working

We now reach out to make contact with the Honored Dead: our ancestors of blood, heart, and spirit.

[let the assembled folk settle into a comfortable position – whether sitting, reclined, or prone on the floor; the lead ritualist will now guide the folk through a journey to meet with the Ancestors, saying:]

Take a moment to relax and get comfortable, closing your eyes and breathing slowly and deeply. *[pause for an appropriate amount of time, then:]* See yourselves surrounded by the Mists of Magic, those Mists that lie Between the Worlds, see the others here with you through the Mists. Move forward through the Mists until you find yourselves on the grounds outside this room, the Mists floating gently just barely above the earth.

See before you the path that leads into the woods. The path that twists and turns and winds its way through the trees and undergrowth to the clearing – the grove – that you have established as a sanctum within the Otherworld. Take a moment to just be, taking in the clearing and becoming attuned to it, before striking off into a section of the clearing on your own, away from the group.

As the presence of the others fades into the distance, you come close to the tree-line…and see a figure approaching from the darkness of the wood. As they get closer, you see it to be one of the Honored Dead, one of the Mighty Ones, one of the Ancestors. They step from the shadows of the forest into the silver light of the Full Moon that bathes the clearing. Take time now to speak with them, commune with them…

[pause for a few minutes to let the participants converse with the Ancestral spirits they encounter, before saying:]

Thank the Ancestor for their time and bid them farewell. They turn and re-enter the forest, disappearing back into the shadows. Turn back yourself and return to the rest of the group. Once everyone is re-assembled, follow the path back through the forest to the Mists, and through the Mists back to where your physical body lies in relaxation. Merge with it.

Take a few deep breaths and come back into the room, into your physical body. Stand up and stretch if need be.

[all participants should take moment or two to stretch and ground themselves, before the ritualist who initially invoked the Ancestors at the beginning of the ritual makes one more offering, saying:]

Mighty Ancestors – Honored and Remembered – we thank you for your presence, your blessings, your wisdom. Please accept this final offering, given in love, honor, and remembrance. *Verði það svo.*

Thanking
[thank the assembled Kindreds in reverse order: Deities, Land-Spirits, and Ancestors]

Closing the Gates

Blessed Moðguð, Vigilant and Steadfast, Keeper of the Way between the Living and the Dead, we call upon you once more to join your power with ours as we close the Gates Between the Worlds.

[give an offering and close the Gates: draw the Two Powers back into your hands, feeling the water and fire turn to ice within you, drawing a counter-clockwise triangle over the Tree, saying:]

May this Tree be just a tree.

[draw a triangle over the Fire, saying:]

May this Fire be just flame.

[draw a triangle over the Well, saying:]

May this Well be just water.

[as you draw the triangles, see the them form from ice, hanging in the air by the Hallows; declare:]

Latið loka hliðunum! Let the Gates be Closed!

[clap your hands firmly together and see the icy triangles shatter, the cosmic powers keeping the Gates open dispersing; and then say:]

Blessed Moðguð, we thank you.

Thanking Inspiration

Noble Askr, First Father of our Folk, You who were Shaped by the Three Brothers, we thank you for your insight and inspiration this night.

Thanking the Earth Mother

Jorð, beauteous and bountiful mother, we thank you.

Closing the Rite

Go now, Children of Earth, in peace with the blessings of the Kindred and a Fire in your Heart. This rite is ended.

July

The Summer Solstice, the zenith of Sunna's yearly power, has come and gone by this time. And though the days are incrementally getting shorter and shorter, there is still much life, vitality, and light throughout the Land. Which makes this a perfect time to establish and strengthen one's bonds with the *Landvættir*.

Working

The focus of this working is primarily the establishment of a good relationship between the group (or the solo practitioner) and the spirits of the Land. While regular offerings (of honey, milk, bread, beer, etc.) are one of the best ways to do accomplish little-by-little over time, one can also build a relationship by recognizing and offering to the *genius loci* (to steal a term from the Romans) of a major feature of your Land or City.

Most cities are generally built around or near a large river – as prodigious amounts of fresh water has been an important necessity of urban life for thousands of years – so if your Land/City has a major river-way than you may want to establish a good relationship with the spirit of that river. Or, should there be an important mountain nearby (or tree or lake or any important feature of the Land) you may want to extend friendly relations to it. Heck, you can even try building good relations with the spirit of the City or town itself. The important part of this working is to better know the Land upon which you live, so researching it and having an intellectual understanding is great, but one should try to cultivate an emotional or spiritual connection, too. And that's what this working aims to do.

Script

Processional

[Insert song/chant here]

Outdweller Entreaty

To all those whose voices do not harmonize with our own, whose purposes may be cross with ours, who may seek to harm and harrow with no legitimate grievance, accept this token of treaty and leave our working be. *[give offering]* Blessed Disir, noble women of our lineages, protectresses and grand-mothers, we ask that you stand watch over this space and make sure that the treaty is upheld. *[give offering]* Praise and thanks be upon on you all. *Verði það svo.*

Purification

[cense and asperse the Folk]

Opening Statement

[ring bells three times to signal beginning of the rite]

We are gathered here this night to celebrate the fullness of Máni's might and main, to re-connect to the cycles of the Miðgarð, and to give worship to the Kindreds. Tonight we seek a connection with the Landvættir, but most especially the Spirit of *[insert name]*. So let us join together as one folk to make our offerings in joy and reverence.

Opening Prayer

The skull of Mighty Ymir stretches out above us.
The bones of Mighty Ymir support the land about us.
The blood of Mighty Ymir flows under and around us.
All things are of His flesh,

Our wyrds woven together,
May we pray with a good fire.

Inspiration

Blessed Idunna, fair wife of Bragi, tender of the Apples of Longevity, we call upon you and your insight into the ways of the Worlds – of their life and cycles – and ask that you inspire us this night with your wisdom and knowledge in exchange for this offering made in honor and gratitude *[give offering]*. Praise and thanks be upon you, Fair Idunna.

Honoring the Earth Mother

The Children of the Earth call out to Blessed Jorð - Birther of Storms, Consort of the Shaper, Mother of All. We who walk upon you, who take sustenance from you, who find comfort and rest within your bosom, remember you this day. *[give offering]* May you find this offering acceptable, for it is given in love and gratitude. Earth Mother, accept this offering!

(Re)Creating the Cosmos

In the primal times, the Great Rimthurs was slain and quartered by the Sons of Búri: his Skull became the Sky, his Blood became the Sea, his Body became the Land. And from his Flesh grew a Great Tree, which connected all of the Worlds. May we recreate that Holy Sacrifice this day as we emulate the ordering of the worlds.

[hallow the Hallows by censing and aspersing them]

Grove Attunement

[perform the Two Powers meditation]

We are shaped from driftwood at the Shore of the Worlds,
Grown from the Land,
Washed in the Sea,
Dried by the Sky.

We are tied together by the gifts of the Three Brothers,
By the weavings of the Nornir.
May we be just and true to each other.
May our worship be pious and pure.
Verði það svo.

The Gates

See now in your mind's a darkened road illuminated by the light of the Full Moon that hangs pregnant and shining, shrouded in a mantle of stars in the empty sky. The scent of grasses and water drifts on the air. You hear the soft padding of footsteps nearby - a dark, indistinct figure approaches on the road. The figure's form resolves into that of a man wearing a thick cloak with a deep, deep hood pulled up hiding his face from the cold. In one hand he carries a tall, thick staff, which gives off a dull *clack!* every time it touches the road.

As he grows closer, you can see within the shadow of his hood, and from within that darkness gleams one, sparkling eye. You recognize him now - the Wise Wanderer, the High One, the Hooded One, the God of the Mysteries: Oðinn.

We call upon him now: Blessed Alfoðr, Shaper of Worlds, and Counselor to those wise enough to listen; you who know all the roads and ways through-out the Worlds, you who befriend those who can aid you, you who know the names and titles and faces of beings neither god nor Man, we call out to you and ask a boon. Accept this offering and join your power with ours, Wisest of the Æsir, as we open the Gates Between the Worlds.

[give offering and open the Gates: pull the Two Powers into your hands, feeling the fire and water mix, and draw a clockwise triangle over the Well, saying]

May this well be the Triple Well.

[draw a triangle over the Fire, saying:]

May this fire be Bifrost's undying flame.

[draw a triangle over the Tree, saying:]

May this tree be mighty Yggdrasil, rising high and low before me.

[see the three triangles – water, fire, and growing wood – hang before in the air and then come together in a valknot, while declaring:]

Latið opna hliðin! Let the Gates be opened!

Forfeður Offering

Blessed Forfeður, you who came before us, you who bore us, you who helped to shape the path that lies ahead. Ancient Wise; Honored Einherjar; You Countless Masses who toiled in obscurity, but upon whose backs our society is built. Meet us at the boundaries. Join us at our Sacred Hearth and be warmed by our good fire. Aid us and guide us as we walk the Elder Ways. Forfeður, accept this offering! *[give offering]*

Landvættir Offering

Noble Vættir, you who inhabit this Land, who lurk in stone and tree and river. Those of the primal wilds, those of the tilled and planted field, those of cobbled stones and bricked-walls: hear our call. May you join us by our fire, may you share your bounties with us as we share ours with you. Meet us at the boundaries. Join us at our Sacred Hearth and be warmed by our good fire. Aid us and guide us as we walk the Elder Ways. Blessed Vættir, accept this offering! *[give offering]*

Guðir Offering

Shining Guðir, you who shaped the Cosmos, you who guard and guide the World's wyrd, you who teach us and bless us with bounty. May your radiance light our hall, may your warmth stoke our fire, and may your presence alongside us this evening make the Long Night that much more pleasant. Meet us at the boundaries. Join us at our Sacred Hearth and be warmed by our good fire. Aid us and guide us as we walk the Elder Ways. Shining Guðir, accept this offering! *[give offering]*

Key Offering

We now recite a portion of the Lay of Stigr, before we make offerings to Blessed Máni:

The news of Stigr's bravery spread near and far,
preceding him, it seemed, as he pressed on.
Whether it was farmers or merchants or migratory birds,
those he met had already heard his name.

At the next town he entered he came to a tavern
and the folk welcomed him warmly.
They bought him drinks, they bought him dinner –
but there was a strangeness that made Stigr cautious.

They called Stigr a hero and lauded him greatly,
even offering to host an eve of celebration.
Stigr realized what worried him about these warm folk:
though mannered and beautiful, they were not Men.

Spirit-folk they were, he found –
though clothed in flesh and cleverly so.
Unsure of this surprising development
Stigr stumbled and stammered among them.

As they prepared to celebrate their heroic guest's presence,
Stigr secluded himselfat the town's humble inn.
Dusk covered the landand colored lamps were lit,
when the townsfolk came for the hero.

The customs of their party were strange 'n' perplexing,
but Stigr's faced showed joy when he saw someone familiar.
It was Eydís he saw surrounded by those fey-folk,
he sought her hand as soon as he could.

Eydís guided him through the eye of the storm,
teaching him the ins, the outs,of the odd folk's ways.
And before him was brought a bright 'n' beautiful maid,
offered as a wife as a way of honoring him.

Eydís counseled him not to consent, for
these folk were tricky even when well-meaning.
So, Stigr politely said "No" to the maid
and stayed near Eydís for the rest of the eve.

In the morn, they made fast from the town,
slipping away as the revelers slept.
Together, finally, Stigr felt elated
to have beauteous Eydís trav'ling by his side.

Blessed Máni, Silv'ry Eye of the Heavens, Brother to the Golden One, and Guide of Humanity through the Dark Night, we honor you this eve'. May your blessings of illumination and guidance be with us through the coming weeks until your face shines bright and full once more. Honored Máni, accept our offerings!

Omen

[make an offering to the Norns, saying:]

Wise Sisters, Tenders of the Great Tree, Weavers of That-Which-Is and That-Which-Is-Becoming. Accept this offering, please, and let me peer into your Sacred Well.

[take the omens, preferably with runes]

The seer for this rite will ask four questions:

- Have our offerings been accepted?
- What do the Forfeður give in return?
- What do the Vættir give in return?
- What do the Guðir give in return?

Calling for, Hallowing, and Affirmation of the Blessings

Holy Ones, we have given in friendship and love, so that you might give in return. Kindreds, we ask that you give us the Blessed Waters: the Waters of Wyrd, the Waters of Wisdom, the Waters of Life!

Mighty Ones, give us the Waters!

Noble Ones, give us the Waters!

Shining Ones, give us the Waters!

[charge the Waters by intoning the rune associated with the specific Kindred during their part of the call-and-response, while pushing energy into the pitcher; when Waters are charged, hold them up to the congregation]

Sjáið vatn lífsins!

Children of the Earth, before you is the holy cup. Do you wish to share in these blessings?

All: We do!

Then, as the waters are poured out, know that they hold blessings for you and this grove and this community. Work well with these blessings, Children of the Earth.

[pass out the Waters to the Folk]

Working

We now reach out to the Honored [insert spirit's name], spirit of [insert feature], as we make this offering [give offering] and humbly ask it to join us.

[let the assembled folk settle into a comfortable position – whether sitting, reclined, or prone on the floor; the lead ritualist will now guide the folk through a journey to meet with the Spirit, saying:]

Take a moment to relax and get comfortable, closing your eyes and breathing slowly and deeply. *[pause for an appropriate amount of time, then:]* See yourselves surrounded by the Mists of Magic, those Mists that lie Between the Worlds, see the others here with you through the Mists. Move forward through the Mists until you find yourselves on the grounds outside this room, the Mists floating gently just barely above the earth.

See before you the path that leads into the woods. The path that twists and turns and winds its way through the trees and undergrowth to the clearing – the grove – that you have established as a sanctum within the Otherworld. A soft, summer breeze lightly shakes the limbs of the trees at the edge of the clearing and the light of the Full Moon shines bright and strong and silvery upon you. Take a moment to just be, taking in the clearing and becoming attuned to it. *[pause for a moment or two]* The light of the Moon wanes and darkens for a breath as a thick cloud passes before it, plunging the clearing into near pitch-black darkness. But, the cloud passes and as the light returns, you find that you're no longer alone.

A spirit stands among your group, old and powerful. See them clearly as they stand before you. *[the lead ritualist can pause at this point, if they desire, and let the participants describe the Spirit or wait until after the journey/ritual is finished to compare experiences]* Greet the spirit and ask whether it seeks to establish relations with you and with the group. [it is recommended that the lead ritualist pause at this point and let the participants describe the Spirit's answer; if the answer is negative, skip to the next block of text describing the return journey; if the answer is positive, continue by saying:] Now ask the spirit if there is any specific offering or act of devotion – within reason – that it would like to receive, as part of the building of relations. As well, is there any specific message that is has for you or the group? [*again, the ritualist can either let the participants answer now, or wait until the end]*

Thank the spirit for its presence this night and bid it farewell. Watch the spirit return to the shadowed tree-line of the surrounding forest until it is out of sight. Turn now and follow the path back through the forest to the Mists, and through the Mists back to where your physical body lies in relaxation. Merge with it.

Take a few deep breaths and come back into the room, into your physical body. Stand up and stretch if need be."

[all participants should take moment or two to stretch and ground themselves, before continuing with the liturgy.]

Thanking

[thank the assembled Kindreds in reverse order: Deities, Land-Spirits, and Ancestors]

Closing the Gates

Blessed Alfoðr, Cunning One, Wise One, Far Traveler, we call upon you once more to join your power with ours as we close the Gates Between the Worlds.

[give an offering and close the Gates: draw the Two Powers back into your hands, feeling the water and fire turn to ice within you, drawing a counter-clockwise triangle over the Tree, saying:]

May this Tree be just a tree.

[draw a triangle over the Fire, saying:]

May this Fire be just flame.

[draw a triangle over the Well, saying:]

May this Well be just water.

[as you draw the triangles, see the them form from ice, hanging in the air by the Hallows; declare:]

Latið loka hliðunum! Let the Gates be Closed!

[clap your hands firmly together and see the icy triangles shatter, the cosmic powers keeping the Gates open dispersing; and then say:]

Blessed Oðinn, we thank you.

Thanking Inspiration

Noble Idunna, fair wife of the Skald of Asgarð, Keeper of the Apples, we thank you for your insight and inspiration this night.

Thanking the Earth Mother

Jorð, beauteous and bountiful mother, we thank you.

Closing the Rite

Go now, Children of Earth, in peace with the blessings of the Kindred and a Fire in your Heart. This rite is ended.

August

Summer wanes toward Autumn under August's *ægis*. Renamed more than two-thousand years ago after the *Princeps Civitatis* of Rome, Caesar Augustus, because it was a month marked by several of his Triumphs, the name "august" means "noble", "majestic", "awe-inspiring", and "venerable." So, it is fitting that during this Moon we seek a deeper connection with the Shining *Guðir*.

Working

The focus of this Moon's working is to establish a patron deity for the group (or, to create ties with a new patron or deepen the bonds with an existent one for solitary practitioners – again, adapt as necessary). The group has met and interacted with the Earth Mother, a Gatekeeper, their Ancestors, a specific Spirit of the Land, and now it is time to create a bond with one of the Deities.

For now, a general offering of alcohol (beer, mead, etc.) should suffice, though any workings done after the initial one should obviously have offerings tailored more towards the tastes of the deity encountered. As well, after the initial encounter with the new patron deity for the group, it is advisable for the group to create an idol of the deity for the focus of religious offerings and any magical workings.

Script

Processional

[Insert song/chant here]

Outdweller Entreaty

To all those whose voices do not harmonize with our own, whose purposes may be cross with ours, who may seek to harm and harrow with no legitimate grievance, accept this token of treaty and leave our working be. *[give offering]* Blessed Disir, noble women of our lineages, protectresses and grand-mothers, we ask that you stand watch over this space and make sure that the treaty is upheld. *[give offering]* Praise and thanks be upon on you all. Verði það svo.

Purification

[cense and asperse the Folk]

Opening Statement

[ring bells three times to signal beginning of the rite]

We are gathered here this night to celebrate the fullness of Máni's might and main, to re-connect to the cycles of the Miðgarð, and to give worship to the Kindreds. Tonight we seek a connection with the Guðir, but most especially one among the shining deities who will be a patron to us. So let us join together as one folk to make our offerings in joy and reverence.

Opening Prayer

The skull of Mighty Ymir stretches out above us.
The bones of Mighty Ymir support the land about us.
The blood of Mighty Ymir flows under and around us.
All things are of His flesh,

Our wyrds woven together,
May we pray with a good fire.

Inspiration

Worlds-renowned Bragi, silver-tongued skald of the Halls of Asgarð, you who delight the gods with wit, wisdom, and a well-turned phrase; I pray that you find this offering acceptable *[give offering]* and that you will bless our speech with honeyed words. Praise and thanks be upon you.

Honoring the Earth Mother

The Children of the Earth call out to Blessed Jorð - Birther of Storms, Consort of the Shaper, Mother of All. We who walk upon you, who take sustenance from you, who find comfort and rest within your bosom, remember you this day. *[give offering]* May you find this offering acceptable, for it is given in love and gratitude. Earth Mother, accept this offering!

(Re)Creating the Cosmos

In the primal times, the Great Rimthurs was slain and quartered by the Sons of Búri: his Skull became the Sky, his Blood became the Sea, his Body became the Land. And from his Flesh grew a Great Tree, which connected all of the Worlds. May we recreate that Holy Sacrifice this day as we emulate the ordering of the worlds.

[hallow the Hallows by censing and aspersing them]

Grove Attunement

[perform the Two Powers meditation]

We are shaped from driftwood at the Shore of the Worlds,
Grown from the Land,
Washed in the Sea,
Dried by the Sky.
We are tied together by the gifts of the Three Brothers,

By the weavings of the Nornir.
May we be just and true to each other.
May our worship be pious and pure.
Verði það svo.

The Gates

See now in your mind's eye the mighty ramparts of a great, walled city. Built of cyclopean blocks of granite, the wall stands strong and tall, capable of rebuffing any host who might dare to breach it. But, along the ramparts walks the figure of a man, his gaze cast ever outward beyond the city's bounds. He is tall and of a noble bearing, with long, white hair that resembles the foam of the sea in its color and motion; his skin is white, as well, pale like alabaster and one could almost mistake him for an albino.

He wears the raiment of a guardsman and carries with him two horns: one clasped in his hand and worn from use, the other slung by his side and pristine as it awaits its purpose. The man squints towards the horizon where he sees figures, small as ants at that distance – moving toward the city. He cocks an ear toward them, nods satisfactorily after a moment, and peals out a call on his weathered horn.

The gates of this great city open and close upon the signal of this man – this noble gatekeeper and vigilant watchman – known as Heimdall.

We call upon him now: Noble Heimdall, Eagle-Eye, Blower of the Gjallarhorn, we call out to you and ask that you open the Gates for us. We come in frið and friendship, and seek to commune with the Kindreds. Accept this offering and join your powers with ours, Vigilant Watchman of the Gods, as we open the Gates Between the Worlds.

[give offering and open the Gates: pull the Two Powers into your hands, feeling the fire and water mix, and draw a clockwise triangle over the Well, saying]

May this well be the Triple Well.

[draw a triangle over the Fire, saying:]

May this fire be Bifrost's undying flame.

[draw a triangle over the Tree, saying:]

May this tree be mighty Yggdrasil, rising high and low before me.

[see the three triangles – water, fire, and growing wood – hang before in the air and then come together in a valknot, while declaring:]

Latið opna hliðin! Let the Gates be opened!

Forfeður Offering

Blessed Forfeður, you who came before us, you who bore us, you who helped to shape the path that lies ahead. Ancient Wise; Honored Einherjar; You Countless Masses who toiled in obscurity, but upon whose backs our society is built. Meet us at the boundaries. Join us at our Sacred Hearth and be warmed by our good fire. Aid us and guide us as we walk the Elder Ways. Forfeður, accept this offering! *[give offering]*

Landvættir Offering

Noble Vættir, you who inhabit this Land, who lurk in stone and tree and river. Those of the primal wilds, those of the tilled and planted field, those of cobbled stones and bricked-walls: hear our call. May you join us by our fire, may you share your bounties with us as we share ours with you. Meet us at the boundaries. Join us at our Sacred Hearth and be warmed by our good fire. Aid us and guide us as we walk the Elder Ways. Blessed Vættir, accept this offering! *[give offering]*

Guðir Offering

Shining Guðir, you who shaped the Cosmos, you who guard and guide the World's wyrd, you who teach us and bless us with bounty. May your radiance light our hall, may your warmth stoke our fire, and may your presence alongside us this evening make the Long Night that much more pleasant. Meet us at the boundaries. Join us at our Sacred Hearth and be warmed by our good fire. Aid us and guide us as we walk the Elder Ways. Shining Guðir, accept this offering! *[give offering]*

Key Offering

We now recite a portion of the Lay of Stigr, before we make offerings to Blessed Máni:

She was gone the next morn when Stigr made
to break fast by their camp's low fire.
Despondent and confused he decided to follow.
He tracked her steps to a city of stained-glass.

Rumors of him flew, prior to his arrival,
to the king's court who demanded Stigr come.
As a friend, he presented himself, no foe to the king;
he simply sought out the sightly Eydís.

'My daughter, she is!' declared the shrewd king,
calling her into the court.
Three tasks he'd need complete to take her hand,
to which Stigr agreed wholeheartedly.

An ancient temple needed repair and renovation;
a monster denned in the forest and needed dealt with;
and a dragon kept hostage the king's ancient diadem.
To all these things, Stigr enthusiastically agreed.

To the temple he came considering his options,
when the dead drew up beside him.
So thankful they were they repaired the holy site,

all within the day that Stigr had.

Stigr made for the forest forthwith,
combing those woods for the monster that couched within.
There he found the dreaded creature
And won its allegiance with charm and reason.
Together they made for the dragon's lair:
an ancient tomb, buried deep and hidden.
The old woman's amulet throbbed warmly as
The duo approached the sleeping dragon.

With the amulet in hand the monster hastened past where
the dragon lay protecting the king's diadem.
Stigr snatched it up - and an unusual sword, too –
as the dragon was distracted by the amulet.

Enraged, the dragon roared its displeasure,
as desp'rately the duo fled its lair.
They parted ways amiably, announcing each as 'friend',
and Stigr, with diadem in hand, stole back to the city.

Blessed Máni, Silv'ry Eye of the Heavens, Brother to the Golden One, and Guide of Humanity through the Dark Night, we honor you this eve'. May your blessings of illumination and guidance be with us through the coming weeks until your face shines bright and full once more. Honored Máni, accept our offerings!

Omen

[make an offering to the Norns, saying:]

Wise Sisters, Tenders of the Great Tree, Weavers of That-Which-Is and That-Which-Is-Becoming. Accept this offering, please, and let me peer into your Sacred Well.

[take the omens, preferably with runes]

The seer for this rite will ask four questions:

- Have our offerings been accepted?

- What do the Forfeður give in return?
- What do the Vættir give in return?
- What do the Guðir give in return?

Calling for, Hallowing, and Affirmation of the Blessings

Holy Ones, we have given in friendship and love, so that you might give in return. Kindreds, we ask that you give us the Blessed Waters: the Waters of Wyrd, the Waters of Wisdom, the Waters of Life!

Mighty Ones, give us the Waters!

Noble Ones, give us the Waters!

Shining Ones, give us the Waters!

[charge the Waters by intoning the rune associated with the specific Kindred during their part of the call-and-response, while pushing energy into the pitcher; when Waters are charged, hold them up to the congregation]

Sjáið vatn lífsins!

Children of the Earth, before you is the holy cup. Do you wish to share in these blessings?

All: We do!

Then, as the waters are poured out, know that they hold blessings for you and this grove and this community. Work well with these blessings, Children of the Earth.

[pass out the Waters to the Folk]

Working

We now reach out to the Shining Guðir as we make this offering [give offering] and humbly ask one of their number for patronage.

[let the assembled folk settle into a comfortable position – whether sitting, reclined, or prone on the floor; the lead ritualist will now guide the folk through a journey to meet with the patron deity, saying:]

Take a moment to relax and get comfortable, closing your eyes and breathing slowly and deeply. *[pause for an appropriate amount of time, then:]* See yourselves surrounded by the Mists of Magic, those Mists that lie Between the Worlds, see the others here with you through the Mists. Move forward through the Mists until you find yourselves on the grounds outside this room, the Mists floating gently just barely above the earth.

See before you the path that leads into the woods. The path that twists and turns and winds its way through the trees and undergrowth to the clearing – the grove – that you have established as a sanctum within the Otherworld. A soft, summer breeze lightly shakes the limbs of the trees at the edge of the clearing and the light of the Full Moon shines bright and strong and silvery upon you. Take a moment to just be, taking in the clearing and becoming attuned to it. *[pause for a moment or two]* The moonlight shimmers and dances before your eyes, and a human form takes shapes within the light as it falls upon the clearing. Another moment and the figure has solidified before you… . *[the lead ritualist can pause at this point, if they desire, and let the participants describe the deity or wait until after the journey/ritual is finished to compare experiences]* Greet the Honored Deity who stands before you all and ask them their name. Thank them for coming and ask if they will be a patron to the group, and then what offerings they desire. Finally, ask them what message they might have for the group. *[the lead ritualist will want to wait until after the working to record these answers]* Thank the deity once more for honoring us with their presence and bid them farewell.

As the deity leaves, they dissolve back into the moonbeam that illuminates the clearing until nothing of their presence remains. Turn now and follow the path back through the forest to the Mists, and through the Mists back to where your physical body lies in relaxation. Merge with it.

Take a few deep breaths and come back into the room, into your physical body. Stand up and stretch if need be.

[all participants should take moment or two to stretch and ground themselves, before the lead ritualist makes one more offering saying:]

Oh, Honored One of the Guðir, we give to you this one last offering. *[make offering]*

Thanking

[thank the assembled Kindreds in reverse order: Deities, Land-Spirits, and Ancestors]

Closing the Gates

Honored Heimdall, Far-Seer, Defender of Asgarð, we call upon you once more to join your power with ours as we close the Gates Between the Worlds.

[give an offering and close the Gates: draw the Two Powers back into your hands, feeling the water and fire turn to ice within you, drawing a counter-clockwise triangle over the Tree, saying:]

May this Tree be just a tree.

[draw a triangle over the Fire, saying:]

May this Fire be just flame.

[draw a triangle over the Well, saying:]

May this Well be just water.

[as you draw the triangles, see the them form from ice, hanging in the air by the Hallows; declare:]

Latið loka hliðunum! Let the Gates be Closed!

[clap your hands firmly together and see the icy triangles shatter, the cosmic powers keeping the Gates open dispersing]

Blessed Heimdall, we thank you.

Thanking Inspiration

Noble Bragi, Skald of Skalds, Poet of Poets,, we thank you for your inspiration this night.

Thanking the Earth Mother

Jorð, beauteous and bountiful mother, we thank you.

Closing the Rite

Go now, Children of Earth, in peace with the blessings of the Kindred and a Fire in your Heart. This rite is ended.

September

September marks the Autumnal Equinox, another milestone on the World's yearly journey through the seasons, with the inevitable goal being the stark chill of Winter. At this time of precious balance between light and darkness, of day and night, of heat and cold, we seek to unite ourselves with the flow of the Cosmos, tying our *wyrd* to Its.

Working

This Moon's working will involve calling upon the Three Sisters – Urðr, Verðandi, and Skuld – who are the primary Nornir,[22] divining their wisdom, and focusing it into a physical talisman. The suggested talisman for this is three female figures standing around a well – something that can easily (if somewhat crudely – no one is expecting you to sculpt like Michelangelo) be created using a polymer-clay such as Sculpey. Once this talisman made, again, let it sit bathed

[22] Lore indicates that there are possibly *tons* of minor nornir, essentially spirits tied to the *wyrd* of individuals from birth until death.

in the light of the Full Moon during it's three nights and afterwards keep it on an altar (should your Grove or homestead have a permanent one) or with your other Hallows (should your group not have any permanent ritual space).

Just remember to handle it carefully and wrap it securely if and when you move it to other locations. After all, your *wyrd* for the coming year is tied to it!

Script

Processional

[Insert song/chant here]

Outdweller Entreaty

To all those whose voices do not harmonize with our own, whose purposes may be cross with ours, who may seek to harm and harrow with no legitimate grievance, accept this token of treaty and leave our working be. *[give offering]* Blessed Disir, noble women of our lineages, protectresses and grand-mothers, we ask that you stand watch over this space and make sure that the treaty is upheld. *[give offering]* Praise and thanks be upon on you all. *Verði það svo.*

Purification

[cense and asperse the Folk]

Opening Statement

[ring bells three times to signal beginning of the rite]

We are gathered here this night to celebrate the fullness of Máni's might and main, to re-connect to the cycles of the Miðgarð, and to give worship to the Kindreds. Tonight we seek a connection with the Nornir, those beings of Fate and Chance and Destiny, the Weavers of the Cosmos' Wyrd. So let us join together as one folk to make our offerings in joy and reverence.

Opening Prayer

The skull of Mighty Ymir stretches out above us.
The bones of Mighty Ymir support the land about us.
The blood of Mighty Ymir flows under and around us.
All things are of His flesh,

Our wyrds woven together,
May we pray with a good fire.

Inspiration

Blessed and Generous Urðr, you who know the Beginnings of Things, whose sight encompasses all that has gone before. I pray that you find this offering acceptable [give offering] and that you will bless us with your insight, such that your wisdom will inspire our words and deeds. Praise and thanks be upon you.

Honoring the Earth Mother

The Children of the Earth call out to Blessed Jorð - Birther of Storms, Consort of the Shaper, Mother of All. We who walk upon you, who take sustenance from you, who find comfort and rest within your bosom, remember you this day. *[give offering]* May you find this offering acceptable, for it is given in love and gratitude. Earth Mother, accept this offering!

(Re)Creating the Cosmos

In the primal times, the Great Rimthurs was slain and quartered by the Sons of Búri: his Skull became the Sky, his Blood became the Sea, his Body became the Land. And from his Flesh grew a Great Tree, which connected all of the Worlds. May we recreate that Holy Sacrifice this day as we emulate the ordering of the worlds.

[hallow the Hallows by censing and aspersing them]

Grove Attunement

[perform the Two Powers meditation]

We are shaped from driftwood at the Shore of the Worlds,
Grown from the Land,
Washed in the Sea,
Dried by the Sky.
We are tied together by the gifts of the Three Brothers,

By the weavings of the Nornir.
May we be just and true to each other.
May our worship be pious and pure.
Verði það svo.

The Gates

See now in your mind's eye an ancient and well-grown forest. Moonlight, silver and bright, filters down through the canopy and the skyward-stretching limbs of trees. In the darkness of the forest, you can see the shape of a woman, cloaked and hooded, walking steadily down a dirt path that is barely more than an animal run in the undergrowth. She carries no lamp and the moonlight barely illuminates the forest enough to see…and yet, this woman does not trip, she does not stumble, every step is planted lightly and confidently, as she maneuvers over and around and past roots, rocks, and other obstacles along the path.

She is Verðandi, who knows the warp and weft all things as they arise in the present moment. We call upon her now: Blessed Verðandi, we call out to you this evening, we ask that you accept this offering and join your powers with ours as we open the Gates Between the Worlds.

[give offering and open the Gates: pull the Two Powers into your hands, feeling the fire and water mix, and draw a clockwise triangle over the Well, saying]

May this well be the Triple Well.

[draw a triangle over the Fire, saying:]

May this fire be Bifrost's undying flame.

[draw a triangle over the Tree, saying:]

May this tree be mighty Yggdrasil, rising high and low before me.

[see the three triangles – water, fire, and growing wood – hang before in the air and then come together in a valknot, while declaring:]

Latið opna hliðin! Let the Gates be opened!

Forfeður Offering

Blessed Forfeður, you who came before us, you who bore us, you who helped to shape the path that lies ahead. Ancient Wise; Honored Einherjar; You Countless Masses who toiled in obscurity, but upon whose backs our society is built. Meet us at the boundaries. Join us at our Sacred Hearth and be warmed by our good fire. Aid us and guide us as we walk the Elder Ways. Forfeður, accept this offering! *[give offering]*

Landvættir Offering

Noble Vættir, you who inhabit this Land, who lurk in stone and tree and river. Those of the primal wilds, those of the tilled and planted field, those of cobbled stones and bricked-walls: hear our call. May you join us by our fire, may you share your bounties with us as we share ours with you. Meet us at the boundaries. Join us at our Sacred Hearth and be warmed by our good fire. Aid us and guide us as we walk the Elder Ways. Blessed Vættir, accept this offering! *[give offering]*

Guðir Offering

Shining Guðir, you who shaped the Cosmos, you who guard and guide the World's wyrd, you who teach us and bless us with bounty. May your radiance light our hall, may your warmth stoke our fire, and may your presence alongside us this evening make the Long Night that much more pleasant. Meet us at the boundaries. Join us at our Sacred Hearth and be warmed by our good fire. Aid us and guide us as we walk the Elder Ways. Shining Guðir, accept this offering! *[give offering]*

Key Offering

We now recite a portion of the Lay of Stigr, before we make offerings to Blessed Máni:

When Stigr returned to Ragnvaldr's hall
he found the king less than happy to see him.
The court was hushed as he approached with the diadem,
which Ragnvaldr received gratefully.

'My apologies, Stigr, for having to state this:
'but, Eydís cannot be yours.
'Promised to another her hand already is,
'to the prince of a potent, rival kingdom.'

Stigr was devastated and would not stand
for this last minute change to their mutual deal.
He offered a challenge to this far-off prince:
single combat, the winner would wed Eydís.

So, the prince was called from so far away
and Stigr passed the days practicing his sword-play.
The ancient blade he'd knicked from the dragon
was always in hand, always at his side.

Eydís would come to him at even-tide,
pleading with Stigr not to play this game.
Though promised to the prince, to Stigr her love was given.
And despair she would, should he foolishly die.

But he'd made his challenge and must keep it,
otherwise, dishonor his name and shame himself.
Distraught and fearful, Eydís would flee –
only to return the next night, and restate her plea.

Finally, the prince arrived, his entourage around him,
eager to meet with Stigr in the melee.
With a sacred oath given that no war would be waged,
no matter the victor, they met swords.

Slash and parry, strikes slapped aside –
so the fight went the warriors circling,
with Stigr finding - in stunning surprise –
he fought so well, it was like the sword wielded him.

The prince fell to his knees, pressing for mercy:
he had no luck 'gainst such a legend'ry blade.
A cheer went up, Eydís embraced Stigr warmly
as Ragnvaldr spoke and recognized his son-to-be.

Blessed Máni, Silv'ry Eye of the Heavens, Brother to the Golden One, and Guide of Humanity through the Dark Night, we honor you this eve'. May your blessings of illumination and guidance be with us through the coming weeks until your face shines bright and full once more. Honored Máni, accept our offerings!

Omen

[make an offering to the Norns, saying:]

Skuld, we make offering to you – you and your Blessed, Wise Sisters. So Wise in those things that have to begin, please lend us your wisdom in return. Accept this offering, please, and let me peer into your Sacred Well.

[take the omens, with runes]

The seer for this rite will ask four questions:

- Have our offerings been accepted?
- What do the Forfeður give in return?
- What do the Vættir give in return?
- What do the Guðir give in return?

Calling for, Hallowing, and Affirmation of the Blessings

Holy Ones, we have given in friendship and love, so that you might give in return. Kindreds, we ask that you give us the Blessed

Waters: the Waters of Wyrd, the Waters of Wisdom, the Waters of Life!

Mighty Ones, give us the Waters!

Noble Ones, give us the Waters!

Shining Ones, give us the Waters!

[charge the Waters by intoning the rune associated with the specific Kindred during their part of the call-and-response, while pushing energy into the pitcher; when Waters are charged, hold them up to the congregation]

Sjáið vatn lífsins!

Children of the Earth, before you is the holy cup. Do you wish to share in these blessings?

All: We do!

Then, as the waters are poured out, know that they hold blessings for you and this grove and this community. Work well with these blessings, Children of the Earth.

[pass out the Waters to the Folk, saving some to asperse the talisman with.]

Working

Blessed Nornir, Triple Sisters, Weavers of That-Which-Is and That-Which-Is-Becoming, we call out to you, again, and make one more offering, *[give offering]* asking that you grace us once more with your wisdom and your blessing.

[take the omens, asking:]

What blessings do the Nornir give us?
What is our Path for the coming year?

What more do the Nornir ask of us?

[asperse the talisman as you say the following:]

Honored Sisters, Tenders of the Tree, Maidens of the Well, we thank you for these blessings and insights, may the holy main of the wyrd you've woven for us be present within and tied to this physical focus for the coming year. Praise and thanks be upon you all.

Thanking

[thank the assembled Kindreds in reverse order: Deities, Land-Spirits, and Ancestors]

Closing the Gates

Blessed Urðr, we call upon you once more to join your power with ours as we close the Gates Between the Worlds.

[give an offering and close the Gates: draw the Two Powers back into your hands, feeling the water and fire turn to ice within you, drawing a counter-clockwise triangle over the Tree, saying:]

May this Tree be just a tree.

[draw a triangle over the Fire, saying:]

May this Fire be just flame.

[draw a triangle over the Well, saying:]

May this Well be just water.

[as you draw the triangles, see the them form from ice, hanging in the air by the Hallows; declare:]

Latið loka hliðunum! Let the Gates be Closed!

[clap your hands firmly together and see the icy triangles shatter, the cosmic powers keeping the Gates open dispersing; and then say:]

Wise Urðr, we thank you.

Thanking Inspiration

Noble Verðandi, we thank you for your inspiration this night.

Thanking the Earth Mother

Jorð, beauteous and bountiful mother, we thank you.

Closing the Rite

Go now, Children of Earth, in peace with the blessings of the Kindred and a Fire in your Heart. This rite is ended.

October

The cold sets in, the nights grow long and darker, and Autumn definitely begins to intimate, like a Stark quoting a mantra, that Winter is coming. At this time, as the easy days of Summer are now behind us and we prepare for the harshness of the Winter to come, we take a moment to remember all the boons and blessings we've had the previous year and give thanks.

Working

The working for this Moon is one of thanksgiving and gratitude, and the prep-work is quite simple: get some paper and a pen, take some time to just sit down and think about the previous year. Then, write down all the things – both good and bad – that you are thankful for. When finished, bring the paper with you to ritual.

Once the working section of the ritual arrives, each member of the group will be expected to voice at least a few of things for which they are thankful. Once done, the paper they brought will be burned in the Fire (should your fire consist of just candles, an iron cauldron or something else suitably non-flammable is recommended to let the papers burn in after they've been lit).

Script

Processional

[Insert song/chant here]

Outdweller Entreaty

To all those whose voices do not harmonize with our own, whose purposes may be cross with ours, who may seek to harm and harrow with no legitimate grievance, accept this token of treaty and leave our working be. *[give offering]* Blessed Disir, noble women of our lineages, protectresses and grand-mothers, we ask that you stand watch over this space and make sure that the treaty is upheld. *[give offering]* Praise and thanks be upon on you all. *Verði það svo.*

Purification

[cense and asperse the Folk]

Opening Statement

[ring bells three times to signal beginning of the rite]

We are gathered here this night to celebrate the fullness of Máni's might and main, to re-connect to the cycles of the Miðgarð, and to give worship to the Kindreds. Tonight we seek to voice our gratitude to the Kindred, for all the blessings, boons, hardships, and obstacles they have given us this past year. So let us join together as one folk to make our offerings in joy and reverence.

Opening Prayer

The skull of Mighty Ymir stretches out above us.
The bones of Mighty Ymir support the land about us.
The blood of Mighty Ymir flows under and around us.
All things are of His flesh,

Our wyrds woven together,
May we pray with a good fire.

Inspiration

Worlds-renowned Bragi, silver-tongued skald of the Halls of Asgarð, you who delight the gods with wit, wisdom, and a well-turned phrase; I pray that you find this offering acceptable *[give offering]* and that you will bless our speech with honeyed words. Praise and thanks be upon you.

Honoring the Earth Mother

The Children of the Earth call out to Blessed Jorð - Birther of Storms, Consort of the Shaper, Mother of All. We who walk upon you, who take sustenance from you, who find comfort and rest within your bosom, remember you this day. *[give offering]* May you find this offering acceptable, for it is given in love and gratitude. Earth Mother, accept this offering!

(Re)Creating the Cosmos

In the primal times, the Great Rimthurs was slain and quartered by the Sons of Búri: his Skull became the Sky, his Blood became the Sea, his Body became the Land. And from his Flesh grew a Great Tree, which connected all of the Worlds. May we recreate that Holy Sacrifice this day as we emulate the ordering of the worlds.

[hallow the Hallows by censing and aspersing them]

Grove Attunement

[perform the Two Powers meditation]

We are shaped from driftwood at the Shore of the Worlds,
Grown from the Land,
Washed in the Sea,
Dried by the Sky.
We are tied together by the gifts of the Three Brothers,

By the weavings of the Nornir.
May we be just and true to each other.
May our worship be pious and pure.
Verði það svo.

The Gates

See now in your mind's eye the mighty ramparts of a great, walled city. Built of cyclopean blocks of granite, the wall stands strong and tall, capable of rebuffing any host who might dare to breach it. But, along the ramparts walks the figure of a man, his gaze cast ever outward beyond the city's bounds. He is tall and of a noble bearing, with long, white hair that resembles the foam of the sea in its color and motion; his skin is white, as well, pale like alabaster and one could almost mistake him for an albino.

He wears the raiment of a guardsman and carries with him two horns: one clasped in his hand and worn from use, the other slung by his side and pristine as it awaits its purpose. The man squints towards the horizon where he sees figures, small as ants at that distance – moving toward the city. He cocks an ear toward them, nods satisfactorily after a moment, and peals out a call on his weathered horn.

The gates of this great city open and close upon the signal of this man – this noble gatekeeper and vigilant watchman – known as Heimdall.

We call upon him now: Noble Heimdall, Eagle-Eye, Blower of the Gjallarhorn, we call out to you and ask that you open the Gates for us. We come in frið and friendship, and seek to commune with the Kindreds. Accept this offering and join your powers with ours, Vigilant Watchman of the Gods, as we open the Gates Between the Worlds.

[give offering and open the Gates: pull the Two Powers into your hands, feeling the fire and water mix, and draw a clockwise triangle over the Well, saying]

May this well be the Triple Well.

[draw a triangle over the Fire, saying:]

May this fire be Bifrost's undying flame.

[draw a triangle over the Tree, saying:]

May this tree be mighty Yggdrasil, rising high and low before me.

[see the three triangles – water, fire, and growing wood – hang before in the air and then come together in a valknot, while declaring:]

Latið opna hliðin! Let the Gates be opened!

Forfeður Offering

Blessed Forfeður, you who came before us, you who bore us, you who helped to shape the path that lies ahead. Ancient Wise; Honored Einherjar; You Countless Masses who toiled in obscurity, but upon whose backs our society is built. Meet us at the boundaries. Join us at our Sacred Hearth and be warmed by our good fire. Aid us and guide us as we walk the Elder Ways. Forfeður, accept this offering! *[give offering]*

Landvættir Offering

Noble Vættir, you who inhabit this Land, who lurk in stone and tree and river. Those of the primal wilds, those of the tilled and planted field, those of cobbled stones and bricked-walls: hear our call. May you join us by our fire, may you share your bounties with us as we share ours with you. Meet us at the boundaries. Join us at our Sacred Hearth and be warmed by our good fire. Aid us and guide us as we walk the Elder Ways. Blessed Vættir, accept this offering! *[give offering]*

Guðir Offering

Shining Guðir, you who shaped the Cosmos, you who guard and guide the World's wyrd, you who teach us and bless us with bounty. May your radiance light our hall, may your warmth stoke our fire, and may your presence alongside us this evening make the Long Night that much more pleasant. Meet us at the boundaries. Join us at our Sacred Hearth and be warmed by our good fire. Aid us and guide us as we walk the Elder Ways. Shining Guðir, accept this offering! *[give offering]*

Key Offering

We now recite a portion of the Lay of Stigr, before we make offerings to Blessed Máni:

Preparations were made for the princess' wedding:
an enormous celebration to ensure its memory.
Servants were set flitting about searching for resources
Which Ragnvaldr insisted upon for his only daughter's wedding.

The day finally came and all the city was festive,
eager to take in the royal nuptials.
The ceremony was presided over by the High Priest,
who offered the ring for the couple to oath on.

A great feast followed and all the city-folk were joyous.
Stigr rose at their table and his voice rang out:
he gave thanks to Eydís and her father, the king,
for their generosity 'n' welcome, their gifts of home 'n' love.

Next he gave thanks to the monster of the woods,
misunderstood by the folk and maligned by their fear.
That wild creature of the Land, who longed for a friend,
and had stood by him in danger within the dragon's lair.

Next he gave thanks to the spirits of the dead,
who'd helped him in the temple in thanks for his aid.
So grateful they'd been for the rest he'd given them –

one must not forget the fate of one's ancestors.

Next he gave thanks to the gods 'n' goddesses,
whose divine inspiration had delivered him from bondage,
that lightless well in which he'd languished.
Without their help he'd not have wed Eydís.

Next he gave thanks to the old man in the cave,
that prisoner of the spirits who'd pointed the way.
Without his aid Stigr would have wandered
aimless and forlorn, forever lost.

Finally he gave thanks to the old woman in the fields.
Whose amulet had proven so shiny a prize that
the dragon's attention had been crucially distracted.
The gift of compassion is a gift that's repaid.

At that the folk cheered for their new crown-prince:
a humble ruler is a good ruler truly,
who values the aid and values the loyalty
of those who willingly offer it.

Blessed Máni, Silv'ry Eye of the Heavens, Brother to the Golden One, and Guide of Humanity through the Dark Night, we honor you this eve'. May your blessings of illumination and guidance be with us through the coming weeks until your face shines bright and full once more. Honored Máni, accept our offerings!

Omen

[make an offering to the Norns, saying:]

Skuld, we make offering to you – you and your Blessed, Wise Sisters. So Wise in those things that have to begin, please lend us your wisdom in return. Accept this offering, please, and let me peer into your Sacred Well.

[take the omens, with runes]

The seer for this rite will ask four questions:

- Have our offerings been accepted?
- What do the Forfeður give in return?
- What do the Vættir give in return?
- What do the Guðir give in return?

Calling for, Hallowing, and Affirmation of the Blessings

Holy Ones, we have given in friendship and love, so that you might give in return. Kindreds, we ask that you give us the Blessed Waters: the Waters of Wyrd, the Waters of Wisdom, the Waters of Life!

Mighty Ones, give us the Waters!

Noble Ones, give us the Waters!

Shining Ones, give us the Waters!

[charge the Waters by intoning the rune associated with the specific Kindred during their part of the call-and-response, while pushing energy into the pitcher; when Waters are charged, hold them up to the congregation]

Sjáið vatn lífsins!

Children of the Earth, before you is the holy cup. Do you wish to share in these blessings?

All: We do!

Then, as the waters are poured out, know that they hold blessings for you and this grove and this community. Work well with these blessings, Children of the Earth.

[pass out the Waters to the Folk]

Working

We now offer our thanks to the Kindreds, for the blessings and the boons they have given us, for the trials and tribulations they set before us to make us stronger, for the love and the wisdom they have offered in generosity all this past year.

[one-by-one, the group shares what things that they are thankful for, offering their pieces of paper to the Fire; as each person burns their paper, the group says:]

Praise and thanks be upon the Kindred for all that they offer to us. Verði það svo.

Closing the Gates

Honored Heimdall, Far-Seer, Defender of Asgarð, we call upon you once more to join your power with ours as we close the Gates Between the Worlds.

[give an offering and close the Gates: draw the Two Powers back into your hands, feeling the water and fire turn to ice within you, drawing a counter-clockwise triangle over the Tree, saying:]

May this Tree be just a tree.

[draw a triangle over the Fire, saying:]

May this Fire be just flame.

[draw a triangle over the Well, saying:]

May this Well be just water.

[as you draw the triangles, see the them form from ice, hanging in the air by the Hallows; declare:]

Latið loka hliðunum! Let the Gates be Closed!

[clap your hands firmly together and see the icy triangles shatter, the cosmic powers keeping the Gates open dispersing; and then say:]

Blessed Heimdall, we thank you.

Thanking Inspiration

Noble Bragi, Skald of Skalds, Poet of Poets,, we thank you for your inspiration this night.

Thanking the Earth Mother

Jorð, beauteous and bountiful mother, we thank you.

Closing the Rite

Go now, Children of Earth, in peace with the blessings of the Kindred and a Fire in your Heart. This rite is ended.

November

As the winds of Winter begin to blow stronger, we are reminded that the mundane aspects of life are just as important as the spiritual, the magical, the mystical. And so, at this time, we remember to focus on the profane as much as we focus on the sacred.

Working

Much like October, this Moon's working is a relatively simple one. In the weeks leading up to the rite, each member of the group is expected to tackle at least one aspect of their mundane life that has been causing them trouble (*e.g.* – doing housework, fixing something, ironing troubles in a relationship, *et cetera*), and during the working section of the ritual, they will report on the outcome (or, at least, their current attempts to resolve the situation) as they speak over a horn filled with the Waters of Life.

The core aim of this working is to show how important our regular day-to-day lives are, and that religion/spirituality should not be an escape from them. We should take the lessons and the blessings that the Kindred offer to us and apply them as fully as is possible and reasonable to our daily lives.

Even if that just means remembering to clean the litter box more, to not antagonize your loved ones, or to be more productive at work.

Script

Processional

[Insert song/chant here]

Outdweller Entreaty

To all those whose voices do not harmonize with our own, whose purposes may be cross with ours, who may seek to harm and harrow with no legitimate grievance, accept this token of treaty and leave our working be. *[give offering]* Blessed Disir, noble women of our lineages, protectresses and grand-mothers, we ask that you stand watch over this space and make sure that the treaty is upheld. *[give offering]* Praise and thanks be upon on you all. *Verði það svo.*

Purification

[cense and asperse the Folk]

Opening Statement

[ring bells three times to signal beginning of the rite]

We are gathered here this night to celebrate the fullness of Máni's might and main, to re-connect to the cycles of the Miðgarð, and to give worship to the Kindreds. Tonight we seek to honor the blessings and the wisdom of the Kindred as they manifest in our day-to-day lives. So let us join together as one folk to make our offerings in joy and reverence.

Opening Prayer

The skull of Mighty Ymir stretches out above us.
The bones of Mighty Ymir support the land about us.
The blood of Mighty Ymir flows under and around us.
All things are of His flesh,

Our wyrds woven together,
May we pray with a good fire.

Inspiration

Blessed Sága, Mistress of the Sunken Benches, weaver of stories and chanter of tales, we call out to you. Please stand with us with us this day as we invite the Kindreds in frið and kinship. Accept this offering given in gratitude and honor, *[give offering]* and share with us your ability to enthrall an audience this day. Praise and thanks be upon you.

Honoring the Earth Mother

The Children of the Earth call out to Blessed Jorð – Birther of Storms, Consort of the Shaper, Mother of All. We who walk upon you, who take sustenance from you, who find comfort and rest within your bosom, remember you this day. *[give offering]* May you find this offering acceptable, for it is given in love and gratitude. Earth Mother, accept this offering!

(Re)Creating the Cosmos

In the primal times, the Great Rimthurs was slain and quartered by the Sons of Búri: his Skull became the Sky, his Blood became the Sea, his Body became the Land. And from his Flesh grew a Great Tree, which connected all of the Worlds. May we recreate that Holy Sacrifice this day as we emulate the ordering of the worlds.

[hallow the Hallows by censing and aspersing them]

Grove Attunement

[perform the Two Powers meditation]

We are shaped from driftwood at the Shore of the Worlds,
Grown from the Land,
Washed in the Sea,
Dried by the Sky.

We are tied together by the gifts of the Three Brothers,
By the weavings of the Nornir.
May we be just and true to each other.
May our worship be pious and pure.
Verði það svo.

The Gates

See now in your mind's eye a darkened, wintry road. Snow falls and obscures your vision, the scent of hearth-fires drifts on the air. You hear the soft crunching of footsteps nearby, a dark, indistinct figure approaches on the road. The figure's form resolves into that of a man wearing a thick cloak with a deep, deep hood pulled up hiding his face from the cold. In one hand he carries a tall, thick staff, which gives off a muffled *clack!* every time it touches the snow-covered road.

As he grows closer, you can see within the shadow of his hood, and from within that darkness gleams one, sparkling eye. You recognize him now - the Wise Wanderer, the High One, the Hooded One, the God of the Mysteries: Oðinn.

We call upon him now: Blessed Alfoðr, Shaper of Worlds, and Counselor to those wise enough to listen; you who know all the roads and ways through-out the Worlds, we call out to you and ask a boon. Accept this offering and join your power with ours, Wisest of the Æsir, as we open the Gates Between the Worlds."

[give offering and open the Gates: pull the Two Powers into your hands, feeling the fire and water mix, and draw a clockwise triangle over the Well, saying]

May this well be the Triple Well.

[draw a triangle over the Fire, saying:]

May this fire be Bifrost's undying flame.

[draw a triangle over the Tree, saying:]

May this tree be mighty Yggdrasil, rising high and low before me.

[see the three triangles – water, fire, and growing wood – hang before in the air and then come together in a valknot, while declaring:]

Latið opna hliðin! Let the Gates be opened!

Forfeður Offering

Blessed Forfeður, you who came before us, you who bore us, you who helped to shape the path that lies ahead. Ancient Wise; Honored Einherjar; You Countless Masses who toiled in obscurity, but upon whose backs our society is built. Meet us at the boundaries. Join us at our Sacred Hearth and be warmed by our good fire. Aid us and guide us as we walk the Elder Ways. Forfeður, accept this offering! *[give offering]*

Landvættir Offering

Noble Vættir, you who inhabit this Land, who lurk in stone and tree and river. Those of the primal wilds, those of the tilled and planted field, those of cobbled stones and bricked-walls: hear our call. May you join us by our fire, may you share your bounties with us as we share ours with you. Meet us at the boundaries. Join us at our Sacred Hearth and be warmed by our good fire. Aid us and guide us as we walk the Elder Ways. Blessed Vættir, accept this offering! *[give offering]*

Guðir Offering

Shining Guðir, you who shaped the Cosmos, you who guard and guide the World's wyrd, you who teach us and bless us with bounty. May your radiance light our hall, may your warmth stoke our fire, and may your presence alongside us this evening make the Long Night that much more pleasant. Meet us at the boundaries. Join us at our Sacred Hearth and be warmed by our good fire. Aid us and guide us as we walk the Elder Ways. Shining Guðir, accept this offering! *[give offering]*

Key Offering

We now recite a portion of the Lay of Stigr, before we make offerings to Blessed Máni:

The years did pass   and with them Ragnvaldr died,
leaving Stigr to ascend   to the throne.
A good ruler, a just ruler   Stigr was revealed to be,
guiding the folk   firmly and wisely.

One day while he hunted   a hawk circled above.
Landing, it called out from the limb of a tree,
stating sad news   for Stigr to hear:
his own father, Aki,   had passed from the World.

Filled with woe   he forsook the hunt,
returning to the city   to repine with Eydís.
With his father gone   he had obligations,
to take care of the Folk   on his father's stead.

Eydís and he agreed   to abdicate the throne,
returning to the people   their political power.
But the folk were scared   'n' feared this change
so great   and so sudden.

They'd not allow the couple   to leave their court,
foolishly incarcerating   them in the throne room.
They languished there and lamented
the foolishness of the city-folk.

In the still of the night,   Stigr woke sudd'nly
startled by the echo   of footsteps in the court.
Among the shadows he   could see the shape of
the old man from the cave,   outlined by moonlight.

'Come and follow,   for I'm here to guide you home,'
he whispered softly, mindful of the sound.
Stigr woke Eydís -   who welcomed the man –

and they followed him from the throne room.

Out through the city they followed the old man,
the streets were empty, the eve' was still.
All the folk were sleeping, the old man supplied,
their flight would go unnoticed until the morning came.

He led them to the forest and through it to the mountains,
and into the tunnels that snaked 'neath the earth.
Out through the old well they emerged in sunlight
and made for Stigr's home, for the old stead of Aki.

Blessed Máni, Silv'ry Eye of the Heavens, Brother to the Golden One, and Guide of Humanity through the Dark Night, we honor you this eve'. May your blessings of illumination and guidance be with us through the coming weeks until your face shines bright and full once more. Honored Máni, accept our offerings!

Omen

[make an offering to the Norns, saying:]

Skuld, we make offering to you – you and your Blessed, Wise Sisters. So Wise in those things that have to begin, please lend us your wisdom in return. Accept this offering, please, and let me peer into your Sacred Well.

[take the omens, with runes]

The seer for this rite will ask four questions:

- Have our offerings been accepted?
- What do the Forfeður give in return?
- What do the Vættir give in return?
- What do the Guðir give in return?

Calling for, Hallowing, and Affirmation of the Blessings

Holy Ones, we have given in friendship and love, so that you might give in return. Kindreds, we ask that you give us the Blessed

Waters: the Waters of Wyrd, the Waters of Wisdom, the Waters of Life!

Mighty Ones, give us the Waters!

Noble Ones, give us the Waters!

Shining Ones, give us the Waters!

[charge the Waters by intoning the rune associated with the specific Kindred during their part of the call-and-response, while pushing energy into the pitcher; when Waters are charged, hold them up to the congregation]

Sjáið vatn lífsins!

Children of the Earth, before you is the holy cup. Do you wish to share in these blessings?

All: We do!

Then, as the waters are poured out, know that they hold blessings for you and this grove and this community. Work well with these blessings, Children of the Earth.

[pass out the Waters to the Folk, save enough to pour into a horn for the working]

Working

We are a thankful for the blessings and lessons that the Kindred give us, and so we now record our efforts into Urðarbrunnr, the Well of Wyrd.

[one ritualist, serving as a valkyrie, will walk the horn around to the other participants as they speak the efforts over the horn; after each, the valkyrie says the following as (s)he takes back the horn:]

May your deeds line the bottom of Urðarbrunnr.

[when all are finished, the Waters will be poured into a blessing bowl – to be poured out later – while the following is spoken by the lead ritualist:]

Blessed Kindreds, hear our words, witness our deeds, may our actions line the Well of Wyrd honorably and with pride. *Verði það svo.*

Thanking

[thank the assembled Kindreds in reverse order: Deities, Land-Spirits, and Ancestors]

Closing the Gates

Wizened Alfoðr, Noble Wanderer of the Nine Worlds, we call out to you once more. Give us the power of your fortuitous foresight, give us the might of your hard-won Mysteries – join your power with ours as we close the Gates Between the Worlds.

[give an offering and close the Gates: draw the Two Powers back into your hands, feeling the water and fire turn to ice within you, drawing a counter-clockwise triangle over the Tree, saying:]

May this Tree be just a tree.

[draw a triangle over the Fire, saying:]

May this Fire be just flame.

[draw a triangle over the Well, saying:]

May this Well be just water.

[as you draw the triangles, see the them form from ice, hanging in the air by the Hallows; declare:]

Latið loka hliðunum! Let the Gates be Closed!

[clap your hands firmly together and see the icy triangles shatter, the cosmic powers keeping the Gates open dispersing; and then say:]

Blessed Oðinn, we thank you.

Thanking Inspiration

Soul-stirring, story-weaving, audience-enchanting Sága: we thank you.

Thanking the Earth Mother

Jorð, beauteous and bountiful mother, we thank you.

Closing the Rite

Go now, Children of Earth, in peace with the blessings of the Kindred and a Fire in your Heart. This rite is ended.

December

December comes and with it Winter reigns supreme, our year-long journey comes to an end.[23] And with that ending, we remember and honor those whose help was integral to this journey.

Working

The working for this final month of Full Moon liturgies focuses back on two figures who are incredibly important in ADF ritual: the Earth Mother and the Gatekeeper. Bear in mind, these titles are just that: titles. And the group (or solitary practitioner) will have ideally struck up a relationship with two spirits that they can "plug in" to those ritual roles when referencing either of them in ritual.[24] So, this

[23] Yes, I know: the lunar calendar has thirteen months. See the following section for the explanation.

[24] As has been said before now – probably *ad nauseum* at this point – the main goal of these liturgies is to provide ideas for practitioners, whether alone or in a group, so if you decide to begin calling upon the specific "Gatekeeper" or "Earth Mother" or

month, we will focus on them in the working, honoring them together, in balance – the sacred and the profane in harmony – one last time for the year.

Obviously, you'll need the Earth Mother representation for this working, and you will need to make a separate representation/idol for the Gatekeeper (which, of course, will need to be exposed to the light of the Full Moon all three nights), as well. Once ready, have appropriate offerings at hand for both the initial invocation of the Earth Mother and Gatekeeper and for the working itself. And then get ready to journey.

---

genius loci spirit into either of those two slots (or *any* slots, really), feel free to do so! Honest: you won't hurt my feelings.

Script

Processional

[Insert song/chant here]

Outdweller Entreaty

To all those whose voices do not harmonize with our own, whose purposes may be cross with ours, who may seek to harm and harrow with no legitimate grievance, accept this token of treaty and leave our working be. *[give offering]* Blessed Disir, noble women of our lineages, protectresses and grand-mothers, we ask that you stand watch over this space and make sure that the treaty is upheld. *[give offering]* Praise and thanks be upon on you all. Verði það svo.

Purification

[cense and asperse the Folk]

Opening Statement

[ring bells three times to signal beginning of the rite]

We are gathered here this night to celebrate the fullness of Máni's might and main, to re-connect to the cycles of the Miðgarð, and to give worship to the Kindreds. Tonight we seek to honor the Earth Mother and the Gatekeeper, both of whom have supported and guided us through the past year. So let us join together as one folk to make our offerings in joy and reverence.

Opening Prayer

The skull of Mighty Ymir stretches out above us.
The bones of Mighty Ymir support the land about us.
The blood of Mighty Ymir flows under and around us.
All things are of His flesh,

Our wyrds woven together,
May we pray with a good fire.

Inspiration

Blessed Sága, Mistress of the Sunken Benches, weaver of stories and chanter of tales, we call out to you. Please stand with us with us this day as we invite the Kindreds in frið and kinship. Accept this offering given in gratitude and honor, *[give offering]* and share with us your ability to enthrall an audience this day. Praise and thanks be upon you.

Honoring the Earth Mother

The Children of the Earth call out to Blessed *[insert name of being]*, whom we call upon as Mother of Us this night. We who walk upon you, who take sustenance from you, who find comfort and rest within your bosom, remember you this day. *[give offering]* May you find this offering acceptable, for it is given in love and gratitude. Earth Mother, accept this offering!

(Re)Creating the Cosmos

In the primal times, the Great Rimthurs was slain and quartered by the Sons of Búri: his Skull became the Sky, his Blood became the Sea, his Body became the Land. And from his Flesh grew a Great Tree, which connected all of the Worlds. May we recreate that Holy Sacrifice this day as we emulate the ordering of the worlds.

[hallow the Hallows by censing and aspersing them]

Grove Attunement

[perform the Two Powers meditation]

We are shaped from driftwood at the Shore of the Worlds,
Grown from the Land,
Washed in the Sea,
Dried by the Sky.

We are tied together by the gifts of the Three Brothers,
By the weavings of the Nornir.
May we be just and true to each other.
May our worship be pious and pure.
Verði það svo.

The Gates

See now in your mind's eye a darkened, wintry road. Snow falls and obscures your vision, the scent of hearth-fires drifts on the air. You hear the soft crunching of footsteps nearby, a dark, indistinct figure approaches on the road. The figure's form resolves into that of *[insert name of being]*.

You recognize them now – the Cunning One, the Helpful One, the One Who has Guided you through the Otherworld these past months: *[insert name of being]*.

We call upon them now: Blessed Guide, Knower of the Ways, we call out to you and ask a boon. Accept this offering and join your power with ours as we open the Gates Between the Worlds.

[give offering and open the Gates: pull the Two Powers into your hands, feeling the fire and water mix, and draw a clockwise triangle over the Well, saying]

May this well be the Triple Well.

[draw a triangle over the Fire, saying:]

May this fire be Bifrost's undying flame.

[draw a triangle over the Tree, saying:]

May this tree be mighty Yggdrasil, rising high and low before me.

[see the three triangles – water, fire, and growing wood – hang before in the air and then come together in a valknot, while declaring:]

Latið opna hliðin! Let the Gates be opened!

Forfeður Offering

Blessed Forfeður, you who came before us, you who bore us, you who helped to shape the path that lies ahead. Ancient Wise; Honored Einherjar; You Countless Masses who toiled in obscurity, but upon whose backs our society is built. Meet us at the boundaries. Join us at our Sacred Hearth and be warmed by our good fire. Aid us and guide us as we walk the Elder Ways. Forfeður, accept this offering! *[give offering]*

Landvættir Offering

Noble Vættir, you who inhabit this Land, who lurk in stone and tree and river. Those of the primal wilds, those of the tilled and planted field, those of cobbled stones and bricked-walls: hear our call. May you join us by our fire, may you share your bounties with us as we share ours with you. Meet us at the boundaries. Join us at our Sacred Hearth and be warmed by our good fire. Aid us and guide us as we walk the Elder Ways. Blessed Vættir, accept this offering! *[give offering]*

Guðir Offering

Shining Guðir, you who shaped the Cosmos, you who guard and guide the World's wyrd, you who teach us and bless us with bounty. May your radiance light our hall, may your warmth stoke our fire, and may your presence alongside us this evening make the Long Night that much more pleasant. Meet us at the boundaries. Join us at our Sacred Hearth and be warmed by our good fire. Aid us and guide us as we walk the Elder Ways. Shining Guðir, accept this offering! *[give offering]*

Key Offering

We now recite a portion of the Lay of Stigr, before we make offerings to Blessed Máni:

The two walked alone all the way back,
neither beset nor besieged on their way.
They enjoyed the quietude, enveloped by the Land,
and Stigr's heart near burst to behold it again.

Though he hadn't known it he'd missed his home,
being gone from it for so long as he had.
Showing Eydís the cave where he'd got the map
and the forest where the spirits had worried him.

And his queen was delighted to see the places where
his many stories had played out.
Stories, they were the most important thing:
all things come down to the stories we tell.

They camped and they foraged, enjoying the solitude.
Eventually they came, as evening fell,
to the full, ripe fields of Aki's stead.
There they found the old woman waiting.

Stigr thank her heart'ly for the amulet she'd given;
after all, it'd won him his beautiful wife.
The old woman informed him that Stigr had inherited
all the wealth 'n' titles of his wise father.

They returned to the stead with the old woman,
and they found Stigr's kinfolk waiting.
They rejoiced when they saw him, they'd waited so long;
with his father dead they'd despaired for the stead.

Stigr again proved quite the prudent leader,
guiding the stead through good times 'n' bad.
Prosperity came and so did progeny,
one day did Eydís birth a boy-child to Stigr.

The stead was fruitful, growing steadily through
the years 'neath Stigr's wise 'n' steady hand.
His boy grew strong, Stigr loved him dearly

and Eydís taught him of her far-off home.

The new year was born, the land-blessing at hand,
and Stigr was to throw a wondrous celebration.
So many were invited,his son so charming,
and an elegant guest caught the youth's eye.

Blessed Máni, Silv'ry Eye of the Heavens, Brother to the Golden One, and Guide of Humanity through the Dark Night, we honor you this eve'. May your blessings of illumination and guidance be with us through the coming weeks until your face shines bright and full once more. Honored Máni, accept our offerings!

Omen

[make an offering to the Norns, saying:]

Skuld, we make offering to you – you and your Blessed, Wise Sisters. So Wise in those things that have to begin, please lend us your wisdom in return. Accept this offering, please, and let me peer into your Sacred Well.

[take the omens, with runes]

The seer for this rite will ask four questions:

- Have our offerings been accepted?
- What do the Forfeður give in return?
- What do the Vættir give in return?
- What do the Guðir give in return?

Calling for, Hallowing, and Affirmation of the Blessings

Holy Ones, we have given in friendship and love, so that you might give in return. Kindreds, we ask that you give us the Blessed Waters: the Waters of Wyrd, the Waters of Wisdom, the Waters of Life!

Mighty Ones, give us the Waters!

Noble Ones, give us the Waters!

Shining Ones, give us the Waters!

[charge the Waters by intoning the rune associated with the specific Kindred during their part of the call-and-response, while pushing energy into the pitcher; when Waters are charged, hold them up to the congregation]

Sjáið vatn lífsins!

Children of the Earth, before you is the holy cup. Do you wish to share in these blessings?

All: We do!

Then, as the waters are poured out, know that they hold blessings for you and this grove and this community. Work well with these blessings, Children of the Earth.

[pass out the Waters to the Folk]

Working

[make sure the Earth Mother and Gatekeeper representations are seated in a visible place on the altar and let the assembled folk settle into a comfortable position – whether sitting, reclined, or prone on the floor; the lead ritualist will now guide the folk through a journey to meet with the two deities, saying:]

Take a moment to relax and get comfortable, closing your eyes and breathing slowly and deeply. *[pause for an appropriate amount of time, then:]* See yourselves surrounded by the Mists of Magic, those Mists that lie Between the Worlds, see the others here with you through the Mists. Move forward through the Mists until you find yourselves on the grounds outside this room, the Mists floating gently just barely above the earth.

See before you the path that leads into the woods. The path that twists and turns and winds its way through the trees and undergrowth to the clearing – the grove – that you have established as a sanctum within the Otherworld. A soft, summer breeze lightly shakes the limbs of the trees at the edge of the clearing and the light of the Full Moon shines bright and strong and silvery upon you. Take a moment to just be, taking in the clearing and becoming attuned to it. *[pause for a moment or two]* The moonlight shimmers and dances before your eyes, and a human form takes shapes within the light as it falls upon the clearing. Another moment and the figure has solidified before you, it is *[the Gatekeeper's name]*.

[the lead ritualist makes an offering to the Gatekeeper, saying:]

O Wise and Far-Traveled, *[insert name]*, we thank you for guiding us throughout this past year and we make this offering in your honor. We ask now that you lead us to the Earth Mother, to a sacred place – a special place – where we can honor you and Her together.

The Gatekeeper beckons you all and turns, leading you off into the forest. Among the dark trees he guides you, over hills and through forested valleys…*[pause for a moment or two]* until you arrive at a sacred spot.

The silver light of Máni shines brightly in this place, illuminating everything it touches with an almost supernal glow. And here, in this spot, you see [insert name of Earth Mother], the Earth Mother.

[*the lead ritualist makes an offering to the Earth Mother, saying:]*

Blessed One, Generous One, Honored and Beloved *[insert name]*. We thank you this night, for all the boons and the support that you have lent us this past year, and make this offering in your honor. May we always be able to find you here when we need you, to give thanks or praise or to take succor in your presence.

The Earth Mother and Gatekeeper stand before you now, side-by-side. Ask them if they have any messages for us. *[pause for a minute or so, to give appropriate time for question and answer]*

Bid the Earth Mother good-bye as *[insert Gatekeeper's name]* leads you back out into the forest. Through the woods you are guided back to our sanctuary, our Grove in the Otherworld. The Gatekeeper takes his leave, fading back into the darkness of the forest…
Turn now and follow the path back through the forest to the Mists, and through the Mists back to where your physical body lies in relaxation. Merge with it.

Take a few deep breaths and come back into the room, into your physical body. Stand up and stretch if need be.

[all participants should take moment or two to stretch and ground themselves, continuing with the rite]

Thanking

[thank the assembled Kindreds in reverse order: Deities, Land-Spirits, and Ancestors]

Closing the Gates

Honored *[insert name of Gatekeeper]*, we call upon you once more to join your power with ours as we close the Gates Between the Worlds.

[give an offering and close the Gates: draw the Two Powers back into your hands, feeling the water and fire turn to ice within you, drawing a counter-clockwise triangle over the Tree, saying:]

May this Tree be just a tree.

[draw a triangle over the Fire, saying:]

May this Fire be just flame.

[draw a triangle over the Well, saying:]

May this Well be just water.

[as you draw the triangles, see the them form from ice, hanging in the air by the Hallows; declare:]

Latið loka hliðunum! Let the Gates be Closed!

[clap your hands firmly together and see the icy triangles shatter, the cosmic powers keeping the Gates open dispersing]

Blessed *[name],* we thank you.

Thanking Inspiration

Soul-stirring, story-weaving, audience-enchanting Sága: we thank you.

Thanking the Earth Mother

Jorð, beauteous and bountiful mother, we thank you.

Closing the Rite

Go now, Children of Earth, in peace with the blessings of the Kindred and a Fire in your Heart. This rite is ended.

Intercalary Moon

"But, wait!" you say, "there are thirteen moons in a lunar year. You've only covered twelve!"

Very true. However, the liturgy for the thirteenth moon is being reserved for ADF Initiates only. So, unfortunately (or fortunately, depending on how one looks at it) everyone else gets a month off.

Perhaps you should use this Moon to test out a liturgy of your own?

The Lay of Stigr

I.

The Land was cold   and the wind blew hard
so it always was   around the new year's birth.
But, beginnings are harsh   - fruit is born slowly –
Whether from the Land   or Man's beating heart.

On a grand farmstead far into the country,
dwelled the household of Aki - an honorable folk
well-known through the Land for their wisdom and wealth,
and their willingness to share with those in need.

A celebration was being held   to bless the land
and mark the boundaries   of Aki's fields.
The folk of the region came for the festivities
And to help with   the hallowing of the land.

The borders were walked,   blessed with incense and water;
offerings were left   for the spirits of the land.
Blessings and gifts would   yield a good bounty
bringing prosperity and weal   to who worked it.

After the blessings   and gifts were given,
the Folk retired   forwith to Aki's stead.
Food was laid out   and drink were ready,
music was made   for the Folk to be merry.

Among the revelers   was Aki's son, Stigr,
first-born of his children   and formidable of mind.
He mingled with the Folk   as a good host should,
dancing and singing, and   drinking with the men.

A young woman caught his eye,   fair and comely,
a far-traveled guest whose   bane was given as 'Eydís.'
Together they talked,   together they ate,

together they drank   and danced merrily.

'Come with me,' she said,   'to my far kingdom.
     'Fortune and fame you'll find.'
As much as he desired it,   Stigr had to decline:
     'My father 'n' folk need me here.'

Shyly, they parted,   she told him to think on it:
come morning's light, the offer would be made, again.
And the feasting continued   far into the night.
Drunk 'n' sleepy was Stigr   when he stumbled to bed.

II.

In morning's light Eydís   made her offer once more;
but, again,   Stigr answered 'No.'
And so she traveled   far from Aki's stead,
with Stigr regretting   his responsibilities.

Swiftly passed the weeks   as Stigr worked the farmstead,
helping his father   and his folk.
The days grew longer   by little increments,
the Sun's light lifting Stigr's spirits some.

But word soon came   of neighbors being harried
by bandits fierce   and fearsome.
Sweeping in from the mountains,   making trouble,
causing worry and   woe for the Folk.

Barbarous men they were,   brash and angry,
itching for a fight   and impudent.
Fields they burned   and farmsteads they razed,
seeking gold   and glory.

Stigr rode out to face them,   when they neared his stead.
His bearing courageous   and his mind cunning,
for the bandits outnumbered him   fourteen to one.
His wits he would need   to win this battle.

In deep-hooded cloak with spear in hand
he met them at the cross-roads.
They heckled and threatened, the harrowers did,
seeing him as easy game to be grabbed.

In a flash the spear flew,
striking the leader from his steed;
from deep in his hood, one eye hidden from sight,
Stigr growled a warning to the warriors.

Fearing the Alfoðr, the bandits all fled,
leaving their bloody, fallen leader to die.
Retrieving the spear, Stigr spoke o the bandit,
forcing an oath to leave he lands 'n' folk alone.

Riding home astride his stout, strong horse,
Stigr couldn't fight the feeling of pride.
It was then that he sighted a strange, hobbling woman
forcing herself to cross the fields.

III.

Stigr hailed the woman and asked if she were well.
Her foot she'd hurt, she answered in response.
Her ankle twisted from falling a gopher hole,
and now she limped lamely on her way home.

The young man was moved
and sympathy forced him from his mount.
He examined the woman, eyeing her ankle,
before offering her a ride back to his stead.

Onto the horse he helped her, gently,
Walking alongside all the way home.
As they traveled, they talked
and Stigr learned about the stranger.

She was a mother and a grandmother,
and she lived not far from there.

On the Land her Folk had lived
from time out of mind, forever it had seemed.

Arriving at the stead, his folk all gathered 'round
they helped the woman with her ankle;
mending and healing, making it better,
and she thanked them for their aid.

'Why are you here? You should be out adventuring,'
she said to Stigr.
'My family,' he said. 'They need me here.
'I dare not disappoint them.'

She produced an amulet and pressed it in his hands,
stating that it was a gift for Stigr's help.
She urged him to follow his heart's desire;
without him, his family would fare fine.

'Go on,' she told him. 'Go find Eydís.
'Go find your heart's fulfillment.'
Stigr was shocked: how did she know of Eydís?
Who was this woman before him?

With that, the woman left leaving Stigr alone
with her amulet and his confusion.
In the next dawn's light he left,
setting out to find his fortune and his lady.

IV.

Several days passed as Stigr did travel
out from the lands of his Folk.
Strange were the lands into which he'd strayed,
following in the wake of the woman, Eydís.

Unknown forests and unknown rivers,
fields and groves that were foreign to him.
It did not take long for him to lose the trail,
not a soul there was from whom to seek guidance.

At night he would hear whispering voices
flitting among the trees of the darkened forests.
On the following morn' he'd find himself confused
unsure of where he'd woken.

More days passed and Stigr pressed on,
catching glimpses of figures from the corners of his eyes.
In the night he saw spirits among the trees,
giggling and mocking as they made him lose his way.

They taunted and teased him and turned him about,
delighting in his helpless, directionless wandering.
One night he stood watch and waited for the spirits,
seeking a way to stop their maliciousness.

Pretending to sleep he waited the spirits out,
then followed them back through the forest.
They led him to a cave - their home, their lair –
within which he found a cage 'n' wizened prisoner.

The old man told him how to banish the spirits,
his own magic bound while he was imprisoned.
Chanting the galdr given to him
Stigr scattered the spirits on the wind.

Freed from the cage the old fellow was grateful
and promised two boons to be paid in return.
Stigr simply asked the wise, old stranger
how he could find Eydís' home.

Smiling, the old man made Stigr a map
showing him which way to travel.
Grateful and elated Stigr bid farewell to the elder
and continued on his course to find Eydís.

V.

With the aid of the map Stigr made good time

traveling through the murky forests.
With the mischievous spirits harassing him no more,
he found navigation fairly easy.

A day and a night passed, and Stigr found himself
not far from where the old man
had marked on the map
where his destination would be.

At dusk he bedded down
'mong the roots of a mighty tree,
but his rest was ripped from him
by the approach of bold, angry spirits.

Brothers they were to the spirits he'd banished
and wrathful they were with Stigr.
They hounded him through the trees,
running him ragged as he fled.

They captured Stigr 'neath a craggy mount
and dragged him by his heels
to an ancient well dug deep within
the rock of that deep-rooted mountain.

They cursed him and crowed at him
and tossed him deep into that treach'rous well.
Stigr fell swiftly, swimming through the darkness
'til he landed in a lump at the bottom.

There he languished, how long he knew not –
maybe hours, maybe days,
the darkness was too deep to tell.
He prayed for help, for deliverance.

He sunk into slumber and when he surfaced
moonlight shone, silv'ry, on a sinuous crack in the stone.
Inspired and elated he worked industriously,
breaking through the wall to an old, worn tunnel.

The tunnel wound lazily through the lightless earth,
though strange mushrooms glowed strikingly on the walls.
Daylight, eventually, dazzled Stigr's eyes
as he emerged, safely 'n' suddenly, in a new land.

VI.

Stigr slowly wanderedthrough woods and fields,
inexplicably unnervedby this unknown land.
Whispers haunted him and flashes of motion weaved through the trees
though he never saw a single person.

Night came and Stigr nestled in some tree roots,
slipping quickly into a sound sleep.
He was startled awake'neath a star-strewn sky
faced with the visage of a barely visible man.

The geist was quite maddened as it got closer to Stigr,
its eyes full of fury and a pale, cold fire.
Stigr scrambled to his feet 'n' staggered into the night,
fleeing from the shadewith fear-frozen blood.

He stumbled 'cross a farm, far from the woods,
and found it inhabited by folk living 'n' kind.
The land, they warned, was haunted by the dead:
restless and angry they all sought revenge.

The problem they knew, lay deep in the woods:
a monument desecrated by mortal hands.
Water from a holy well and the fruits of honey, bottled,
he'd need for the necessary cleansing.

Mead they gave him, to help his noble quest,
and told him where a sacred well sat
nestled stout and ancient 'neath a hoary Ash.
Stigr did set out, fearing the roaming dead.

He found the Ash and the well that fed it,

and filled his skin though his nerves were skittish.
Through the wood he traveled with hase
seeking the monument that moved the dead so.

Stigr braved the wilds and the winding paths,
dodged the draugar and the dreadful geists,
ventured forth through the dark, dread forest
and made it to the unclean monument.

He washed it with the holy water
and poured mead to the many gods.
The darkness lifted and the dead grew quiet,
and the land seemed to lay peaceful.

VII.

The news of Stigr's bravery spread near and far,
preceding him, it seemed, as he pressed on.
Whether it was farmers or merchants or migratory birds,
those he met had already heard his name.

At the next town he entered he came to a tavern
and the folk welcomed him warmly.
They bought him drinks, they bought him dinner –
but there was a strangeness that made Stigr cautious.

They called Stigr a hero and lauded him greatly,
even offering to host an eve of celebration.
Stigr realized what worried him about these warm folk:
though mannered and beautiful, they were not Men.

Spirit-folk they were, he found –
though clothed in flesh and cleverly so.
Unsure of this surprising development
Stigr stumbled and stammered among them.

As they prepared to celebrate their heroic guest's presence,
Stigr secluded himselfat the town's humble inn.
Dusk covered the landand colored lamps were lit,

when the townsfolk came for the hero.

The customs of their party were strange 'n' perplexing,
but Stigr's faced showed joy when he saw someone familiar.
It was Eydís he saw surrounded by those fey-folk,
he sought her hand as soon as he could.

Eydís guided him through the eye of the storm,
teaching him the ins, the outs,of the odd folk's ways.
And before him was brought a bright 'n' beautiful maid,
offered as a wife as a way of honoring him.

Eydís counseled him not to consent, for
these folk were tricky even when well-meaning.
So, Stigr politely said "No" to the maid
and stayed near Eydís for the rest of the eve.

In the morn, they made fast from the town,
slipping away as the revelers slept.
Together, finally, Stigr felt elated
to have beauteous Eydís trav'ling by his side.

VIII.

She was gone the next morn when Stigr made
to break fast by their camp's low fire.
Despondent and confused he decided to follow.
He tracked her steps to a city of stained-glass.

Rumors of him flew, prior to his arrival,
to the king's court who demanded Stigr come.
As a friend, he presented himself, no foe to the king;
he simply sought out the sightly Eydís.

'My daughter, she is!' declared the shrewd king,
calling her into the court.
Three tasks he'd need complete to take her hand,
to which Stigr agreed wholeheartedly.

An ancient temple needed repair and renovation;
a monster denned in the forest and needed dealt with;
and a dragon kept hostage the king's ancient diadem.
To all these things, Stigr enthusiastically agreed.

To the temple he came considering his options,
when the dead drew up beside him.
So thankful they were they repaired the holy site,
all within the day that Stigr had.

Stigr made for the forest forthwith,
combing those woods for the monster that couched within.
There he found the dreaded creature
And won its allegiance with charm and reason.

Together they made for the dragon's lair:
an ancient tomb, buried deep and hidden.
The old woman's amulet throbbed warmly as
The duo approached the sleeping dragon.

With the amulet in hand the monster hastened past where
the dragon lay protecting the king's diadem.
Stigr snatched it up - and an unusual sword, too –
as the dragon was distracted by the amulet.

Enraged, the dragon roared its displeasure,
as desp'rately the duo fled its lair.
They parted ways amiably, announcing each as 'friend',
and Stigr, with diadem in hand, stole back to the city.

IX.

When Stigr returned to Ragnvaldr's hall
he found the king less than happy to see him.
The court was hushed as he approached with the diadem,
which Ragnvaldr received gratefully.

'My apologies, Stigr, for having to state this:
'but, Eydís cannot be yours.

'Promised to another her hand already is,
'to the prince of a potent, rival kingdom.'

Stigr was devastated and would not stand
for this last minute change to their mutual deal.
He offered a challenge to this far-off prince:
single combat, the winner would wed Eydís.

So, the prince was called from so far away
and Stigr passed the days practicing his sword-play.
The ancient blade he'd knicked from the dragon
was always in hand, always at his side.

Eydís would come to him at even-tide,
pleading with Stigr not to play this game.
Though promised to the prince, to Stigr her love was given.
And despair she would, should he foolishly die.

But he'd made his challenge and must keep it,
otherwise, dishonor his name and shame himself.
Distraught and fearful, Eydís would flee –
only to return the next night, and restate her plea.

Finally, the prince arrived, his entourage around him,
eager to meet with Stigr in the melee.
With a sacred oath given that no war would be waged,
no matter the victor, they met swords.

Slash and parry, strikes slapped aside –
so the fight went the warriors circling,
with Stigr finding - in stunning surprise –
he fought so well, it was like the sword wielded him.

The prince fell to his knees, pressing for mercy:
he had no luck 'gainst such a legend'ry blade.
A cheer went up, Eydís embraced Stigr warmly
as Ragnvaldr spoke and recognized his son-to-be.

X.

Preparations were made for the princess' wedding:
an enormous celebration to ensure its memory.
Servants were set flitting about searching for resources
Which Ragnvaldr insisted upon for his only daughter's wedding.

The day finally came and all the city was festive,
eager to take in the royal nuptials.
The ceremony was presided over by the High Priest,
who offered the ring for the couple to oath on.

A great feast followed and all the city-folk were joyous.
Stigr rose at their table and his voice rang out:
he gave thanks to Eydís and her father, the king,
for their generosity 'n' welcome, their gifts of home 'n' love.

Next he gave thanks to the monster of the woods,
misunderstood by the folk and maligned by their fear.
That wild creature of the Land, who longed for a friend,
and had stood by him in danger within the dragon's lair.

Next he gave thanks to the spirits of the dead,
who'd helped him in the temple in thanks for his aid.
So grateful they'd been for the rest he'd given them –
one must not forget the fate of one's ancestors.

Next he gave thanks to the gods 'n' goddesses,
whose divine inspiration had delivered him from bondage,
that lightless well in which he'd languished.
Without their help he'd not have wed Eydís.

Next he gave thanks to the old man in the cave,
that prisoner of the spirits who'd pointed the way.
Without his aid Stigr would have wandered
aimless and forlorn, forever lost.

Finally he gave thanks to the old woman in the fields.
Whose amulet had proven so shiny a prize that
the dragon's attention had been crucially distracted.

The gift of compassion is a gift that's repaid.

At that the folk cheered for their new crown-prince:
a humble ruler is a good ruler truly,
who values the aid and values the loyalty
of those who willingly offer it.

XI.

The years did pass and with them Ragnvaldr died,
leaving Stigr to ascend to the throne.
A good ruler, a just ruler Stigr was revealed to be,
guiding the folk firmly and wisely.

One day while he hunted a hawk circled above.
Landing, it called out from the limb of a tree,
stating sad news for Stigr to hear:
his own father, Aki, had passed from the World.

Filled with woe he forsook the hunt,
returning to the city to repine with Eydís.
With his father gone he had obligations,
to take care of the Folk on his father's stead.

Eydís and he agreed to abdicate the throne,
returning to the people their political power.
But the folk were scared 'n' feared this change
so great and so sudden.

They'd not allow the couple to leave their court,
foolishly incarcerating them in the throne room.
They languished there and lamented
the foolishnessof the city-folk.

In the still of the night, Stigr woke sudd'nly
startled by the echo of footsteps in the court.
Among the shadows he could see the shape of
the old man from the cave, outlined by moonlight.

‘Come and follow,   for I’m here to guide you home,’
he whispered softly, mindful of the sound.
Stigr woke Eydís -   who welcomed the man –
and they followed him from the throne room.

Out through the city   they followed the old man,
the streets were empty,   the eve’ was still.
All the folk were sleeping,   the old man supplied,
their flight would go unnoticed   until the morning came.

He led them to the forest   and through it to the mountains,
and into the tunnels   that snaked ‘neath the earth.
Out through the old well   they emerged in sunlight
and made for Stigr’s home,   for the old stead of Aki.

XII.

The two walked alone all the way back,
neither beset   nor besieged on their way.
They enjoyed the quietude,   enveloped by the Land,
and Stigr’s heart near burst   to behold it again.

Though he hadn’t known it   he’d missed his home,
being gone from it   for so long as he had.
Showing Eydís the cave   where he’d got the map
and the forest where the   spirits had worried him.

And his queen was delighted to see the places where
his many stories   had played out.
Stories, they were   the most important thing:
all things come down to the stories we tell.

They camped and they foraged,   enjoying the solitude.
Eventually they came, as evening fell,
to the full, ripe fields of Aki’s stead.
There they found   the old woman waiting.

Stigr thank her heart’ly   for the amulet she’d given;

after all, it'd won him his beautiful wife.
The old woman informed him that Stigr had inherited
all the wealth 'n' titlesof his wise father.

They returned to the stead with the old woman,
and they found Stigr's kinfolk waiting.
They rejoiced when they saw him, they'd waited so long;
with his father dead they'd despaired for the stead.

Stigr again proved quite the prudent leader,
guiding the stead through good times 'n' bad.
Prosperity came and so did progeny,
one day did Eydís birth a boy-child to Stigr.

The stead was fruitful,growing steadily through
the years 'neath Stigr's wise 'n' steady hand.
His boy grew strong, Stigr loved him dearly
and Eydís taught him of her far-off home.

The new year was born, the land-blessing at hand,
and Stigr was to throw a wondrous celebration.
So many were invited,his son so charming,
and an elegant guest caught the youth's eye.

Appendix I: "Freyr Learns the Virtues"

***Note**: ADF promotes a variant on the Heathen Nine Noble Virtues as a system of ethical standards to cultivate within one's life: wisdom, piety, vision, courage, integrity, perseverance, hospitality, moderation, fertility. A few years back, I created a set of prayer-beads and a set of Virtue prayers to go with them. The following narrative was created to give the prayers a framework.*

I. Expulsion

There was a time, when Freyr Ingvi was in his youth, that he caused his father, Njorðr, much consternation and many headaches. His wild, raucous behavior and lack of thought for others as he indulged his own whims was turning Noatun upside-down and inside-out. Finally, having reached the limit of his patience, the great, marine Ván called his son before him and told him that until he learned to comport himself with ethics and virtue and some semblance of decency that he would be expelled to the Miðgarð to learn from Men, who at that point held themselves much better than young Freyr did.

Distraught and turned out from his father's home, Freyr Ingvi ventured out into the lands of Men.

II. The Farmer

It was not long before Freyr came upon someone in his travels. As he made his way through the countryside of Miðgarð, he met an old farmer resting upon his tractor. The young god was hungry and asked the farmer if he had food. The farmer gladly shared what food he had with him with the stranger, and as they ate Freyr asked the farmer why he worked so hard at raising his crops and tending to his fields when there were easier ways of getting food.

The farmer thought for a moment, and then replied, "I love this land that I live on and work. I want to see it flower and prosper, bursting forth with life. That's piety, I'd say, friend. Loving something beyond yourself, loving something so much that you're willing to give of yourself in order to see it bettered." Freyr Ingvi asked how the farmer remembered that love, how he kept it going from day to day.

The farmer replied: "Those times when being pious becomes hard, I remind myself through prayer:

May I feel the warm flame of Piety within me.
May I allow it to blossom and grow,
Shining forth into the world with my love for the Kindreds.
For my family and friends.
For the very cosmos itself.

"When I say that prayer, it reminds me what it is to be pious."

Freyr thanked the farmer for his food and for his insight, and asked for directions to the nearest town. The farmer told him where to go and bid him a safe journey, and as Freyr departed, he whispered a soft blessing and felt the land become effulgent with fertile life.

III. The Fisherman

As Freyr traveled through the fields and countryside, he eventually came to a simple road winding its way through the trees, crops, and high grasses. Following this road, the land slowly dropped away on one side, and a large river came into view. The young god walked along road that mirrored the winding course of the river, and after a while he saw a figure standing on the bank.

It was a man holding a long pole, with which he would periodically cast, wait, reel back-in, and recast a long line into the slow-moving waters. As Freyr approached closer to the fisherman, he could see the line snap and fall into the waters. "Drat!" the fisherman called out, reeling the broken line back in.

The fisherman was sitting on the bank, mending the broken line, as Freyr came within speaking distance. "Why not give up?" the young god asked, his eyes scanning the ground around the fisherman, which was bare aside from his box of tackle.

"A man's got to eat," the fisherman replied.

"But how do you keep going on? You've caught nothing and your line is broken."

"Patience, my boy! It's a virtue," the fisherman smiled. "That and perseverance. When the way gets rocky and the journey hard, I close my eyes and say to myself:

May I have the strength to Persevere.

May I not let temporary failures become final defeats.

Holy Ones, give me the courage to press on, despite all obstacles.

"That helps calm my mind and heart and remember what needs to be done."

Freyr nodded thoughtfully, and then helped the fisherman finish mending his line. The man thanked him and gave the young god a few coins for his effort, before Freyr Ingvi continued on his way.

IV. The Priest

The young god kept walking and as he traveled down the road, he began to notice the sun's quickening descent in the west. Impatient to reach town before nightfall, he sped up his pace as much as he could without breaking out into a full run. He continued in this way for a while, his shadow lengthening before him, until he heard a voice call out.

"Ho, boy! What is your rush?"

Freyr Ingvi stopped and looked off to the side of the road, where he saw an older gentleman sitting beside a campfire. "What business is it of yours, old man? But, if you must know, I seek to make it to the next town before night falls."

"Well, you'll tire yourself out long before that happens. The next town over is more then ten miles off and already Lady Sunna prepares to bed down for the night." The old man replied, stoking the burning branches of his small fire with a long stick. "Here, share my fire for the night and continue your travels in the morning. You'll be the better for it."

The young god snorted softly, but after a moment's consideration he approached the old man's fire and sat down. "So, what brings you to the side of this road, sir?" he asked the old man.

"I am a traveling *goði*," the old man said. "And, as I said: Sunna has just about put her horse away for the evening, so I felt it best that I do the same. It wouldn't do to push myself and continue traveling through the night. As I always remind myself:

May I be centered and Moderate in all things.

Let the light of wisdom shine within me
And guide my actions every day.
May I know when to work, may I know when to play.

"And, thus, I knew it was time to stop working and rest for the evening."

Young Freyr smiled, nodding as he did so. "You make a good point, sir. I'd much rather fall asleep with the warmth of a fire at my side and good company, than cold and alone."

"As would I," the *goði* concurred. The two men shared food and conversation together, taking shifts at watch as Máni traveled through the starry heavens. When Freyr woke in the morning, the goði was gone, but he had left the young god a small package of food by the cooling embers of the previous night's fire.

V. The Mayor

By late-morning, Freyr saw the rising peaks of the town's houses, shops, and buildings. They grew larger and larger on the horizon as the sun climbed to its zenith and then prepared for her slow descent, as Freyr's shoes put more and more asphalt behind him. It was late-afternoon by the time that the young god entered the town proper, taking in the sights and sounds of the quaint village.

As he wandered through the town's square, idly window-shopping and people-watching as he walked, Freyr was stopped by a middle-aged man sitting at a table outside one of the town's small diners. "Afternoon, stranger," the man said. "I haven't seen you around before, what brings you to our fair town?"

"What, are you the town's sheriff?" Freyr snorted in reply.

The man shook his head. "Nope. I'm her mayor. And I like to greet any new visitors and residents that I happen upon with an open hand and a smiling face."

The young god felt his cheeks redden and apologized. "I'm simply traveling through," he said. "But, I must say, that your town is quite beautiful from what I've seen."

"Well, thank you!" The mayor replied jovially. "I and the other townsfolk have put in more work than can be explained to make this town - our home - as nice as it can be. But it's all been worth it."

"Wow," Freyr said. "How did you find the fortitude to keep going? I'm sure you must've wanted to give up more than once."

"Aye," the mayor said, nodding. "But if you walk through the park across the street, you'll find a commemorative obelisk in the center. And upon that, is carved these words:

Blessed Kindreds,
May the fertile energies of Creativity flow through me.
May I create without ravaging and insatiably consuming.
May I help to reinforce the cosmic order of the Holy Ones,
Bringing beautiful, new forms into existence
While helping the old pass away in their time.

"Those words gave us the courage and perspective to remember what we were working for during those times of weariness and despair."

Freyr nodded thoughtfully as the mayor spoke, and thanked him for his words and his welcome before continuing on through the town.

VI. The Soldier

As Freyr wandered through the town, he eventually came upon a large celebration, the focus of which seemed to be a young man in a military uniform. Freyr drifted among the groups of people, helping himself to some of the food and beverages that were laid out, as he had not eaten since leaving his road-side camp. Eventually, he made his way to the uniformed young man, striking up conversation.

"I am not from here," the young god said, "and I feel compelled to ask: why the festivities?"

"I've been called off to war. This is my going-away party."

Freyr looked confused. "But, why leave? All your friends and family are here. Besides, you could die, why risk that?"

The young man smiled. "Because I value peace, and sometimes one must fight and sacrifice to make sure that peace survives. And if I'm honest with myself, I could do no less to make sure that my friends and family are safe and sound and able to enjoy that peace. It's like a prayer that my grandfather taught me:

Blessed Kindreds,
Give me courage to see myself wholly,
With all my virtues and vices laid out before my eyes.
May I have the strength to be honest with myself,
So that I might be honest with others.
May I have the Integrity to always keep my word.

"In those moments that I want to run and hide from what I know is right, I remember that, and I remember the oaths that I've sworn and my duty to uphold them."

Freyr nodded, thoughtful, but did not have time to reply before the young man moved on.

VII. The Mother

The young god continued to wander around the gathering, taking in the festivities. As he did, he noticed a young woman with two small children in tow. She was alone, that much was clear, as Freyr could see that she had a singular presence about her. The kind of centered control that a seasoned parent, and a lone one at that, maintained amidst the tiny hurricanes of chaos drifting about them. As Freyr stood watching, one of the two children ran passed the young god, bumping into his leg, as he played tag with his sibling. The young mother chastised the two children for making trouble and apologized to him for their rudeness.

"Don't worry," Freyr responded, before asking: "They seem like a handful, how do you do it?"

The woman smiled. "Lots of love. Lots of patience. The occasional shot of whiskey." They both chuckled at that. "But, no, it's mostly love."

"I'm sure that it makes it easier to have another pair of hands to help when things get rough."

The woman's face fell slightly. "I wouldn't know. The kids' father left a year or so after Dylan - the youngest - was born." Freyr began to apologize, but the mother cut him off. "No, it's okay. With the grace of the gods I get through each day, without their strength and guidance I don't know how I would do it."

"'Guidance'?" Freyr asked.

The young mother nodded. "When I feel lost and don't know how to proceed I pray to the gods, asking:

Blessed Kindreds,
Open my eyes to See the Path before me.
Give me guidance to follow, so that I might lead.
Give me spirit to press on.
Give me Vision to help the cosmos and its beings proper.

"At the very least, it helps me calm down and not choke the life of my darling babies," the woman said with an ironic smile. Her eyes went wide before she abruptly darted passed Freyr, yelling out: "Samantha, don't you dare yank on that table-cloth!"

VIII. The General

As Freyr watched the young mother run off after her children, an older man in uniform came up to stand beside him. "Poor girl," the man said, "it'll be a fine day when she finds a *good* man to love her and help her." He nodded to Freyr Ingvi and thrust out his hand in greeting. "General Benjamin Ayers."

"Ingvi Njorðrsson," Freyr returned the handshake.

"I don't believe I've met you before, son," the General said.

"I'm passing through town. I saw the festivities and came to see what was going on."

The General smiled. "Ah. Well, I hope you're having a good time. I pulled out all the stops for this. I wanted to make sure my son had some good memories before going off to war."

Freyr tilted his head to the side. "But…I'm a complete stranger…?"

The General's smiled broadened. "So? I was raised with a healthy sense of hospitality. Unless someone proves themselves unworthy of that generosity, you do what you can to provide for them. No matter who they are. After all, you never know when one of the gods might be about in the land."

Freyr said nothing.

The General continued. "As a boy, whenever I was selfish and greedy, my mother would make me repeat this to myself:

Blessed Kindreds,
May I be a generous host and a gracious guest.
Let the spirit of ghôsti, *of Hospitality, well up within me.*
May I share my wealth and love with my kith and kin,
Weaving the threads between us that much closer.

"It always reminded me that there was a bigger world beyond myself, and that it was important to be mindful of others."

Freyr nodded as he took in the General's words. The older man clapped him on the shoulder, beaming jovially. "Well, enjoy yourself, son. Be sure to try the pulled pork sandwiches, they're absolutely delicious!" And with that, the General moved off into the crowd of party-goers.

IX. The Chaplain

Freyr wandered through the party, to its edges, finding a seat at an empty table. He thought heavily upon the General's words, turning them over in his mind. His ruminations were interrupted by the approach of a middle-aged man, wearing a military uniform that was becoming more and more pervasive as Freyr observed the festivities.

"You okay, friend?" the man asked.

Freyr nodded. "Yes, yes. I'm fine."

"It's just that you looked troubled about something," the man replied.

"No, I'm fine," Freyr responded. He looked the man over once. "You're in the military as well? Are you serving with the young man who is being shipped out?"

The man nodded his head. "Aye. I'm the chaplain for his unit."

Freyr paused. "Doesn't that mean that you're not allowed to carry weapons? How can you go into battle so…*naked* like that?"

The man smiled. "Well, I won't lie, it can be terrifying at times. But one has to acknowledge the fear and push passed it, otherwise it controls them and dictates their actions."

Freyr seemed impressed. "It must take a lot of mental discipline to be able to do that."

The man nodded. "It does. Sometimes, the fear takes a hold of you and you can't shake it. That's why a lot of people use mnemonics, like prayers, to help steady their hearts and their heads. I always repeat this one to myself when I need to keep my head:

Blessed Kindreds,
Fill my heart with Courage.
May I face my fears.
May I surmount them and keep them from impeding me.

"At the very least it helps clear my head and help me think somewhat more rationally when things are stressful."

Freyr thanked the chaplain for his insightful words and set off from the party.

X. The Magician

The young god wandered to the outskirts of the town just as the sun was setting, his head and his heart whirling with all of the new information he had taken in over the previous several days. He sat down at the side of the road, watching cars fly by without even a glance in his direction, trying to make sense of things.

As the sun slid lower toward the horizon, a figured appeared from the direction of the countryside, walking along the road. Freyr didn't move as the man approached closer and closer, until he stood next to him, looking down at the seated god. "Why the long face, *kemo sabe*?"

"What does it matter to you?" Freyr grunted in reply.

The man shrugged. "Well, it's not every day that one finds a god with a troubled air about him, sitting by the side of the road."

Freyr stared up at the man in surprise. "How did you know…?"

The man smiled. "I'm a *vitki*, a magician. It's my business to know these kinds of things. I am one of the 'wise', after all."

Freyr grunted thoughtfully. "Well, if you're so wise, perhaps you can help me. I was sent here by my father to learn about virtue and ethics and wisdom, and though I've certainly been taught a lot by the men and women I've met, I don't know what to make of it all."

The magician was silent for a moment, thoughtful. Finally, he spoke: "Wisdom and knowledge, the expansion of understanding, are never easy. Sometimes, what it takes is a lot of contemplation and quiet reflection. Perhaps these words will help you:

Blessed Kindreds,
Help me to find Wisdom, Crown of All the Virtues.
May I feel its fullness and humility within me.
May I let its insight guide me.
May I let its hunger drive me toward virtue.
Blessed Kindreds,
Help me to kindle its flame within my breast,
So that I might have a light to guide me through all my days."

The magician patted Freyr gently on the shoulder. "I'm sure that you will find understanding in time, good Ingvi. Good luck."

And with that, the magician continued on his way.

XI. Return

Freyr sat by the side of the road for nine days and nine nights. Contemplating the lessons and the insights he had gained during his time of Miðgarð, and reciting the prayer that the magician had taught him, he barely noticed the passing of the days. And as the last night passed into day, the dawning of Sunna on the eastern horizon saw a similar dawning of understanding in the young god's mind. He realized what it was that his father had wanted him to learn: responsibility, strength, mindfulness of others, humility.

Leaping to his feet, Freyr made his way from the world of Men and back to Noatun, where he was warmly greeted by his father and the other deities.

Appendix II: Glossary

- **Ægis** (“ay-jiss”): Latin – “protection, guidance”; originally taken from the Greek aegis, referring to the shield of Athena made from a goat-skin.
- **Æsir** (“aye-sear”): Old Norse – one of the primary tribes of Norse deities, most often associated with the developments of civilized human life.
- **Alfar** (“al-far”): Icelandic – “elves”, singular “Alfr”; a class of deceased human ancestors generally associated with barrow-mounds and familial lands.
- **Alfoðr** (“all-fother”): Old Norse – “All-Father”, a by-name of Oðinn.
- **Alvíss** (“all-veese”): Old Norse – “All-Wise”, one of the Dvergar; tried to best Thor in a challenge of wits in order to win the hand of the Thunderer’s daughter.
- **Ansuz** (“ahn-sooze”): Proto-Germanic – “deity, mouth”, one of the runic symbols of the Elder Futhark.
- **Áss** (“ace”) Old Norse – one of the male members of the Æsir.
- **Asgarð** (“az-garth”) Old Norse – “the garden of the Æsir”, one of Nine Worlds, most often associated with the deities, whether Æsir or Vanir.
- **Askr** (“ask”) Old Norse – “Ash”, the First Man.
- **Ásynja** (“ay-sinya”) Old Norse – one of the female members of the Æsir; plural: “Ásynjur”.
- **Beltaine** (“bell-tay’n”) Old Irish – “May”.
- **Berkano** (“burr-kahn’oh”) Proto-Germanic – “birch”, one of the runic symbols of the Elder Futhark.
- **Bífrost** (“bee-frost”) Old Norse – “shimmering path”, the rainbow bridge connecting the Miðgarð with Asgarð.
- **Borr** (“bohr”) Old Norse – “son”, the son of Búri and father of Oðinn.
- **Bragi** (“brah-gee”) Old Norse – likely connected to bragr, “poetry”; the Skald of the Æsir and husband to Iðunna.
- **Búri** (“boor-ee”) Old Norse – the father of Borr and grandfather of Oðinn.

- **Daimon** ("day-moan") Ancient Greek – "a god, goddess, divine power".
- **Dises** ("dee-says") Old Norse -
- **Dísir** ("dee-sear") Old Norse – "minor female deities", singular "Dís"; generally believed to be the deceased female ancestors of a family line.
- **Disting** ("diss-ting") Old Norse – a festival traditionally held in late February or early March honoring the dísir and other female powers.
- **Dvergar** ("d'were-gar") Old Norse – "dwarf."
- **Ehwaz** ("eh-w'ahz") Proto-Germanic – "horse", one of the runic symbols of the Elder Futhark.
- **Einherjar** ("eye'n-her-yar") Old Norse – "the spirits of warriors who died bravely in battle."
- **Élivágar** ("Eh-lih-vow-gahr") Old Norse – "Ice Waves", the primeval rivers formed from the warming of Niflheim's icy-wastes by the heat of Muspelheim.
- **Embla** ("Ehm-blah") Old Norse – uncertain, possibly "Elm"; the First Woman.
- **Eostre** ("Yo-straw") Northumbrian Old English – most likely the name of the goddess of the dawn among the Germanics, as her name is cognate to the Greek Eos, the Roman Aurora, and the Vedic Ushas; the modern English word "Easter" is a direct continuation of the Old English (West Saxon) form of her name, "Eastre."
- **Etin** ("Eh-tin") Middle English – "giant"
- **Fenrir** ("Fehn-rear") Old Norse – "fen-dweller", a monstrous wolf and a child of Loki; was bound by the Guðir with a magical chain, during which Tyr lost his right hand for lying to Fenrir.
- **Forfeður** ("Four-feather") Icelandic – "ancestors"
- **Freyja** ("Fray-yah") Old Norse – "Lady", cognate to German "frau"; twin sister to Freyr (Ingvi) and daughter of Njorð; one of the Vanir.
- **Freyr Ingvi** ("Fray Ing-vee") Old Norse – "Lord Ing"; twin brother to Freyja and son of Njorð; one of the Vanir.
- **Frigga** ("Frih'g-gah") Old Norse – uncertain, cognate to Sanskrit prīyā́ ("wife"), also related to Swedish fria ("to

propose for marriage"), Old Saxon fri ("beloved lady"), and Icelandic frjá ("to love").

- **Frið** ("frih'th") Old English – "peace; freedom from molestation, protection; safety, security."
- **Frið-stead** ("frih'th sted") Old English – an area set aside as sacrosanct where no weapon could be drawn, blood spilled, nor could one relieve oneself; usually temples were set up within the bounds of frið-steads.
- **Galdr** ("gall-der") Old Norse – "spell, incantation", usually a song or poetic composition.
- **Garm** ("Gahr'm") Old Norse – "rag", a large dog that guards the gate to Helheim.
- **Garð** ("Gahr'th") Old Norse – "garden"
- **Gefjon** ("Geh'f-yawn") Old Norse – one of the hand-maidens of Frigga.
- **Ghôsti** ("G'oss-tee") Proto-Indo-European reconstruction – concerned the interconnected relationship between persons (both individuals and groups), and between humans and deities; the words guest and host have their roots in this word.
- **Ginnungagap** ("Gih-noon-gah-gap") Old Norse – "mighty gap", the primal void that existed before the creation of the manifest cosmos.
- **Gjallarhorn** ("G'yah'll-er-horn") Old Norse – "yelling horn", the horn of Heimdall that will be blown to signal to the beginning of Ragnarök.
- **Gleichentag** ("G'lie-ken-tah'g") German – "even-day", a modern term used for the Autumnal Equinox.
- **Goði** ("go-thee") Old Norse – "priest"; plural "Goðar", feminine "Gyðia".
- **Gullveig** ("gull-v'eye'g") Old Norse – uncertain, possibly "Gold-drunk."
- **Guðir** ("goo-th'ear") Icelandic – "deities"
- **Gyðia** ("g'ih-th'yah") Old Norse – see Goði
- **Hamingja** ("ham-ing-yah") Old Norse – "luck".
- **Hamr** ("ham") Old Norse – "shape".
- **Hati** ("hah-tee") Old Norse – "he who hates, enemy", the wolf that chases Máni through the heavens; full name is "Hati Hróðvitnisson".

- **Húsvættir** ("h'oos-v'eye-tear") Icelandic – "house-spirits"
- **Heimdall** ("high'm-doll") Old Norse – uncertain, possibly "the one who illuminates the world"; guards Asgarð.
- **Heiðr** ("High'th) Old Norse – "shining"
- **Helbindi** ("hell-blihn-dee") Old Norse – "all-blind", a by-name of Oðinn.
- **Hella** ("hell-lah") Old Norse – also called "Hel", the goddess of death and the underworld (likewise named "Hel" or "Helheim" – "Hel-home").
- **Hoenir** ("Ho-near") Old Norse – one of the Æsir, shaped Askr and Embla alongside Oðinn and Loðurr, gave humanity "reason".
- **Imbolc** ("Im'melk") Irish – "in the belly", refers to the pregnancy of ewes.
- **Iðunna** ("Ee-thoon'nah") Old Norse – Ásynja who cultivates and guards the apples of immortality, the wife of Bragi.
- **Jörð** ("Yorth") Icelandic – "earth", a Jötynja but friendly to the Æsir and the mother of Thor and Meili by Oðinn.
- **Jotnar** ("Yot'nahr") Old Norse – "giants"
- **Jotunheim** ("Yo-ton-high'm") Old Norse – "giant-home"
- **Jotun** ("Yo-ton") Old Norse – "giant"
- **Jötynja** ("Yeh-tin-yah") Old Norse – female giant, singular
- **Jötynjur** ("Yeh-tin-yur") Old Norse – female giants, plural
- **Kaunaz** ("Cow-nah'n") Proto-Germanic – "ulcer", one of the runic symbols of the Elder Futhark.
- **Kvasir** ("Kuh'vah-sear") Old Norse – a god from whose blood the Mead of Inspiration was brewed.
- **Lammas** ("Lah-mass") English – "loaf-mass"
- **Landvættir** ("Land-v'eye-tear") Icelandic – "land-spirits"
- **Latið opna hliðin** ("Lah-teethe oh'p-nah h'leethe-in") Icelandic – "Let the Gates be open"
- **Latið loka hliðunum** ("Lah-teethe loh-kah h'leethe-uhn-uhm") Icelandic – "Let the Gates be closed"
- **Laufey** ("L'ow-fay") Old Norse – "leafy-island"; the mother of Loki
- **Loki** ("Low-key") Old Norse – Jotun blood-brother to Oðinn and friend to Thor, associated with fire.

- **Lughnassadh** ("Loo-nah-sah") Irish – "the Feat of Lugh"
- **Mabon** ("Mah-bohn") – a relatively modern (circa 1970) term used in Wicca for the Autumnal Equinox.
- **Main** ("May'n") – spiritual strength or potency.
- **Máni** ("Mah-nee") Old Norse – the spirit/deity of the Moon
- **Maitag** ("M'eye-tah'g") German – "May Day"
- **Mannaz** ("Mah-nah'z") Proto-Germanic – "man", one of the runic symbols of the Elder Futhark.
- **Mörnir** ("M'air-near") Old Norse – "giantesses"
- **Mimir** ("Me-m'ear") Old Norse – "the rememberer, the wise one"
- **Might** ("M'eye'ght") – physical strength or potency.
- **Miðgarð** ("M'eethe-garth") Old Norse – "the middle-garden", the world inhabited by Humanity.
- **Móðguðr** ("M'othe-goothe") Old Norse – "furious battler", a giantess who guards the bridge to Hel's Hall.
- **Mundilfari** ("Moon-dill-far-ee") Old Norse – possibly "the one moving according to particular times", the father of Sunna and Máni.
- **Muspelheim** ("Moo-spill-h'eye'm") Old Norse – "Muspell's Home", the home of the Muspelli, or fire-giants, who will lay waste to the cosmos during Ragnarök.
- **Niflheim** ("Niff'l-h'eye'm") Old Norse – "Mist-Home"
- **Nerðus** ("Ner-thoos") Proto-Germanic – a goddess of the Earth attested to by Roman historian Tacitus, it is possible that she is related to the Vanic god, Njorðr, or is possibly the same (hermaphroditic) being.
- **Njorðr** ("N'yor'the") Proto-Germanic – "force, power", one of the Vanir, a god of the sea and sea-travel, the father of Freyr Ingvi and Freyja.
- **Nóatún** ("Noah-ton") Old Norse – "ship-enclosure", the home of Njorðr.
- **Nornir** ("No'r-near") Old Norse – possibly related to the verb "to twine", the deities/beings associated with Wyrd.
- **Ostara** ("Oh-star-ah") Old High German – the continental version of Eostre.

- **Óttar** ("Oh-tar") – in Norse myth, he is a follower of Freyja whom the goddess temporarily disguised as her boar.
- **Oðinn** ("Oh-thin") Old Norse – "the ecstatic one", eldest of the Æsir and god of magic, wisdom, writing, and victory.
- **Perthro** ("Pear-throw") Proto-Germanic – unknown meaning, one of the runic symbols of the Elder Futhark.
- **Ragnarök** ("Rag-nah-r'oak") Old Norse – "final destiny of the gods"; in Norse mythology, the end of the current world-age after which the cosmos will be reborn.
- **Ratatosk** ("Rat-a-tosk") Old Norse – "rat-tooth", the squirrel who lives on Yggdrasil.
- **Hrímthurs** ("Ream-thurss") Old Norse – "rime giant"
- **Rúnatyr** ("Roon-a-tear") Old Norse – "god of the runes/mysteries", a by-name of Oðinn.
- **Samhain** ("Sow-wan") Irish – "Summer's End", the traditional name of the festival marked in the modern day as "Halloween."
- **Sága** ("Sow-gah") Old Norse – possibly "seeress", the goddess of storytelling.
- **Seiðkona** ("say'the-koh-nah") Old Norse – a female practitioner of the magical art of seiðr.
- **Sif** ("S'ih'f") Old Norse – the goddess of the grain and wife of Thor.
- **Sjáið vatn lífsins** ("S'y'ow'th vah-tin leaf-sins") Icelandic – "Behold the Waters of Life"
- **Skald** ("scald") Old Norse – a practitioner of a Skaldic poetry.
- **Skaði** ("Sk'ah-thee") Old Norse – "shadow", the goddess of the wintry wilds, of giant-origin.
- **Skinfaxi** ("Skin-fax-ee") Old Norse – "shining mane", the horse associated with either Sunna or the personification of Day.
- **Sköll** ("Skell") Old Norse – "treachery", the wolf that chases Sunna through the Heavens.
- **Sowilo** ("So-we-low") Proto-Germanic – "sun", one of the runic symbols of the Elder Futhark.
- **Stigr** ("St'ih'g") Old Norse – "path"
- **Sunna** ("Sun-nah") Old High German, Old Norse – the spirit/deity of the Sun.

- **Svartalfheim** ("S'w'art-ale'f-h'eye'm") Old Norse – "home of the black elves", the realm of the Swartalfar/Dvergar.
- **Thor** ("Th'oar") Old Norse – "thunder"; the god of lightning, storms, fertility, and protection.
- **Thurisaz** ("Th'ur-ih-sah'z") Proto-Germanic – "giant", one of the runic symbols of the Elder Futhark.
- **Tiw** ("Too") Old English – "god"; see "Tyr" below.
- **Tyr** ("Tear") Old Norse – "god"; the god of inter-"national" justice, honor, and law.
- **Ur-Etin** ("Er-eh'tin") – "primal giant"
- **Ur-Goð** ("Er-go'the") – "primal god"
- **Ur-Jotun** ("Er-yo'ton") – "primal giant"
- **Uruz** ("Oo'r-ooze") Proto-Germanic – "aurochs", one of the runic symbols of the Elder Futhark.
- **Vættir** ("V'eye-tear") Icelandic – "spirits"
- **Valaskjálf** ("Vah'lahss'k-y'ow'l'f") Old Norse – "the Shelf of the Slain", one of Oðinn's halls in Asgarð.
- **Valknot** ("Vall-knot") Old Norse – "knot of the slain", a symbol consisting of three inter-woven triangles associated with Oðinn.
- **Valkyries** ("Vall-k'ear-ee's") Old Norse – "choosers of the slain", female spirits associated with Oðinn and Freyja who would guide the battle-slain to their respective halls in Asgarð.
- **Van** ("V'ahn") Old Norse – a deity of the Vanir.
- **Vanaheim** ("V'ahn-nah-h'eye'm") Old Norse – "Vanir-Home".
- **Vanir** ("V'ah-near") Old Norse – one of the two principle tribes of deities.
- **Verði það svo** ("V'air-thee th'ah'the s'voh") Icelandic – "So be it."
- **Vitki** ("Vih't-key") Old Norse – "wise one", a magician.
- **Viðarr** ("Vee-thar") Old Norse – possibly "wide ruler"; a son of Oðinn.
- **Völsa þáttr** ("V'ell'sah th'ow-ter") Old Norse – a short story found in a chapter of Óláfs saga helga within the Flateyjarbók.
- **Völsi** ("V'el-see") Old Norse – a severed and preserved penis (usually equine), used ritually for blessing.

- **Woden** ("Woah-den") Old English – the Anglo-Saxon version of Oðinn.
- **Wyrd** ("Weird") Old English – "fate"
- **Wyrm** ("Worm") Old English – "dragon, snake"
- **Yggdrasil** ("Ee'g-drah-seal") Old Norse – "Terrible's Mount", a name for the World Tree.
- **Ymir** ("Ee-m'ear") Old Norse – the primordial giant, eventually slain and butchered by Oðinn, Vili, and Vé to create the cosmos as it is today.
- **Yule** ("Y'ool") Old Norse – a festival held during the winter season, generally around the time of the Winter Solstice.

Appendix III: Recommended Reading

- Corrigan, Ian. *Sacred Fire, Holy Well: A Druid's Grimoire.* (Tredara Hearth Publishing, 2006).
- Gundarsson, Kveldulf. *Elves, Wights, and Trolls: Studies Toward the Practice of Germanic Heathenry*, Vol. I. (iUniverse Inc., 2007).
- ----------. *Teutonic Magic*. (Thoth Publications, 2007).
- ----------. *Teutonic Religion*. (Llewellyn Publications, 1993).
- Gundarsson, Kveldulf, ed. *Our Troth, Volume I: History and Lore*. (BookSurge, LLC., 2006).
- ----------. *Our Troth, Volume II: Living the Troth*. BookSurge, LLC., 2007)
- Paxson, Diana. *Taking Up the Runes*. (Weiser Books, 2005).
- Serith, Ceisiwr. *A Book of Pagan Prayer*. (Red Wheel/Weiser, 2002).

For this and other books, as well as all your ritual needs, check out
The Magical Druid

http://www.magicaldruid.com/

For ritual and other work that might excite you, check out
Three Cranes Grove, ADF

http://www.threecranes.org/

www.ingramcontent.com/pod-product-compliance
Lightning Source LLC
LaVergne TN
LVHW020527100826
845148LV00010B/1369

* 9 7 8 0 6 1 5 8 8 0 2 4 2 *